The Angel in the Marketplace

The Angel in the Marketplace

*Adwoman Jean Wade Rindlaub
and the Selling of America*

ELLEN WAYLAND-SMITH

The University of Chicago Press

Chicago and London

The University of Chicago Press, Chicago 60637
The University of Chicago Press, Ltd., London
© 2020 by Ellen Wayland-Smith
Published 2020
Printed in the United States of America

29 28 27 26 25 24 23 22 21 20   1 2 3 4 5

ISBN-13: 978-0-226-48632-1 (cloth)
ISBN-13: 978-0-226-48646-8 (e-book)
DOI: https://doi.org/10.7208/chicago/9780226486468.001.0001

Library of Congress Cataloging-in-Publication Data

Names: Wayland-Smith, Ellen, 1966– author.
Title: The angel in the marketplace : adwoman Jean Wade Rindlaub
    and the selling of America / Ellen Wayland-Smith.
Description: Chicago : University of Chicago Press, 2020. |
    Includes bibliographical references and index.
Identifiers: LCCN 2019053531 | ISBN 9780226486321 (cloth) |
    ISBN 9780226486468 (e-book)
Subjects: LCSH: Rindlaub, Jean Wade, 1904–1991. | Businesswomen—
    United States—Biography. | Women in the advertising industry—
    United States—History—20th century. | Advertising and women—
    United States—History—20th century. | Advertising—United
    States—History—20th century.
Classification: LCC HF5810.R56 W39 2020 | DDC 659.1092 [B]—dc23
LC record available at https://lccn.loc.gov/2019053531

♾ This paper meets the requirements of ANSI/NISO Z39.48-1992
(Permanence of Paper).

Contents

Odd Adman Out

Who Was Jean Wade Rindlaub?

In 1977, long before *Mad Men*, Patricia Tierney revealed the life of a sheep among the wolves of Madison Avenue in the 1960s.[1] Girls had to work twice as hard for half as much pay, she confesses in *Ladies of the Avenue: The Advertising Agency Jungle . . . Defoliated by an Insider, a Successful Woman Copywriter*, and even the most feminist-minded among them used their sex as well as their brains to advance. "A girl doesn't have to use sex to get ahead," Tierney quips, "but if nature was more generous with your endowments below the neck than above, you needn't consider it a handicap."[2] Mary Wells Lawrence, who spun off from a major ad agency to found her own firm in 1966, echoed Tierney's gimlet-eyed take in her 2002 autobiography, *A Big Life in Advertising*, as did Wells Lawrence's protégée Jane Maas in her memoir *Madwomen: The Other Side of Life on Madison Avenue in the '60s and Beyond*.[3] And, of course, in 2007 the television series *Mad Men* burst onto the scene with its moral center Peggy Olson: girl-next-door turned corporate powerhouse, Peggy rises up the advertising ranks through a mix of sexual savvy, smarts, and raw ambition. Some said Jane Maas was "the real-life Peggy Olson," while others suggested she was modeled on Wells Lawrence.[4]

All of these adwomen, real and fictional, take a tongue-in-cheek attitude toward the sexism they endure in the workplace, as well as the inanity of much of their industry's advertising to women. All's fair in love and work, Tierney reasons, noting that the nascent feminist movement found few sympathizers among lady advertisers in the '60s and '70s: "They have become such experts at using their wiles to get their ways," she muses, that "they're convinced there's no need to resort to the whip." Wells Lawrence made headlines when she sexed up the airline industry, painting Braniff Airways' fleet candy colors and marketing its stewardesses as high-class strip-tease artists. And Maas played on sexist stereotypes, pragmatically accepting in her work for Dove dishwashing liquid and Maxim coffee that any advertising aimed at women would have to be sexist to succeed; once second-wave feminism hit, she just as pragmatically consigned those classic ads to the ashcan of history. "I have always thought that our husband-pleasing strategy killed Maxim," she commented coolly. "As feminism came in, husband-pleasing went out."[5]

The feminist narrative of a Wells Lawrence or a Maas or an Olson is the archetypal one of a feisty girl deliciously beating men at their own game, a female Horatio Alger protagonist battling her way through the sexist workplace jungle to perch atop the advertising tree. They are all proto–Sheryl Sandbergs, leaning in to get their piece of the corporate pie—whatever feminist ideals have to be sacrificed in the process.

But before them all was Jean Wade Rindlaub. Her approach was different from Tierney's or Wells Lawrence's or Maas's, and she certainly was no model for Peggy Olson. Yet she was, according to Tierney, one of the "most successful ladies ever in advertising," who "probably sold more soap, more soup, more cake mixes, and God knows what else than any other single human on earth."[6] In 1920 at the age of sixteen, Jean took a job as secretary to the head of the Advertising Department at Armstrong Cork, a flooring manufacturer in her hometown of Lancaster, Pennsylvania; ten years later she was offered a copywriting position at the prestigious Madison Avenue firm of Batten Barton Durstine and Osborn. There, she rose through the ranks to become the company's first woman vice president in 1944, and the first woman named to the executive board in 1954. Along the way, she churned out award-winning, sales-generating advertisements for all things domestic: Oneida silverware, North Star blankets, Betty Crocker cake mix, Campbell's soup, Chiquita bananas.

Yet Jean didn't resemble any of the female archetypes in the popularizing portraits of the era and the industry, her story shaped

FIGURE 1. Portrait of Helen Jean Wade as a young woman, n.d.

neither by sex nor the proverbial "casting couch." Jean was resolutely unsexy. Tierney refers to her as "one of the most physically unattractive females you would want to lay your eyes on," specifying that she was "short, dumpy, and dark with outcroppings of hair where there was really no need for them." Even by her own assessment, Jean was not office eye candy. "I was short and fat," Jean once admitted in an anonymous article in which she explained why she rushed to wed the first man who asked her, imperfect as he was: "I hadn't enough money or social position or charm or beauty to make me a matrimonial catch." Any marriage was better than no marriage, in Jean's eyes, so she "said 'yes' quick!"—and urged other young women to do the same. Jean always rejected the label of "career" woman, describing her Madison Avenue post as simply "a job she liked," and one that she never allowed to displace her "primary job" of wife and mother.[7]

Unlike Tierney or Maas, Jean had no ironic distance from her chosen profession. "If I were twenty again," a forty-four-year old Jean announced in a 1948 speech to a women's advertising club, "I'd believe in advertising. This is one firm faith that has grown through the years." That is because, Jean claimed, advertising is a vital cog in the mechanism of "the American business system" on which our national moral and material well-being depended. "Advertising has accepted its primary social responsibility of contributing to the effective mass production and economic distribution of the products of American industry, . . . [which] has done so much in the way of material things for the comfort and happiness of its people."[8] Jean had unblinking faith in the American Christian corporate order and the strict domestic gender divisions on which it was built. Unlike the home-resistant and home-busting heroines of lady advertiser lore, Jean was the most fervent believer in the white picket fence dream. She even once called her suburban homestead "a little piece of heaven."

Jean believed that the humble American home of soup and soap and cakes not only was the moral Christian center of American life; it also depended on another, larger structure: free-market capitalism. The interdependence of the two structures—the feminine home as safe haven from the competitive masculine market—had been axiomatic in American culture from the onset of industrialization in the nineteenth century. During the Victorian era, the dutiful wife and mother was esteemed an "angel in the house," exerting her virtuous control over all under her roof. With the growth of consumer culture in the 1910s and '20s, however, women were increasingly invested with a household's purchasing power and expected to apply their angelic influence not just in the home but in the marketplace as well.

The banker V. Everitt Macy in 1917 called free-market capitalism "the industrial and commercial structure which is the indispensable shelter of us all," and that Americans were duty-bound to protect.[9] Jean concurred: she believed it was her God-appointed work to keep both these homes safe.

The arc of Jean's professional life is a lens through which we can trace the larger evolution of American capitalism and the key role that women played in consolidating it at each step along the way. From the rise of corporate capitalism at the turn of the twentieth century, through the New Deal's bid to temper the power of big business and the eventual triumph of "free enterprise" in the postwar consumer boom, Jean was there to sell the "American business system" to women consumers. At key points throughout the country's history—during the Progressive Era at the dawn of corporate capitalism, and then again during the New Deal of the 1930s and '40s—a more inclusive, less atomistic vision of the capitalist project appeared possible. At each of these points, the nation ultimately backed away from large-scale structural reform. This peculiarly American resistance to economic regulation and socialization would not have been possible without the support of women.

What Jean's career from the 1920s through the 1960s allows us to see with particular clarity is how a range of cultural narratives—advertising aimed at women, prominent among them—worked powerfully to shape women's emotional and economic behavior in support of the free-market system. Jean provided housewives with an accessible emotional vocabulary and an uplifting, happily-ever-after storyline by which to understand their market behavior.

"Sentimentality is the mark of dishonesty, the inability to feel," James Baldwin once wrote. It betokens "an aversion to experience" and is "always, therefore, ... the mask of cruelty."[10] We cannot understand the popularity of free-market faith in America—and the cruelty that often attends its reign—without understanding the appeals it has historically made to Christian belief specifically and magical thinking more broadly. From our Puritan forebearers' sanctification of profit as a sign of God's blessing, to Norman Vincent Peale's *The Power of Positive Thinking* and the wealth-attracting power of sheer will, Americans have always genuflected before the inscrutable power of the free market to distribute favors both earthly and heavenly. That the market is righteous is a national article of faith.

Sentimentality is a subgenre of magical thinking. When faced with the complexity and contradiction of lived experience, the sentimentalist takes refuge in a vague ideal such as human brotherhood, or the sanctity of freedom, or maternal devotion. This is the pull of "human interest" stories. The self-congratulatory swell of emotion we feel in response to local, folksy tales of the "triumph of the human spirit" works to suspend belief in (or attention to) the larger collective ills that plague us. For the sentimentalist, the verities of the human heart are timeless, universal, and, as such, resistant to any evidence to the contrary.

Jean understood this and put what she called "heart-tug" at the center of her advertising strategy.[11] Men's eyes are drawn to newspaper headlines "about war and Washington," Jean once tutored a group of pharmaceutical executives. And women? "[They] read the ones about somebody's baby or somebody's missing bride or somebody's pet squirrel," she assured her audience. "Your customer's world is a very small world, . . . carefully bounded by the four square walls of her family circle."[12] Tapping into these domestic sentiments was key to moving merchandise. "When you can tell your story logically in a warm and heart-tugging way," Jean urged, "you have a powerful [sales] weapon."[13] Jean breathed new life into the Victorian sanctification of the home, crafting an ideal of love-and-kisses, heart-tugging domesticity tailored to the psychic needs of twentieth-century American women—and the free-market economy.

So why hasn't her story been told before?[14] For starters, collaborators are not as immediately attractive as rebels. Why follow the story of a woman who embodies and enables the dominant white male narrative that *Mad Men* is premised on disrupting with its quirky, rebellious, home-breaking females? Jean is more Betty Draper than Peggy Olson. Yet it is precisely in its very over-the-top domestic sentimentalism, the almost campy earnestness of its free-market faith, that Jean's advertising career reveals what Peggy's cannot: the fundamental evasiveness, if not outright dishonesty, at the heart of the white patriarchal free-market edifice as it emerged at midcentury. In critiquing the advertising industry's rampant sexism but leaving largely intact the corporate values within which it operated, previous "feminist" accounts of women breaking advertising's glass ceiling have missed the deeper scoop. Jean's story gives it to us, unvarnished.

After forty-three years in the advertising business, upon retiring in 1963 Jean took up the volunteer work that, in the nineteenth century, was the usual fare for progressive-minded women who sought to do "community housekeeping": the traditional Christianity-infused mission of uplifting the poor, the hungry, the huddled masses. And once she turned her mind to it, joining Lyndon B. Johnson's War on Poverty and the civil rights movement, Jean began to take a dimmer view of her previous faith in private initiative and private capital as a cure for the world's ills. It was precisely because her aim now *wasn't* "leaning in"—to get her just desserts, her part of the pie—but communal caretaking that she became, ultimately, more critical of advertising than did any of its better-publicized heroines.

In the long arc of her fervent faith, followed by the sneaking suspicion that it might have been misplaced, Jean's story reveals the darker underpinnings of the corporate order for which she was once such a willing foot soldier. Jean believed in the gospel of the free market—until she didn't. The tale of her belief and eventual disenchantment is the "Mad Women" story that hasn't yet been told.

1

A Tale of Two Gospels

Helen Jean Wade was born on February 9, 1904, in Lancaster, Pennsylvania. It was the year Theodore Roosevelt assured US control of efforts to dig the Panama Canal, one of the most complicated feats of engineering ever attempted. It was the year Eugene V. Debs clinched the presidential nomination of the recently formed Socialist Party, pledging a new movement for solidarity among the working class to fight the iron grip of capital. It was the year Henry Ford climbed behind the wheel of his latest Red Devil automobile and, zipping across an ice track carved into Lake St. Clair, Michigan, broke the reigning speed record: 91.37 mph.

But the origins of Jean's story stretch further back. From one perspective, the narrative of her life was set in motion on the day in 1893 that her father, Robert Mifflin Wade, decided to sign up for a class at the Wilkes-Barre Business College. He graduated soon after with a degree from the Commercial Division as well as three months' training in shorthand and typewriting under his belt.[1]

Robert's family were farm people, Scotch-Irish and Pennsylvania Dutch, and knew the satisfactions but also the strain of manual labor. He had worked, at various times, as a coal miner, a railroad worker, a lumberjack, and a hand at a plate glass factory. His was backbreaking, often unrelenting labor. The summer he worked on the railroad as part of a "paddy gang," he once recounted, "I got up at four o'clock every morning and, after getting my lunch packed, walked one-and-a-half miles and rowed a boat across the Allegheny

FIGURE 2. Portrait of Jean's father, Robert Mifflin Wade, n.d.

River before going to work at seven o'clock, and every evening . . . went through the same performance to get home again."[2]

The timber and glass, coal and iron he helped to churn out of mill, factory, and mine were the raw materials of a brave new American world. The train tracks he labored to build knit the country and its expanding markets together at unprecedented speed. In America's urban centers, skyscrapers rose up, steel and glass palaces out of the pages of a futurist fairy tale. The skyscrapers were designed to meet a skyrocketing demand for office space—offices where the complex business of administering the modern production and distribution of goods could be managed by a phalanx of lawyers, accountants, recordkeepers, typists, and stenographers. Robert had sensed a turning of the tides. He had dedicated himself to producing the hard, raw materials of modernity. But the future, he wagered, belonged to paperwork—and he wanted a part of it.

After graduating from Wilkes-Barre Business College, Robert hit the pavement in search of clerical work. A letter of recommendation from one of his professors declared him an "earnest student of sound talents and excellent attainments," "thorough and conscientious in his studies."[3] His brother Joseph Marshall Wade dashed off a letter to him on October 3, 1895, with fifteen dollars enclosed. "Get yourself a pair of pants and a good tie of modern design," he instructed him. "It don't pay to look too plain." He went on to urge his brother to keep himself washed and clean shaven, and to get regular exercise. "You must make it a part of your business to keep a clean head."[4] In 1896, Robert, Joseph, and their brother William founded their own commercial school, the Wade Pennsylvania Business and Short-hand College, whose mission was to churn out the steady stream of paper pushers required to meet the labor needs of an increasingly incorporated America. "Business as it is now conducted could not do without this army of deft workers any more than it could spare the railroads," a 1903 brochure from the college assured prospective students.[5]

And increasingly, this new middle-class army of salaried profes-sionals, clerical workers, and salespeople was populated by young women. "White-collar" work at the turn of the century offered an acceptable path of employment for middle-class girls of limited means as well as working-class girls hoping to climb the social lad-der. The 1903 brochure, after running through the advantages that a business education could provide an ambitious young man, has-tened to add that women were equally likely to benefit from a busi-ness education. "Stenography has given ladies, who have to work, a refined occupation for which they are well adapted," the brochure declared. "Thousands of them are now employed in the various lines

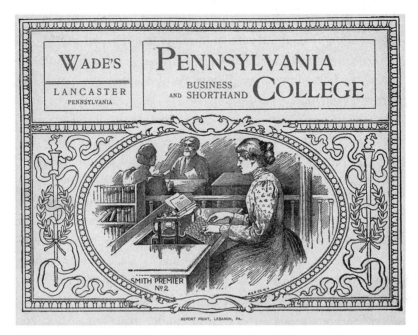

FIGURE 3. Cover of a brochure for the Pennsylvania Business College, 1903. Robert Wade was co-owner of Wade's Pennsylvania Business and Shorthand College, founded in 1896. Jean was a graduate of the school and taught there for one year before taking a position as secretary to the head of the advertising department at Armstrong Cork, a local flooring manufacturer, in 1920.

of business. . . . There are firms that employ several hundred ladies."[6] On the booklet's cover: an engraving of a neatly coiffed and dressed young woman seated at a desk, clicking away at the keys of a Smith Premier typewriter.

Jean attended public school for only two years, before her father decided it would be more efficient to educate her himself at his business college. In 1915, at the age of eleven, she was awarded a Certificate of Efficiency from the Remington Typewriter Company for typing 50 words a minute. She was the youngest pupil ever to receive a certificate of proficiency from the Gregg Shorthand Company. She picked up bookkeeping, letter writing, and business math with equal speed. In short, Jean soon proved herself a paperwork prodigy. In 1915, the institution of the "advertising agency" was still in its infancy. But Jean's eventual choice of career as an advertiser, helping to grease the wheels of a corporate capitalist machine that grew beyond the most fantastic expectations of its turn-of-the-century exponents, was a natural extension of her father's work.

This work was successful in America in part because it fit so seamlessly into the traditional religious fabric of American culture. As the industrial and market revolution of the 1830s and '40s blazed relentlessly ahead, upending centuries-old patterns in social and economic life in its quest to make America over in its image, it braided multiple, frequently contradictory threads pulled from the country's Puritan past. "Business Is King," proclaimed one of Robert's brochures—a declaration whose faint tinge of religious enthusiasm was no accident.[7] Almost half a century later, at the height of the Cold War, Jean would deliver a speech to fellow advertisers conferring a sacred status on their public taste making: "It is a frightening thing, an awesome thing," she mused, "to know that we are holding in our hands not only the wellbeing of [an] individual can of soup or box of cake mix but we are serving as . . . [guides] to a confused, driven, harried, helpless, crazy, mixed up world." In a rhetorical mode more fitted to the pulpit than the boardroom, she concluded her oration: "Are you big enough for that? Are you strong enough for that? Are you brave enough for that? . . . Have you *prayed* enough for that?"[8]

The belief that free-market capitalism will deliver us from evil has been—and continues to be—key to the story we tell ourselves about America. Jean Wade Rindlaub worked tirelessly to convince American women that in their purchasing power, they held the keys to the long-awaited Kingdom.

The idea that wealth, work, and salvation were inextricably linked in an individual Christian's life was a core tenet of Protestant theology and *a fortiori* of Puritan American culture. According to Max Weber's thesis, the forbidding Jehovah of Calvinism left man on earth to work out his salvation for himself, aware that his place among the heavenly elect or the eternally damned was predetermined and that nothing he did could alter it. To devote himself single-mindedly to his work and to fruitful multiplication—whether of children or of capital—was the closest this lonely Christian might come to proof of salvation.

But it was not enough simply to be diligent in one's calling. To ignore providential chances to increase one's profit, and thereby multiply the glory of God, was equally a sign of theological backsliding. Weber quotes the seventeenth-century Puritan theologian Richard Baxter: "If God show you a way in which you may lawfully get more than in another way (without wrong to your soul or to any other), if you refuse this, and choose the less gainful way, you cross one of the ends of your calling, and you refuse to be God's steward, and to accept His gifts and use them for Him when He requireth it." Profit was an absolute good, in and of itself, and the profit motive therefore above reproach. Nor did the successful businessman need to trouble his conscience about material inequality here on earth. The distribution of earthly favors, like the distribution of heavenly favors, was entirely in the hands of Divine Providence, "which in these differences, as in particular grace, pursued secret ends unknown to men."[9]

This theological model joining salvation to rugged individualism, both spiritual and economic, worked well in a setting where economic independence and property ownership was the norm, and formed the basis of the white American male's political identity. Up through the antebellum period in America, the majority of white men were self-employed property owners or could reasonably expect to become such, once released from indenture or apprenticeship. Access to capital—and thus grace—appeared roughly democratic. George Washington was fond of quoting the Old Testament prophet Micah's vision of the New Jerusalem as a world of abundance and equality in which "each man shall sit under his vine and fig tree," "and none shall make him afraid." Washington took the passage as a fitting symbol for the republican "paradise" of America, where gentleman farmer and small producer alike could rest secure in his property (and prosperity).[10]

The coming of the Industrial Revolution, which heightened inequities between owners and workers, unsettled this theological and economic orthodoxy. No one saw the radically altered nature of the American theological landscape more clearly than the Unitarian pastor and Marxist *avant la lettre*, Orestes Brownson. As early as 1840,

Brownson limned the coming battle between "wealth and labor," lambasting the emerging factory system as the antithesis of a Christian order of things. Brownson called on true Christians to recognize the hopeless position of a laboring class who "own none of the funds of production, neither houses, nor shops, nor lands, nor implements of labor, being therefore solely dependent on their hands," and with no chance of accumulating capital.[11]

In denying the worker access to capital, Brownson claimed, the wage system stunted his spiritual growth as well, denying him "that free scope . . . to unfold himself in all beauty and power, and to grow up into the stature of a perfect man in Christ Jesus." Brownson insisted that in the new context of modern capitalism, it was not individual but systemic faults that were the root of sin: "No man can be a Christian who does not refrain from all practices by which the rich grow richer and the poor poorer, and who does not do all in his power to elevate the laboring classes, so that one man shall not be doomed to toil while another enjoys the fruits." In a justly ordered society, Brownson insisted, "each man shall be free and independent, sitting under 'his own vine and fig tree with none to molest or to make afraid.'"[12]

The communitarian critique of competitive free-market capitalism would not win the day, however. Mainstream antebellum republican thought eschewed any whiff of class conflict, deriding it as a "European import irrelevant to a society of 'self-made men.'"[13] "Free labor" republicanism insisted that, in a country that was as open and afforded as much mobility as the United States, it was still possible for a man to jump from the working class to the owning class. Anyone with a little pluck, diligence, and an eye for the main chance could succeed; as Abraham Lincoln once famously said, if a man failed to make it into the entrepreneurial class, "It is not the fault of the system . . . but because of either a dependent nature which prefers it, or improvidence, folly, or singular misfortune." The inability to advance economically was an individual failure, not a social one.[14]

This economic bootstrap narrative, backed by a stern Protestant work ethic, was an article of faith in Jean's household as she was growing up. Of Scotch-Irish Presbyterian stock, Robert Wade was a deeply religious man, trained as a child to hold a "reverential respect" for the village pastor. Whenever his mother spotted the minister coming down the country road past their house, she would immediately send Robert out to dispatch a chicken in the backyard. Before the pastor's "horse was unhitched and in the stable, the chicken was . . . boiling in a pot."[15] As an adult Robert was a church elder and a member of the Brothers of the Presbytery; on the side, he dabbled in biblical commentary. He wrote church lectures on many themes, but devoted the most extended of these to the topic closest his heart: the relationship between faith and economic prosperity.

Robert Wade's meditations are as clear an expression of the Protestant prosperity gospel as one might hope to find in the archives of a provincial nineteenth-century businessman. In one speech titled "Our Duty to the Poor," Robert cited scriptural evidence to argue that Christ took the side of the poor, not as against the rich but to help the poor to help themselves. For, Robert specified, the causes of poverty were to be sought nowhere other than in the character of the poor man himself. "What is property?" he asked. "It is the product of intelligent skill, of thought, applied to material substance. All property is raw material that has been shaped to uses by intelligent skill." "When intelligence is low," he reasoned, "the power of producing property is low." It stands to reason, then, that the ignorant will always be tools in the industrial machinery, and the intelligent will be "the master workmen and capitalists." In addition to ignorance, "the appetites and passions" of men were equally responsible for poverty. Those who blamed the government, the power of the trusts, or insufficient capital for their own lack of prosperity needed to turn inward, for "it is the demon of laziness . . . , drunkenness, gluttony, and wastefulness" that truly explains their want of fortune.[16]

The poor, then, needed "moral and intellectual culture," not alms; a hand up, not a hand out. The Gospel was "a new power that is kindled under men that will lift them from ignorance and degradation and passion into a higher realm," he asserted, and he who knew not the word of God was "poor indeed." In preaching to the poor, Christ taught them "how to develop their outward condition by developing their inward forces." By telling the poor that, as sons of God, they held the power within themselves to "grow . . . into the likeness of [their] father," Christ was "preaching prosperity to them."

In true Puritan fashion, Robert scoffed at those who suggested that the coming Kingdom of God would be a world of leisure. The "vine and fig tree" camp should be taken with a grain of salt. "It was not to bring in a golden period of fruitfulness when men would not be required to work, that men should lie down on their backs under the trees, and that the boughs should bend over and drop fruit into their mouths," that Christ came to earth, he explained. "No such conception of equality and abundance entered into the mind of the Creator."

In a Sunday school lecture, Robert read a passage from Numbers where the Israelites, delivered out of Egypt, are still wandering in the desert. (He paused in his narration to make the odd comment that the golden tabernacle housing the ark of the covenant likely cost "a million dollars.") Moses dispatches twelve spies to travel to Canaan and bring back a report on the land and its inhabitants. Joshua and Caleb alone among the spies have enough faith in God's blessing to recommend they take it by force: "If the LORD delight in us, then He will bring us into this land, and give it unto us—a land which floweth with milk and honey" (Numbers 14:8).[17]

Robert highlighted Joshua and Caleb as models of Christian inspiration and the fighting spirit Christian soldiers must adopt to make progress in the world. He closed out the rousing lecture by drawing an analogy between the Israelites poised to take the Promised Land and America: "Dear friends we stand tonight very much in the same situation as the Children of Israel did when they stood on the border of the land of Canaan. A world of opportunity lies before us, the richness of which has never been equaled in the history of the world." And at the last minute, this triumphant taking swerved into a triumphant business deal: "Talk about inspiration," he mused. "We businessmen subscribe for a little magazine called 'Inspiration,' but if you will take the Bible and study the life of the young man Joshua, . . . you will get more inspiration to the square inch than you can get from a square yard of such a magazine." And just to be clear on the link between the hand of grace and material profit, Robert added: "If you study [the story of Joshua] from a mere business point of view it will be worth hundreds of dollars to you."[18] Outward success was a direct reflection of how profitably one had turned to account the "inward forces" and the "new power" that the Gospel has kindled in the souls of men. Profit, Robert knew, was a sign of providential grace.

By the end of the nineteenth century, the republican vision of America as a nation of small independent producers and farmers was beginning to strain credibility. The emergence of a permanent industrial working class flew in the face of America's prized image of itself as a classless society. Equally worrisome, the rise of the big corporate trusts threatened America's founding republican commitment to keeping economic and political power broken up and broadly diffused. During the merger movement of the 1880s and '90s, giant combinations in industry and finance such as Rockefeller's Standard Oil and J. P. Morgan's banking empire emerged as the largest consolidated units of capital and power in the country, making even state governments appear puny by comparison. There arose a groundswell of revolt against this new form of aggregate capital that looked poised to do away with the earlier model of Yankee individualism and free enterprise. From many quarters people looked to the federal government to bust the trusts, to break up or regulate this sinister new form of "collectivism."[19]

Still, many saw the breathtaking changes brought by large-scale industrial capitalism as heralding a utopian future of better living for all. The magic of mass production and speedy distribution via the nation's ever-expanding railways and canals seemed to confirm that a New Jerusalem, a land of peace and plenty not unlike Washington's fig-tree idyll, was still a live possibility. Of course, America had always been imagined as a land of abundance (when it wasn't imagined as a wilderness).[20] In the 1605 play *Eastward Ho!*, a character rhapsodizes of Virginia: "Why, man, all their dripping pans are pure gold, . . . and for rubies and diamonds they go forth on holidays and gather 'em by the seashore to hang on their children's coats."[21] With the rise of industrial production and modern modes of transport, this abundance—now in the more prosaic form of cheap, mass-produced consumer goods—suddenly seemed as if it might be within everyone's grasp, a universal bounty heretofore only glimpsed in myth and fable.[22]

No one was a more tireless early spokesperson for the power of corporate capitalism to spread the blessings of abundance than the economist Simon Patten, who was named to the faculty of the University of Pennsylvania's fledgling Wharton School of Business in 1887. In 1907, Patten argued that the developed world, having definitively passed from a "scarcity economy" into a "pleasure or surplus economy," could now go about planning and rationalizing the "equitable distribution of [our] surplus."[23] Corporate capitalism, he said, was key to these distribution efforts. Patten conceded that businessmen of the past had been "isolated" individuals whose "primitive," scarcity-driven instincts led them to pursue their own narrow self-interest. But the shift to an abundance economy and the resulting corporate merger movement, whereby bigger combinations of capital facilitated the efficient flow of goods, had changed all that. By inducing businessmen to take the "large view," corporations incentivized cooperation rather than selfish striving. "The growth of large-scale capitalism," Patten determined, "has resulted in the elimination of the unsocial capitalists."[24]

Patten's rose-colored vision of corporate capitalism as the royal road to more equitable distribution of the blessings of abundance found a ready audience, particularly among Protestant clergy and Progressive intellectuals. On the one hand, liberal Protestant leaders or "Social Gospel" advocates in the first decades of the new century were sympathetic to Orestes Brownson's prescient account of the ravages of unregulated capitalism. In his 1912 book *Christianizing the Social Order*, Protestant minister Walter Rauschenbush points out that thinking of salvation and Christian duty in individualist terms was the product of particular historical circumstances that, in the age of corporate capital, no longer exist. "The Golden Rule is not really adequate" for the needs of modern society, he argues. "It is indeed love we want, but it is socialized love." Political and social equality and freedom mean very little, he suggests, without economic equality.[25] Yet the Protestant establishment stopped short of calling for an overhaul of the capitalist system and the privileged legal and economic status it granted corporations. Instead, they looked hopefully toward corporations as allies, not antagonists, in the "progressive" quest for abundance. Corporations would help engineer the coming Kingdom of God where all would enjoy the fruits of modern productivity and, at long last, the lion would lie down with the lamb.[26]

In this, they echoed leading Progressive intellectuals and journalists. Walter Lippmann, Herbert Croly, and economist-cum-political commentator Walter Weyl, typified a strand within turn-of-the-century liberal thought popularizing the idea that standardized national consumption would raise living standards across the board and weave together an increasingly fractured population. In his widely read 1912 book *The New Democracy*, Weyl asserted cheerfully not only that expanding abundance was key to eradicating poverty in America, but that it would bring with it a new and higher national morality: "Democracy means material goods and the moral goods based thereon."[27] Like Patten, Weyl looked to corporations as good-faith partners in the communal pursuit of prosperity, further strengthening "big" business's reputation as steward of the public trust.[28]

The emerging class of corporate magnates were quick to endorse this benevolent, managerial spin on their core mission. As Roland Marchand has argued, corporations from the 1880s through the 1920s took painstaking efforts to craft their public images as responsible, stable, progressive "institutions" on a par with the church and state. Procorporate sentiment helped produce the cultural ideal of the "business-statesman," a leader whose hand in directing the economy was every bit as crucial as the hand of the politician.[29] Adman Elmo Calkins, in his 1926 book *Business the Civilizer*, was eager to confirm that business had left behind its mercenary, antisocial origins and had gained a Progressive conscience. He attributed the uptick in the overall corporate conscience to the high "character of the men who have gone into [business]" since the turn of the century, most of whom are "graduates of the colleges and universities." While at an earlier time this elite would have entered the learned professions, Calkins argues that "such men now realize that business is the true field of high adventure . . . [and] have taken their brains and their ideals" into it—with uplifting results. "The large point of view, good will, fair play, welfare work, are all results of a higher code of business ethics as surely as they are the source of greater profits." Ethics and profits were, far from being contradictory principles, partners in bringing about the Good Society.[30]

Such disparate stakeholders, from captains of industry to Protestant clergy to Progressive journalists, were united in their almost worshipful trust in efficiency as the key to progress, both moral and material. By the end of the nineteenth century, the thermodynamic concept of "mechanical efficiency," the drive to maximize the energy input-output ratio of a machine, had blended into the idea of commercial efficiency, or the drive to maximize return on investment. The businessman and the engineer could now tinker with both dollars and energy to ensure maximum productivity. Mechanical and commercial efficiency were accepted as good in and of themselves, "progressive" tools in the forward march of civilization. By osmosis, this cheerful faith began to bleed into the social sciences and even theology. Society was imagined as a well-oiled, frictionless mechanism, and "social efficiency" extolled as the ultimate product of a well-tuned industrial, commercial, and spiritual system.[31]

Yet the very looseness of these "cooperative" corporate catchphrases meant they could signify a wide range of things to a wide range of people. "Cooperation" could refer to anything from a genial but unenforced spirit of "give and take" between managers and employees, to actual ownership and control of the means of production by the workers. Similarly, industrialists and businessmen could claim that they were providing high-quality "service" to their customers by bringing the best products to market at the lowest possible cost. The ambiguity of these terms would provide cover as corporations continued exploitative practices under the guise of benevolent "teamwork" and wealth creation for all.[32] A naïve liberal faith in this new "harmony of interests" managerial state helped hammer the final nail in the coffin of more socialized visions of how labor and capital might relate.

Federal legislation enacted between 1901 and 1921 under the presidencies of Theodore Roosevelt, William Howard Taft, and Woodrow Wilson did work to pose a critical counterweight of sorts to the concentrated power of the trusts. The Sherman Antitrust Act of 1890, followed by the Clayton Antitrust Act and the formation of the Federal Trade Commission in 1914, sought to blunt the outsized economic and political power of combined capital. But ultimately, despite their passionate rhetoric, these administrations, too, were committed to maintaining a system judged too big to fail. And they worked, accordingly, as much to accommodate corporate capital as to keep it in check.[33]

As joint owners of the Pennsylvania Business College in Lancaster, Robert Wade and his brothers cannily navigated America's changing work ecology. As the demand for stenographers and typists grew, so did the demand for easily accessible and affordable training. In 1885, the number of students enrolled nationally in commercial education courses was roughly 47,000; by 1900, that number had nearly doubled to 81,000 students.[34] The Pennsylvania Business College offered a variety of on-site and correspondence courses. Typewriting and stenography were popular, as was the comprehensive "Commercial Course" centered on accounting and bookkeeping, with additional training in business writing, business law, spelling, arithmetic and rapid calculation. Graduates, the Wade brothers promised, went on to work in the offices of "all the great Railroads and Transportation Companies, Federal and State Governments, Banks, Manufacturing Companies, Trading Companies, Insurance, Lumber and Mining Companies, Commission Houses, and a lot of other business firms too numerous to mention."[35]

The college's catalogs were a model for what would form the heart of procorporate rhetoric for at least another half century, aligning the corporation with a vague commitment to national "teamwork" or, in its overtly evangelical forms, "brotherhood," while simultaneously underscoring business's role as the purveyor of higher living standards. On the ennobling qualities of business pursuits, the Wades quoted Andrew Carnegie, who once pronounced that the modern businessman acts not merely in self-interest—"the dividend which [he] seeks today is not alone in dollars"—but in pursuit of moral development, providing "abundant room for the exercise of man's highest power, and of every good quality in human nature." The modern businessman earns, in addition to mere dollars, the satisfaction of knowing he is helping to carry civilization and human happiness ever forward.[36]

Predictably, the college's voluminous promotional and descriptive literature reflect the Wade brothers' conviction that theological and economic striving worked hand in hand. Their pamphlets and brochures are peppered with appeals to prospective students not to let their hidden potential lie dormant, not to miss the opportunities for profit and advancement Providence places in their paths. In 1909, one pamphlet throws down the gauntlet to public school teachers to "increase your educational attainments and thereby *double your earning power.*" Teaching is fine, J. M. Wade declares, if all you want is a reliable paycheck—but ambitious folks yearn for more. While "our salvation is our work," he acknowledges, we are obligated to select work that allows us to develop our God-given potential. "If we want to come up to the full measure of our possibilities," he suggests, "we must select work that is educative, that offers progression, that will develop as well as compensate us."[37] By investing in business and stenography training, he says, students will profit both materially and spiritually. Failing to invest in one's spiritual and material betterment when the opportunity presents itself is not only foolish, it is also sinful.[38]

The college's pamphlets are generously sprinkled with upbeat jingles and quotes reminding readers to seize their chance or lose it forever. The incipit to one pamphlet is an unattributed ditty entitled "Opportunity": "'Tis a long, weary road to the bye and bye,/and a 'sometime' that seldom arrives;/Why not take the pathway that leads thro' today,/Make each day the 'now' of our lives?" "Go forth into the future and with a stout heart and purpose prepare for the next deal," another maxim counsels. "You can be defeated only by yourself."[39]

Robert Wade was not the only businessman of the Gilded Age to associate Gospel-fueled power and profit. The 1880s and '90s witnessed an explosion of Jesus biographies, not a few of which echoed the luck-and-pluck, rags-to-riches narratives that saturated dime store fiction of the same period. Eager to shed the effeminate, long-faced Jesus of the Victorians, biographers repurposed the Savior as a muscled, can-do man of action. The Reverend T. Dewitt Talmadge, after a rugged tour of the Holy Land, composed a 600-page life of a relatable Jesus, a Jesus that men could turn to for quick and easy advice amid the hustle and bustle of modern economic life. Talmadge undertook this labor at the suggestion of a fellow passenger on his steamer bound for the Orient who encouraged him to "write a life of Christ which a businessman . . . may profitably take up and in the few minutes before [he leaves for work] and after he returns, read in snatches and understand." That the title of Talmadge's biography, *From Manger to Throne*, could almost double as the title for a Horatio Alger novel is no accident.[40]

The connection between "Gospel power" and business profit was popularized in the first decades of the twentieth century not only by clergy but by businessmen as well. Among the most popular of these authors was Orison Swett Marden, self-made man and author of such inspirational titles as *The Masterful Personality* and *Prosperity—How to Attract It*. Marden was an advocate of Christian "New Thought," close cousin to Christian Science, and shared the latter's belief that the path to health and wealth lay simply in "right thinking." Only by exiling mental doubt and "encouraging our friend thoughts," Marden urges, do we "unlock the door to the great within [ourselves]" and reach our full potential.[41] Marden's idiom is tinged with a proto–New Age pantheism, larded with exhortations to his readers to "cultivate . . . the consciousness of your oneness with the Source of all prosperity, the Source of the All-Supply." Yet his theology is the direct, if heterodox, descendant of the Puritan doctrine of grace as "inner power" that man has a duty to develop to its fullest. One of the greatest tragedies in life, Marden sermonizes, is to fail to "answer for the talent [the Almighty] has given us." If we listen for His voice in our soul, he suggests, and "do our best in whatever situation we are placed," then "new power will be developed with every forward step we take."[42]

As a devout Presbyterian, Robert Wade probably thought Marden's appeals to God as the All-Supply sounded pagan. But as businessman, he recognized a fellow traveler, and his college pamphlets accordingly quote liberally from Marden's inspirational magazine, *Success*. The Wade brothers borrow Marden's swooning prose to assure their prospective students that a business education is both an insurance policy against poverty and a chance to take part in the ever-expanding, "dazzling" commercial life of the nation, "a story that reads like a romance."[43]

Yet for all their seize-the-day wisdom and tantalizing descriptions of the businessman as swashbuckling adventurer, the Wade brothers' pamphlets are careful to caution prospective students that the economic conditions that made possible a Rockefeller or a Carnegie no longer exist in America. One catalog explains the changed business ecology and the managerial revolution of the new century, whereby the small businesses of yore are swallowed up by national corporations, "owned, not by those operating them, but by people unskilled in the particular lines required to manage them." As a result, "the opportunity now to persons of small capital, or none at all, is in a salaried position" in the ranks of that "corps of trained, salaried men, most of whom do not own a single share of the[ir] company's stock."[44] The promotional literature doesn't call attention to the fact that a white-collar worker in a salaried position may toil away an entire lifetime without ever acquiring any capital or economic independence to speak of—the very promise that, for centuries, had guaranteed the dignity of (white) labor.

This failure to recognize that the social and economic realities of corporate capitalism were incompatible with the rugged individualism of the earlier proprietary-competitive capitalism was endemic in early twentieth-century America. The relations between labor and capital, and indeed the very nature of capitalism and property itself, had radically shifted since the end of the Civil War. Yet American culture lagged, continuing to romanticize the ideals of individual freedom, independence, and initiative as keys to economic success. The Wade brothers' promotional pamphlets embody this disconnect with particular clarity.[45]

One Pennsylvania Business College graduate who heeded the Wade brothers' challenge to maximize return on her God-given talents was Helen Jean Wade. After completing her education, she briefly took up a position as a teacher there. But Jean knew that, in the words of her alma mater, this job was little more than a kind of idleness, and that she could better employ her expansive energies elsewhere. In 1920, at the age of sixteen, she was hired as secretary to the head of the Advertising Department at Armstrong Cork, a local flooring manufacturer. She had eagerly answered when opportunity knocked. Now, heeding her father's advice, she was poised to step forth into the future and "prepare for the next deal."

Among the most consistently kept of Jean's records are her personal finance ledgers. The earliest of these notebooks dates from 1922, when she was eighteen; the whole series—through 1929—offers a fascinating glimpse into the day-to-day life of a young unmarried white-collar woman in the American provinces. Jean recorded her expenses under a number of broad categories: "Home"; "Gifts/Charity"; "Luxuries"; "Necessities." Every month in the "Home" column she has penned in a neat "45," presumably what she contributed to the family coffers for food and lodging. That was a sizable portion of her monthly salary, which in 1923 was $139. She kept herself neat and tidy, presentable at work, as regular entries in the "Necessities" column indicate: "Hair," "Gloves," "Hat," "Dresses Cleaning" and, once, a fifteen-cent shoe shine. Scattered here and there are the few "Luxuries" she allowed herself: a thirty-cent ice cream sundae; a twenty-cent pair of earrings; a one-time splurge for a "Book on Bridge," $1.50.[46]

But by far the most populated column, month after month, is that for "Gifts/Charity." In addition to weekly or biweekly generic contributions to "Church," "Sunday School," "Missions," "Near East," and "Red Cross," every month brought its own allotment of special charitable cases that read like something out of a Dickens novel. "Deaf Mute Home" ($5); "Tuberculosis Society" and "Map for Sunday School Teaching" ($1 each); "Poor Family" ($10); and "Leper Fund" ($2.50). In spite of her father's rather stern attitude toward the poor and ill fortuned, the young Jean devoted a large portion of her free time—and an even larger portion of her monthly paycheck—to help balance the favors so unequally parceled out at birth by an inscrutable God.

The American theological landscape at the turn of the century thus presented two intertwined, often contradictory narratives about the relationship between economic abundance and Christian faith. On the one hand, profit could be tied to the "progress"—and prosperity—of the solitary pilgrim making his way toward God. On the other hand, profit could be the "progressive" vehicle by which the collective industrial mechanism distributed its blessings to all. Jean's upbringing, both professionally and religiously, placed her squarely at a crossroads. If Robert Mifflin Wade's economic theories retained a Calvinist flavor, exalting the solitary Christian soldier-businessman whose treasures were a sign of individual grace, they could also be flipped, gesturing toward the expansive economic vision of the Progressives. Jean would blend the two visions in her lifelong efforts to influence women's consumption: the masculine field of individual capitalist Christian striving was the sacred vehicle that would bring about a Peaceable Kingdom of maternal plenty for all.

2

The Angel in the Marketplace

Proficient in shorthand, typewriting, and bookkeeping, Jean flourished in her new position at Armstrong Cork. A 1927 photograph of a board-appointed Policy Committee shows Jean the lone woman amid seven tweedy executives. The caption explains her inclusion: "Miss Jean Wade, Secretary of the Committee." Her dark hair pulled back into a neat, tight bun, her hands folded in her lap, she stares directly into the camera with her habitual half-smile.[1]

While her fluency in typing and shorthand undoubtedly made her an excellent note taker, her work for the company went well beyond taking dictation. She edited the company's house organ, the *Armstrong Jobber*, and wrote retail copy and catalogs. Between 1926 and 1929, she wrote a number of publicity articles on linoleum for trade and other journals, among them "A Decorator Plans a Young Girl's Room" for *Young Ladies' Journal* and "A Background of Beauty Helps to Sell Hats" for the *Dixie Milliner*.[2] Jean was able to bridge the gap between the masculine world of manufacturing and the feminine world of interiors, offering a "woman's point of view" to help Armstrong market to female consumers. One issue of the *Armstrong Jobber* featured an interview and photo spread with J. W. McCoy, executive at a home furnishings company, who had recently built a house and floored it entirely in linoleum. "These floors are practical as well as beautiful," the article boasted, and "Mrs. McCoy finds them very easy to clean."[3] As Jean once quipped, her work at Armstrong turned her into a combined stenographer, typist, bookkeeper, copy writer, and editor who had, in fact, "done practically everything in an office but run an elevator."

Culturally, Jean's position as a young professional working woman selling the perks of domesticity was a tricky one to inhabit in the 1920s. On the one hand, postwar working women, with the wind of the Nineteenth Amendment in their sails, were poised to break aging Victorian stereotypes about what "proper" femininity looked like. Jean's almost ferocious ambition, as she threw herself into her corporate position, aligned her with feminist calls for woman's right to have a place in the public, as well as in the domestic, sphere. On

FIGURE 4. A 1932 BBDO advertisement for Armstrong Linoleum. As a copywriter for the trade and industrial department, Jean may have had a hand in developing it.

the other hand, Jean's prodigious professional energy was directed almost entirely at convincing consumers of the sweetness of home and hearth—the very feminine values her role as a white-collar woman professional threw open to question.

As it turns out, this contradiction was neither new nor particularly surprising. As the entire work ecology of the United States shifted in the late nineteenth century to wage labor, including salaried white-collar positions, more and more women were drawn out of the private sphere of the home into the public domain of the office. Jean's decision to make domesticity her profession was one of a wide range of balancing acts that early twentieth-century Americans, women in particular, performed in dealing with the new economic and social configurations of corporate capitalism.

Jean Wade was by no means the first woman to figure out that preaching the virtues of homemaking to middle-class Americans could be a viable career path. Catharine Beecher and her sister Harriet Beecher Stowe, of *Uncle Tom's Cabin* fame, are commonly credited as the first nationally recognized practitioners of the domesticity genre, with the 1869 publication of their advice manual, *The American Woman's Home, or, Principles of Domestic Science; Being a Guide to the Formation and Maintenance of Economical, Healthful, and Christian Homes.* There, the Beecher sisters set themselves the task of explaining why the home—and the woman presiding over it—was the moral center of American life. Unlike men, who "toil for wealth, honor and power, . . . mainly for earthly, selfish advantages," a woman was the "chief minister" of the Christian home, "the aptest earthly illustration of the kingdom of heaven." Through her self-sacrificing labor and patient instruction, the wife-mother taught "all under her care to lay up treasures, not on earth, but in heaven."[4]

Many Americans were appalled by the ethos of unregulated capitalism that the Industrial Revolution unleashed in the 1840s and '50s. The brutal market logic dictated that to succeed a man had to be willing to ride roughshod over his neighbors. The domestic sphere, where the old communal values of selfless sacrifice and Christian charity still held sway, emerged as a counterweight. Men could labor in the sweat of their brow in the public sphere; women would henceforth do the moral housekeeping of instilling Christian virtue in the home's inhabitants and providing a private haven from the ravages of a market economy. Morality was conveniently compartmentalized: the new economy might eat workers up and spit them out; it might transform face-to-face personal relationships into impersonal ones defined by cash; but the home provided a place to hide from industrial capitalism's ugliness: to repent for hurts inflicted or find compensation for hurts incurred.[5]

Charging that America's strength as a democracy depended on the proper moral upbringing of its citizens, the Beecher sisters were appalled that women were not adequately trained to take up their "natural" professions and that domestic labor was so universally degraded. Feminine "apprenticeship" in housekeeping within the confines of the home was unsystematic at best, riddled with error and inefficiency at worst. The principles of domestic science, like those of engineering or law or any other masculine profession, needed to be codified and taught in public educational institutions. Catharine herself had founded the Hartford Female Seminary in 1823, where she had insisted that traditional male subjects such as Latin and geometry be taught alongside what she called "domestic economy."

Certainly, at the dawn of civilization, women had been tasked merely with clothing and feeding their families, tending to the base wants of the body and no more. But "as society gradually shakes off the remnants of barbarism," the woman's sphere of influence demanded a level of intelligence and strength no less than that of male professions. "No statesman, at the head of a nation's affairs, had more frequent calls for wisdom, firmness, tact, discrimination, prudence, and versatility of talent" than the housewife, they asserted.[6] *The American Woman's Home*, accordingly, sought to educate its women readers: it dispensed scientific lessons on everything from lung anatomy and the importance of well-ventilated kitchens, to a treatise on the chemistry of yeast and tips on efficient dish washing. The Beecher sisters never disputed that woman's proper place was in the home. Rather, they argued that female domestic labor deserved to be treated as a profession in its own right alongside male occupations.

If the Beechers sought to maintain separate spheres while professionalizing the domestic duties that naturally fell to the second sex, other women at the turn of the century were moved to carve out more public roles for themselves. Newly liberated by industrialization and mechanization from the more time-consuming tasks of household labor, middle-class American women joined clubs by the thousands. While many of these clubs were literary and social in character, others were overtly reform-minded and sought to put women's natural "housekeeping" skills to work in the larger community. Social work, as a kind of feminine caretaking writ large, was largely eschewed by men, and women found in it a crack through which they might slip into the public sphere.[7]

The settlement house movement provided educated, middle-class white women in search of a career the perfect chance to engage in meaningful public work while still heeding the Beecher sisters' call to "care for God's children." Jane Addams's Hull House, founded in Chicago in 1898, demonstrated that middle-class women could join forces to help ameliorate the crushing burden of poverty among workers living in congested, unsanitary tenement housing. While social workers initially billed their work as a moral duty of private citizens, they soon recognized the structural problems that kept people mired in poverty demanded public and political, rather than piecemeal and private, solutions. The result was women lobbying for federal regulation of business as well as the creation of social safety nets, in a process that has been called "the domestication of the state."[8] Indeed, women activists were key to pushing the nascent Progressive movement, otherwise led by an all-male cadre of statesmen, businessmen, and public intellectuals, to seek publicly mandated solutions to what had been seen as private problems: poverty, crime, malnutrition.

By 1920, women had shown themselves a force to be reckoned with in the public sphere.[9] Yet the ideal of domesticity and the essentially private function of the "real" woman was not so quick to surrender.

An heir in spirit to the Beechers, Christine Frederick, a housewife and self-styled "home efficiency expert," argued for the primacy of woman's domestic destiny but agreed that homemaking could be "professionalized." In her 1912 manual, *The New Housekeeping: Efficiency Studies in Home Management,* Frederick explained that the drudgery of childcare and housekeeping had left her hopeless until she figured out that the very same "industrial efficiency" measures currently being applied to factory and office production could, with profit, be imported into the home. "For once I found a use for some of the college training I had despaired of ever putting into practice," Frederick wrote. Doing so not only streamlined housework to leave her more leisure time to devote to mental pursuits, but was in itself of "keen mental interest"—"quite the same, I am now sure," she enthused to her reader, "as the tasks of the business and industrial world which men tackle with zest and results."[10]

But perhaps most important, Frederick updated the Beechers' ideal of professionalized domesticity to fit the new economic conditions of mass production and corporate capitalism at the onset of the twentieth century. *The New Housekeeping* educated readers on the changing nature of the American economy, as it shifted its emphasis from production to consumption. Christine's husband, George Frederick, an early public relations and advertising executive, wrote a history of American business dating this shift to the first decade of the twentieth century. The rise of mass production and increasingly efficient national distribution networks pressured manufacturers to create, rather than simply meet, demand for their product: what he termed "market-mindedness" as opposed to "production-mindedness." Successful companies of this period realized that selling and advertising was no longer "a department of the business—*it was the business.*" "The top-executives of such companies had but one main task—to create and maintain demand and good will for its goods, and to provide distribution."[11]

The Beechers' detailed instructions on how to make soap or properly ventilate a kitchen thus gave way to Christine Frederick's lectures on the importance of understanding the nuts and bolts of supply and demand and product distribution. "Today, in Podunk,

Mich., or Flagstaff, Ariz., the men are wearing the same styles of collar and tie as are seen on Fifth Avenue, New York City," she observed. The fact that the "woman in Tallahassee" used the "same peanut-butter, neckwear and flatirons" as her sister in the metropole meant that now, more than ever, a woman's duty was to understand "this highly complex machinery of distribution" and to use her purchasing power to influence the quality and quantity of products on the market. If the Beechers' imagined the home as a space apart from the market, Frederick taught homemakers that their purchasing choices fed into a larger economic and social nexus; they would henceforth exercise their moral influence through their pocketbooks.[12]

Housewives, Frederick wrote, were "the great purchasing factor in modern life," and their most important duty was to educate themselves on their "proper relation . . . to the business world which makes and sells." She must thoroughly educate herself on her important role in "the drama of distribution," the complex mechanics of getting an article from the factory to the purchaser in the most efficient and cost-effective way. Only by understanding and putting her weight behind such long-term cost benefit practices as advertising, the one-price system, and competitive branding would the housewife be fulfilling her true domestic duty. Frederick patiently explained how the use of brands ultimately resulted in lower costs and greater, more reliable distribution. The homemaker, then, must understand "the point of brands and trademarks and the evil of substitution." The act of giving in to cut-rate and inferior substitutes for the brand name article, Frederick likened to a train jumping the track: "it cripples the whole distribution system," she warned, and—as if that weren't enough—"is a confession that your judgement is defective." The woman who refused to educate herself, Frederick lectured, "is driving the family and the nation into a wrong economic balance which makes panics, unhappiness, and lack of character and worth."[13]

The housewife's strict attention to her purchasing power and its effects would, in addition to ensuring better products at cheaper prices, also guarantee ethical production standards and fair labor practices. The best manufacturers, she argued, were beginning to realize that mistreating workers was inefficient; paying a living wage was the best way to guarantee good work. Women must then "insist that the goods we buy are made or manufactured under proper conditions." "The economic relation of the woman to the rest of the world," she concluded with moral urgency, "is a terribly real thing and a live responsibility."[14] Frederick's insistence that smart buying was women's moral duty, weeding out "unsociable" capitalists, was a line straight out of Simon Patten's cheerful corporate mantra. Frederick infused women's consumption with new moral weight: in their choice of soap or breakfast cereal, women were not only fulfilling their domestic duty toward their families—and modeling feminine virtue—but were contributing to the broader goal of "community housekeeping." Insofar as her purchasing power kept afloat the larger "shelter" of America's "industrial and commercial structure," to quote banking magnate V. Everitt Macy, she was doing her gendered part to keep the American ideals of life, liberty, and the pursuit of happiness alive.

For much of the early twentieth century this domesticated model of the woman consumer's exercise of "citizenship" competed with a more radical vision of how consumers might be political actors and effect change in the public sphere. In this version, women denied access to direct political power banded together to use economic leverage to demand reform from government and business.[15] Working-class Jewish immigrant housewives in New York organized rent strikes and meat boycotts throughout the first decade of the twentieth century. To their efforts were joined those of the more stolidly middle-class National Consumers League, a women's organization that sought to enforce "ethical consumption" by endorsing only products guaranteed to have been manufactured under humane working conditions.[16]

Yet whenever activist women sought systemic, public reforms under the banner of advancing "maternal" values, or actively withheld their purchasing power to hold capital to account, Frederick and others like her stood at the ready with a more ladylike alternative: similar civilizing results could be achieved, they argued, through trickle-down redistribution, leaving intact the free-market model. Frederick's privatized model of women's political activism was the domestic equivalent of what corporations attempted in negotiations with labor: to take structural, directly political critiques of capitalism off the table, to be dealt with in private, reformist negotiations between "partners."

And indeed, women consumer rights activists and social reformers during the Progressive Era and beyond were routinely labeled "unfeminine," accused of wanting to demolish the patriarchal home and the American values of industry, freedom, and private Christian virtue for which it stood. This hysterical gendering of economics and the state/private debate peaked in the wake of the Russian Revolution of 1917 and the Bolshevik rise to power in 1919, which touched off a Red Scare panic in the United States.[17] The national press reported that the Bolsheviks, after stripping citizens of private property and nationalizing industry and resources, had nationalized women as well: all unmarried women over eighteen were reportedly forced to register at a "Bureau of Free Love," where they became the communal property of lustful revolutionary men. These tales of true womanhood tragically defiled joined reports of newly emancipated Bolshevik women flooding the schoolroom, the law courts, and the government in a thoroughly unnatural, mannish power grab. The resulting gender and economic anarchy was proof positive, for many Americans, of what might happen if the traditional patriarchal authority of the private home were to be intruded on by the state.[18]

In their role as "community housekeepers," American women who sought to enlist the state on behalf of corporate capitalism's castoffs fell under suspicion of being Bolshevik infiltrators. As a result, as Kim E. Nielsen has shown, this convergence of antiradicalism and antifeminism in the 1920s "severely limited the ability of progressive women to promote social welfare legislation," including a constitutional amendment restricting child labor, a bill providing for state-funded healthcare and education for women and children, and the creation of a federal department of education.[19] The fearful specter of an army of bureaucratic "nannies"—unnatural, childless women—taking over a whole arm of the federal government to "nationalize" family life was a powerful ideological device for the forces of social conservatism—as it still is today.

Yet in the face of American culture's segregation of middle-class men and women's spheres, a growing class of border crossers were muddying the distinctions between public and private: namely, women office workers—of whom Jean was a textbook example. The great "merger movement" of the 1890s, with corporate behemoths swallowing up small firms, revolutionized the American office. The increased volume of business and geographic reach of national and international markets required more accurate recordkeeping and more voluminous correspondence—as Jean's father and uncles, in founding the Pennsylvania Business School, had astutely realized. Where a small firm had traditionally employed a handful of office workers—clerks, copyists, a bookkeeper—the sheer size of the corporation required its division into separate departments, along with the labyrinthine subdivision of clerical labor within each of those.

US Treasurer General Francis Elias Spinner is commonly credited with hiring the first systematic corps of female clerks in response to a severe shortage of male workers during the Civil War. This early experiment in hiring women for government office work was deemed a success—not least because women could be paid a fraction of the wages demanded by their male counterparts—and thus opened the door to continued hiring of women by postwar businesses. The majority of women were hired for mechanical and routinized labor, including the job of copyist or scrivener.[20] The fact that women dominated light manufacturing, such as textiles and papermaking, paved the way for their integration into the modern office behind the new white-collar "machinery" of telephones, typewriters, and adding machines. In 1880, women accounted for 40 percent of all stenographers and typewriters in the United States; by 1930, they had driven their male counterparts almost entirely out of the market, cornering 95 percent of these positions.[21]

From the beginning, these working girls presented an ideological puzzle. Opponents of their presence in the workplace worried, predictably, that middle-class women's moral purity would be sullied by contact with the masculine sphere of rough-and-tumble commerce. On the flipside, advocates for women workers argued that their angelic virtue would provide an elevating influence in the office.

It was by developing this latter image, in which the female office worker combined the domestic roles of helpmeet, moral muse, and efficient administrator to a male employer, that professional women gained legitimacy.[22]

The more low-skill, mechanical jobs, such as typist and stenographer, remained tainted by working-class bias; these women office workers were stereotyped as loud, frivolous, flighty, and overly sexualized. Even more damaging, they were suspected of being "gold diggers," using office work as a ploy to snag a middle-class husband. The higher position open to women was that of secretary or private stenographer working directly under the supervision of a male executive. Often jokingly referred to as "gal Fridays" or "office wives," these jobs were also sexualized but genteelly so; they were coded solidly middle class. The role of private secretary provided women the opportunity to bend gender stereotypes to their advantage: competence and efficiency made a secretary a helpmeet; middle-class charm and grace made a secretary a pseudocompanion or "wife" rather than a purely sexualized underling.

To succeed in a white-collar job, a woman in the first decades of the twentieth century thus had to perform a very specific kind of femininity.[23] By entering the workplace, women were suspected of denaturing themselves and required to prove that they could still be reliably classified as women rather than ersatz men. At the same time, if they hewed too closely to domestic feminine codes of "parlor etiquette," they risked confirming the suspicion that the parlor was, precisely, where they belonged. Women clerical workers may have moved into the public space of the office. But they did so as purveyors of the civilized feminine virtue characteristic of the private home.

Jean was able to perform the role of feminine white-collar worker to perfection. When she was hired by Armstrong Cork in 1920 she bypassed the "steno pool" altogether and jumped immediately into the position of private secretary. This gave her not only the "borrowed prestige" of being the wingwoman to a male executive but an opportunity to showcase her talents beyond mere mechanical prowess as a typist. And yet, Jean managed never to offend or to come off as unladylike or "forward." Indeed, in her ruminations on women's success in the office, she was quick to peg aggressiveness as the deadliest of office girl sins. Once she had passed into the executive seat herself, Jean noted the qualities she looked for in a female job candidate: personal cleanliness ("I like her to look fresh"), "friendliness," and deference. "The girl I like comes in quietly, smiles pleasantly, . . . [and] sits where I tell her," she specified. She abhorred what she called those "very aggressive females" who presumptuously pull up a chair next to her, "snuggling in" rather than keeping a respectful distance.[24] Jean no doubt modeled the neat, efficient, respectful feminine ideal in the ten years she worked at Armstrong Cork.

Jean gave a lot of thought to women in business. At the height of her career, she was continually invited to give speeches to women's professional organizations and clubs. For the magazine *New York Woman,* she once proposed writing a weekly advice column for young businesswomen called "To Girls on the Way Up," pitched as "a combined Emily Post–Dorothy Dix job on business problems."[25] In all of these ventures, Jean diverged very little, if at all, from the stereotypes surrounding women office workers since the 1880s and '90s. Jean liked to divide working women into three categories. "There are women who take advantage of being women," Jean suggested—who think their status as women entitled them to a little less work, a little more sympathy. These were the women who played, improperly, on the "parlor" codes of feminine weakness and male chivalry to gain an advantage in the workplace. "Luckily," she observed, in her experience this was a "small group." On the other extreme were those women who "ride the soapbox for the cause of women": who yap, yap, yap about unfair treatment and unequal pay and, unfortunately, "make themselves a good bit of a nuisance." Finally, there was that group of women who were just right: who accepted that women had their "special sphere" in business, as in life, and who were too busy "doing a good job" to waste time in calling attention to their "plight" as a minority.[26]

Jean didn't deny that gendered disparities existed, only that those working women who did "the cause of women [the most] good" would be content with the ample opportunities for pay, achievement, growth, and "spiritual satisfaction" offered by a job well done.[27] In another speech to women in the Advertising Department at Dupont, Jean told of a coworker at the end of her career who claimed that if she could give professional women one piece of cautionary advice, it would be that they "create most of their own troubles by taking themselves too darn seriously." Jean suggested going one step further and adopting the two words of counsel she had once heard a male colleague offer to women in business: "Shut up!"[28]

Yet in her rise up the corporate ladder, Jean didn't so much shut up as simply devise strategies that would feminize, and thus mute, her professional ambition. One profession that was wide open to "girls on their way up" in the 1920s was the burgeoning field of advertising. Because women held the purse strings in most American households—accounting for 96 percent of sales in dry goods, 67 percent of food stuffs, and 67 percent of automobiles[29]—getting "the woman's point of view," ad agencies reasoned, was essential to crafting effective copy. They hired accordingly. Most women were offered jobs as either copywriters, working under male account heads, or as research assistants, sent out into the "field" to collect data. While their sex secured them jobs, early women copywriters occupied an ambiguous position within the ad agency: part professional, part "visiting ethnographic subject," as one historian notes.[30] A 1927 agency ad aimed at procuring corporate clients declared that the value of "the woman in advertising" was not in her copywriting per se but in her daily chatter with the other office "girls" on such subjects as garter runs, fabric swatches for armchairs, and the proper height of kitchen sinks. This firsthand sociological data helped imbue the firm's eventual advertisements with "a thousand and one intimacies," and thus a patina of feminine authenticity.[31]

Over her career, Jean was happy to give her two cents on "the woman's point of view" and proved herself exceptionally able to read the desires of the "average housewife" and then write copy that targeted her. Yet Jean's vision of how to put her femininity to productive—and nonthreatening—professional use expanded far beyond the ethnographic. From the early years of the profession, advertising agencies sought to craft an image of themselves as key partners in the great drama of modernization and the quest to create a society of abundance. By matching producers with consumers, they argued, advertising helped rationalize the market and made it more efficient—bringing lower prices and better living to all.[32] This was consonant with the progressive image that most corporations were eager to establish for themselves in the early years of the twentieth century. The "service ideal" became a corporate mantra in this era, as industries claimed they were benevolent institutions engaged in equal partnership with consumers to bring about ever higher standards of living.[33]

And "service" was something a professional woman could claim to do without stepping on any masculine toes. As Simone Weil Davis has argued, the advertising industry in the 1920s solidified its professional reputation by instituting a kind of ideological division of labor between the masculine and feminine branches of the business, an arrangement Jean took advantage of. In garnering its investors profits and return, advertisers spoke the masculine language of cold hard cash but wrapped it in the more socially acceptable feminine promise of social harmony and plenty.[34] Private profit and public service were not only compatible, but the pursuit of the first was, in fact, the surest means of achieving the second. Jean's religious upbringing, which stressed the inseparability of material and moral profit, made her ideally suited to this gendered role.

The idea that a woman could exercise public power through her private purchasing decisions was one to which Jean pledged unflagging faith; she would recur to it again and again throughout her career, whether in presentations to clients, in-house memos, or motivational speeches. In her speech at Dupont, Jean stressed that advertising was not about the vulgar business of getting people to spend money. Rather, it was about helping them to save money by making distribution more efficient and keeping costs down, a prime example of American democracy in action: "In that greater function advertising renders a public service that makes it a closely-knit part of our entire economic system," she assured them. "So that makes your job and mine important—they are part of the American pattern of living, a demonstration of free people making a democracy work."[35] The inseparability of material and moral "goods," a founding article of early twentieth-century Progressive faith, would gain increasing traction in the decades to follow, a ready-to-hand alibi whenever the corporate order's good faith was called into question.

Indeed, Jean actually took exception to the idea that advertisers needed to prove their status as "good citizens" *other* than by providing the basic service of rationalizing the market and keeping America's economic engines well oiled. In a memo to agency heads Charlie Brower and Ben Duffy in 1948, Jean complained about the recent vogue in advertising for championing specific "social causes." "Advertising that speeds the distribution of basic products from manufacturer to consumer *is* exerting a social force in a healthy and responsible way," she insisted. "I resent the implication that the only way to prepare advertising worthy of an award is to prepare so-called 'unselfish' advertising on something someone has decided is a social cause."[36] Jean saw value enough in that greater economic efficiency of the (masculine) market on which all of (feminine) civilization depended.[37]

Yet even as she proved her corporate and advertising bona fides at Armstrong Cork, Jean never abandoned her conviction that a woman's greatest satisfaction in life was to be a devoted wife and mother. Her attention to maternal caretaking is evident in her account keeping. Beyond her extensive financial contributions to "community housekeeping" causes—gifts to the sick and the poor—Jean's accounts reveal a young woman scrupulous about performing the rituals of feminine caretaking within her private circle as well. "Flowers Sick," presumably flowers purchased to cheer up ailing friends and family, is a recurring expense in her account books throughout the 1920s. "Gift for Mother," "Pin for Betty Anne," "Plates—Gift for Mary," "Sunday School Gifts," offer additional glimpses into a private life devoted to pleasing others. Then, in 1927, a new name appears in the expenses column: "Willard." "Willard's Gift" is entered on December 28, 1927; in February 1928, he pops up again as "Willard—Dance."[38] This was Willard Rindlaub, a fellow Lancaster resident and engineering student. He would eventually propose to Jean, and she would jump at the offer.

Jean went on to publish an anonymous account of her courtship and marriage to Willard in *Young People's Magazine*. In "Don't Wait—Marry the Man," Jean cautioned girls not to be too choosy when looking for a mate, lest they miss out on the "enduring togetherness" that marriage builds—"gloriously, happily, contentedly, complainingly, exhaustedly"—over a lifetime. She confessed that when Willard was courting her, she worried he was not brilliant enough, rich enough, cultured enough to be a star match. But she knew her own shortcomings as well. "I was short and fat," she admitted. "I was good at a job or a speech—a complete flop at a dance or a party."[39] Willard may have been poor and socially awkward and gangly, but he was also honest and warm and dependable. Jean "[said] 'yes' quick!"—and urged her young readers to do the same, promising they will "end up oh, so deeply thankful every day for the blessed good fortune that you married the man!"

The photographs from Jean and Willard's wedding in 1930 bear out her description of him. Tall, stiff and serious, he looks uncomfortable in his suit. Jean, with her twinkling black eyes and habitual Mona Lisa smile beneath a neat white lace bonnet, comes up only to his breastbone. Immediately after their marriage, Willard took a job at Bell Telephone Laboratories in New York City. The couple bought a modest colonial-style house in West Englewood, in the New Jersey suburbs.

Armstrong Cork partnered with the Madison Avenue firm BBDO to do their advertising. Jean, as secretary to the head of Armstrong's ad department, had become the de facto point person between the two companies. Jean's boss, "impressed by her energy and ability," set her the task of "thinking up things for [BBDO] to do, new projects, new tasks, new areas of work, work, work," as a colleague later reminisced. Jean's indefatigable quest to make the advertising group "earn their commission" soon made her a familiar name in BBDO's Madison Avenue headquarters.[40] And so, when the newly wed Jean relocated to New Jersey, it was not entirely surprising that she should find an office home in the industrial and trade copywriting department at BBDO.

In 1934, Jean's first child, John, was born. Like all working mothers, Jean was faced with a choice: quit her job to take up childcare or

FIGURES 5 AND 6. Jean married Willard Rindlaub in 1930; shortly after, the couple moved to New York, where Willard took a job as an engineer at Bell Laboratories, and Jean was hired in the copywriting department of the Trade and Industrial Division at Batten Barton Durstine and Osborn (BBDO).

outsource childcare to continue with her job. Luckily for Jean, her maiden Aunt Mary—whose name is among those appearing most frequently in Jean's account notebooks—agreed to come live with them and look after the new baby, freeing Jean to pursue her profession. Four years later, Jean gave birth to a daughter, Anne. Once again,

FIGURES 5 AND 6. (*continued*)

Aunt Mary was able to stand in as stay-at-home mother. "I hadn't any large career ambitions," Jean was quick to inform an interviewer for a *Herald Tribune* profile much later when asked about how she had handled her "double life" as mother and adman. "But I liked my job and it liked me," so the arrangement with Aunt Mary suited everyone well.[41]

3

A Clean Rinse and a Fresh Start

The Magic of Soap

Jean was a regular contributor to BBDO's series of promotional pamphlets, the *Wedge*. Aimed at potential corporate clients, the columns were often written in the voice of a chummy businessman—a tone Jean excelled in mimicking. One of her columns, "The Story of Susy," was an encomium to advertising told from the point of view of an adman. On his daily subway commute, our narrator always sees a "drab little girl," "someone's office girl, probably," scuttling in and out of the train. "Susy," as he nicknames this familiar stranger, is irredeemably mousy: baggy clothes, stringy hair, "skin that tired color city skins grow." Her case appears hopeless.

But one day, something changes. Susy's skin has become "cream-smooth" and glowing; her gray eyes are suddenly visible beneath artfully applied shadow. Her hair, too, is transformed: arranged in a "soft, friendly swirl," and she had "learned, somewhere, how to make it gleam, sparkle, come alive." The transformation is not merely a matter of appearances; improved looks go hand in hand with improved life prospects. The narrator guesses that Susie must have "gotten a better job" as a result of her makeover, as evidenced by a set of spanking-new clothes that give an added "lift" to her new face. Finally, one fine morning Susy appears with a beau at her side: "I saw them coming down the steps that morning—a pair of husky brogues pacing her small, pleased feet. She was laughing up at him—he was looking down at her. From that day they rode together—alone in a noisy world," "the still gleam of a diamond on [her] hand."

This fairy-tale ending, the narrator assures us, was made possible thanks to advertising: "friendly, helpful advertising" that taught Susy "about soap, about makeup, about how to care for her hair and nails." "Miracles! Fairy Tales! Cinderella and Prince Charming," the narrator concludes with satisfaction. "Yes, there are miracles awakening, miracles of transformation, miracles of lives coming into their own all around us every day . . .—through that magic that is advertising." The piece ends with a postscript promising, with a wink, that BBDO can perform similar "makeovers" on any company's lagging sales numbers, making "business dreams come true."[1]

The origin of the "makeover" as a staple in beauty magazines is often traced to a 1936 *Mademoiselle* article, "The Made Over Girl," featuring real-life nurse and magazine reader Barbara Phillips. Phillips wrote to the editors asking for tips on how to "make the most" of her plain looks; the magazine team took their subject directly in hand and published dramatic before, during and after photos of their "Cinderella" beauty regimen: a recipe for turning plain girls into princesses. The piece was so popular that *Mademoiselle* made it a regular feature.[2]

That Jean should cast the story of advertising as a tale of miraculous metamorphoses—whether of Susies or of corporate bank accounts—is no accident. By the time Jean was writing the majority of her copy for cosmetic companies in the 1930s, the advertising industry had long established itself as playing a crucial role in the larger chain of national product production and distribution.[3] In his sweeping 1929 history of advertising from ancient Babylonia on, industry pioneer Frank Presbery waxed poetic about advertising as a progressive, rationalizing force. Properly deployed, advertising would not only evenly distribute earthly goods to the masses, but would make knowledge universally available as well. "If everybody had all the knowledge that exists and is available, and applied it, there would be very little unhappiness," Presbery concludes sunnily.[4]

But American advertising—and cosmetic advertising, in particular—traces its origins to the decidedly less-than-rational hodgepodge of science, magic, and faith that formed the culture of medicine and "wellness" in the late nineteenth century. The first efforts at national advertising were launched by patent medicine manufacturers, whose elixirs, pills, drops, and ointments promised customers miraculous physical and mental transformations. For all of its purported down-to-earth rationality, the advertising industry had deep roots in magical thinking. This was a past it would never completely leave behind: that was, in fact, integral to its cultural success. The advertiser's promise of salvation through consumption blended rationality and magic, scientific progress and dreams into a remarkably potent tonic.

"Patent" medicines—so-called because in seventeenth- and eighteenth-century England, one had to acquire a government license to peddle them—had a guaranteed place on every apothecary's shelf in colonial America. Such English imports as Daffy's Elixir, Dr. Bateman's Pectoral Drops, and a specially patented "Oyl extracted from a Flinty Rock for the Cure of Rheumatick and Scorbutick and other Cases" were stocked side by side with the druggist's more standard *materia medica*.[5]

Nineteenth-century medicine lagged notably behind other scientific fields, with the average doctor's practical knowledge barely advanced beyond the medical wisdom of the second-century Greek physician Galen. Galen's "humoral" theory hypothesized that the body was composed of four substances: blood, phlegm, black bile, and yellow bile. Sickness resulted from an imbalance in these elements. The average physician's principal weapon for fighting illness—induced vomiting/diarrhea and copious bleeding of patients with lancets and leeches—remained of dubious aid. Those desperate to see themselves and their loved ones well were naturally tempted by alternative remedies.

Before the scientific revolution, science and magic—including the science of healing—were separated by only the finest of lines. Medicine men were stock characters at carnivals, markets, and fairs, peddling their cures alongside palm readers, acrobats, magicians, and animal trainers. Indeed, the pairing of "showmanship and dental surgery" was a bizarrely popular genre, spawning a number of dentist-puppeteers and dentist-acrobats who, presumably, found that, in the absence of anesthesia, their surgery went more smoothly when performed on distracted patients.[6] They and their heirs attracted an audience as much for their entertainment value as for their medical adventuring.

In this vein, nineteenth-century American patent medicine manufacturers mounted elaborate "Medicine Shows," sent out to travel the highways and byways of the country. The Wizard Oil Company, founded by magician John Hamlin, is illustrative of the genre, whose popularity peaked in the 1870s and '80s. The Chicago-based company combined a canny modern distribution model with the ancient lure of spectacle: Hamlin sent out fleets of horse-drawn wagons, emblazoned with colorful ads for Wizard Oil and equipped with a stage and parlor organ. The performers not only conducted open-air entertainments and point-of-service sales but stocked village pharmacies throughout the midwest with bottles of Wizard liver pills, cough remedy, and liniment oil.[7]

Despite the appeal of these theatrical extravaganzas, American patent medicine manufacturers got their greatest boost from the rapid spread of literacy and print media in the nineteenth century. In 1800, the United States counted 20 daily newspapers; by 1860, that number had shot to 400, thanks in part to steam-powered presses and cheaper paper.[8] Patent medicine companies were among the earliest and most cash-flush investors in the new advertising medium. True to form, patent medicine print advertisements were flamboyant and theatrical. "There is no Sore it will Not Heal, No Pain it will not Subdue," promised one newspaper advertisement for Hamlin's Wizard Oil. "The Great Medical Wonder . . . Magical in its Effects," the company assured health-conscious consumers. "The bones are sold with the beef," sighed one small-town editor when readers objected to the quantity of advertising in the paper. He knew that without ad revenue, the paper would require a paid circulation of two thousand, rather than its current two hundred, to survive.[9]

Nor did the patent medicine companies confine themselves to newspaper ads. The introduction of photo-engraving and chromolithography meant that advertisements and other printed promotional materials could be made more eye-catching. Medicine firms ran off handbills, pamphlets, posters, trade cards and, perhaps most effective, almanacs. The traditional almanac was intended for use as a calendar, but it could also contain general reference material, horoscopes, recipes, and cartoons and jokes, making its annual publication something of a literary event. No other printed sources were issued in such large editions, with the possible exception of the Bible. While patent medicine companies began by taking out ad space in popular almanacs, they soon realized printing and distributing their own almanacs provided better exposure. By the 1890s, all of the major patent medicine companies were distributing their own almanacs—replete, of course, with generous plugs for their healing remedies—free of charge to drugstores across the country.

Trade cards were another means by which advertising slipped, often unnoticed, into the American home. Indeed trade cards were, according to one historian's estimate, the most ubiquitous form of advertising in America in the 1880s.[10] These palm-sized three-by-five cards, engraved with the name and address of a product and an accompanying picture, created brand loyalty and a feeling of "ownership" in the customer. The fact that the pictures were printed in color was both a delight and a novelty to the average nineteenth-century reader, and the cards quickly spawned a collecting craze. Young women and girls, in particular, organized them into scrapbooks, cutting, pasting, and collaging the images into playful patterns; ads for tea, soap, shoes, and sewing thread side by side with plugs for Dr. Grosvenor's Liveraid and Lydia Pinkham's Female Vegetable Compound.

By the dawn of the twentieth century, there was no village so remote, no backwater so forsaken that the patent medicine industry hadn't penetrated it, spreading its garish, cheerful gospel of good health through mass mailings; trade cards in scrapbooks; almanacs piled high on drugstore counters; posters plastered on fences and billboards and barns. But the American unconscious had been primed, perhaps, for this riotous explosion of therapeutic messages by the religious fervor that had swept the country in the 1830s and '40s. During the Second Great Awakening, revivalist preachers canvassed the nation, holding forth in local pulpits and in open-air "camp meetings," calling for believers to step forward and accept Jesus Christ as their Lord and Savior. The promise of rebirth and spiritual rejuvenation through Christian faith overlapped with the rhetoric of medical "miracles" common among patent medicine hawkers.

These public spectacles of conversion entailed their own kind of theater—and magical thinking—with prospective converts frequently overcome by sobs, moans, fainting spells, and bouts of hopping and shouting as the Holy Spirit did its appointed work. Indeed, one minister who became alarmed at the carnivalesque aura attaching to religious revivals, John Fanning Watson, penned an 1819 pamphlet entitled *Methodist Error; or, Friendly Christian Advice to Those Methodists, Who Indulge in Extravagant Emotions and Bodily Exercises.* In it, he warned readers that these "noisy Christians" prone to "falling down, jumping up, clapping hands, and screaming" were, far from bearing witness to the miracle of transformative grace, committing a "gross perversion of true religion." Despite their different genres, the acrobatic dentist, banjo-strumming medicine salesman, and leaping Christian bore an uncanny family resemblance. All promised rejuvenated bodies and souls to an audience in search of health.[11]

For proof that Christian conversion narratives and patent medicine could comfortably cohabitate within nineteenth-century wellness culture, consider the life of one itinerant evangelist preacher, Lorenzo Dow. Known for his shaggy, unkempt appearance, in imitation of the apostles, Dow larded his apocalyptic sermons with plugs for his patented Dow's Family Medicine (reportedly a mixture of Epsom salts, water, and nitric acid, recommended for all nature of "bilious derangements"). One doctor, Benjamin Dolbeare, wrote a posthumous testimonial to Dow in 1836, claiming that he, "in science, had no rival; in piety, religion and morals, no equal," and that "it appears that hardly anything short of inspiration could have led to the discovery of such a remedy, so wonderful [is it] in its effects."[12]

The Reverend Watson's suspicion that an element of superstition and even black magic lurked within the Christian conversion experience was not unfounded. On the eve of the American Revolution, only 15 percent of the American population belonged to a formal church. In his famous 1782 *Letters from an American Farmer*, Hector St. John de Crèvecoeur remarked that the average American's religious training was so poor and mixed that "religious indifference [is] . . . one of the strongest characteristics of the Americans."[13] What *was* widespread, in the absence of strict Christian dogma, was a hodgepodge of occult practices held over from Europe, including astrology, alchemy, and divination. While the eighteenth-century Enlightenment spirit had done much to dampen such superstitious habits in America, folk magic continued to be popular into the nineteenth century, especially in rural areas. In many cases, folk magic blended indifferently with orthodox Christian beliefs.[14]

The European folk practice of divination—or seeking buried treasure through occult means, such as dreams, divining rods, mineral balls, or "seer stones"—continued to flourish in the New World and was not uncommonly imbued with Christian meaning. Treasure seeking was located, as one scholar has noted, "at the murky intersection of material aspiration and religious desire," and could serve as a reassuring physical token of divine election. Joseph Smith Jr. got his first inkling that he might be God's prophet when, at the age of fourteen, he began helping neighbors seek out lost property or find buried treasure with the aid of his "seer stone." It was with the help of this same divining tool that Smith later discovered the spiritual payload of the Golden Tablets—and by which he was able effectively to transmute the profane mud of pagan treasure into the institutional gold of the Church of Latter Day Saints.[15]

During her childhood, Jean Wade was steeped in this uniquely American blend of Christian-pagan prosperity folklore. In that worldview, God's "power" is an influx or inspiration that, if we believe in it firmly enough, will deliver both spiritual and material fruits. The cleaned-up brand of Christianized, self-help wisdom that Robert Wade preached did not truck with the more obvious magical claptrap of Wizard Oil and seer stones and divining rods. But at its heart, there lodged a similar sturdy faith in "miracles of transformation." Jean was a successful adwoman because she instinctively combined the roles of carnival barker, minister, therapist, and life coach that could guide Americans on their quests for better living and better health. She had come by it naturally.

Home medicine in the early modern period fell within woman's proper sphere. Women were expected to tend to "domestic" illness and injuries, from cuts to stomach aches, and often had recourse to recipe books of "home physic" in healing. "Cosmetical physic," means of improving or beautifying the body, were a subcategory of these home remedies. One of the most popular ladies' recipe books in seventeenth-century England was Sir Hugh Plat's *Delightes for Ladies, To Adorne their Persons, Tables, Clothes, and Distillatories with Beauties, Banquets, Perfumes and Waters.* The cosmetic recipes were often equal parts chemistry, magic, and astrology, such as this one for the removal of freckles: "Wash your face in the wane of the moon with a sponge morning and evening with the distilled water of Elder leaves, letting the same dry into the skin." An updated freckle-removal recipe from 1876 omitted reference to the lunar calendar, but retained elder flower as an active ingredient, now mixed with the slightly more scientific-sounding "sulphate of zinc."[16]

It was not until after World War I that "face paint"—the use of face-altering color such as rouge, lipstick, and eye pencil—became acceptable for middle-class American women. Through much of the nineteenth century and into the first decades of the twentieth, any cosmetic that crossed the line from "improving" to "painting" a woman's face was condemned. A popular ladies' recipe book of 1876, Madame Bayard's *The Art of Beauty, or Ladies' Companion to the Boudoir* allowed that certain powders to lighten the skin (perfumed chalk, crushed mother of pearl) were permissible, but that in general, "no borrowed charms can equal those of 'A woman's face, with Nature's own hand painted.'"[17]

This ban on face paint stemmed from the presumed connection between a woman's external appearance and her inner virtue. For a woman to mask her God-given face was a particularly vicious type of deception because it would hide not merely her physical qualities but mislead others as to the state of her inner soul as well. Alexander Walker, a Scottish physiologist, proclaimed that "goodness and beauty in woman will . . . be found to bear a strict relation to each other; and the latter will be seen always to be the external sign of the former." That men are naturally attracted to beautiful women was essential, according to Dr. Walker, as "individual happiness" and nothing less than the "amelior[ation] of the species" depended on a man's choice of a morally upright reproductive mate. A woman with a painted face would leave her suitors in agonizing doubt as to whether she was truly virtuous or just putting on a show.[18]

But if appearance-altering face and body paint was stigmatized, products that promised to "cleanse" and thus "transform" the skin from the inside out were another matter. Indeed, it was precisely because of the presumed link between a clean face and a clean soul that these products' appeal was so powerful. By 1885, no one thought it particularly odd that the Reverend Henry Ward Beecher should publicly endorse Pears' Soap, announcing that "if Cleanliness is next to Godliness, then Soap must be considered as a Means of Grace."[19]

Women's magazines from the 1880s up through World War I featured advertisements for a wide variety of soaps, creams, and powders that were judged to be "skin improving" rather than skin covering or masking. In part, the rhetoric of cleanliness worked because it resonated with a wide range of "clean living" health and reform regimens that were popular in the nineteenth century, from hydropathy (water cure) to temperance to vegetarianism. These movements imagined the human body as a porous organism whose health depended on strict regulation of inputs and outputs, guarding against attack by toxins and foreign bodies.

Hydrotherapy, which by the end of the century counted thousands of adherents and dozens of treatment centers nationwide, operated on the principle that cold water taken internally and applied externally conferred a host of health benefits. In his 1850 medical treatise *Hydropathy for the People*, Dr. William Horsell counseled daily vigorous cold-water sponge baths as of "the greatest value to persons suffering from gout . . . , nervous irritability, or weakness of the skin, etc."[20] In our artificial state of civilization, Dr. Horsell clarified, we fear exposing the skin to the natural healing elements of air and water, instead keeping it jealously wrapped up. The result is that our "skins become clogged, . . . until at length we get crusted over with a substance similar to Roman cement." "Open pores" and a "vigorous skin" are essential to "complete restoration" of bodily health.[21]

The water cure mantra was echoed in cosmetic literature. The skin, Madame Bayard averred in *The Art of Beauty*, is among the most important of organs and the principal means for purifying our bodies. The pores exude daily "a multitude of useless, corrupted, and worn-out particles," by which "the greater part of all the impurity of our bodies is removed." Clogged pores result in "acidity and corruption of our juices," she said, and are the "secret source" of disease.[22] Partly in response to a contemporaneous push for sanitation reform, and tied to the spread of indoor plumbing, the market for soap exploded between 1890 and 1920.[23] Soap ads, using water-cure rhetoric, routinely compared the skin to a living, breathing entity whose vigorous natural process of absorption and evacuation were impeded only at grave peril.

In the quest to differentiate themselves from competitors—as well as to drum up new markets—soap advertisements in the *Ladies' Home Journal* during the 1910s and '20s were keen to teach consumers that household soaps, for use with laundry and dishes, were not to be confused with toilet soaps. Jap Rose soap, for instance, advertised with the tag line "Give Nature a Chance!," warning that the woman who used "opaque, sediment depositing" household soaps on her skin was asking for complexion trouble. Only "transparent" Jap Rose soap would "loosen impurities" and "let the air in."[24] Ivory soap alone resisted product differentiation, marketing a single soap product for toilet, kitchen, and laundry, but offering detailed instructions on how to use it in each context.[25]

Almost without exception, soap manufacturers crafted their advertisements around the principle that proper cleansing helped the skin and scalp perform its "natural" biological functions. With assiduous attention, the user's inner beauty (and thus moral virtue) could be coaxed to shine through. Packer's Tar Soap, for instance, promised that regular use would not only cleanse but "quicken the blood supply, increase the scalp's nutrition, and thus aid nature in keeping your hair alive and beautiful."[26] Packer's also claimed for itself the honor of being "first assistant of good Dr. Nature," bringing "quickened life to your glands."[27] Woodbury's and Pears' soaps echoed this pseudoscientific, vitality-obsessed language. Beautiful hair starts with a "vigorous" scalp, they assert, since it is here that the nutrition-rich "network of blood vessels," "fat glands," and "color supply pigment cells" lie nestled. Stimulating massage plus lather plus water flushes out "dead cells" and "dust," leaving "the pores clear and free to do their work."[28] In a stroke of off-label marketing genius, Sunkist citrus fruits even got in on the cleansing game. Sure, soap helped flush out sediment, but who was to say that soap wouldn't itself become a kind of second-order sediment? Only the fresh-squeezed juice of a lemon, Sunkist offers helpfully, "cuts the alkali in the soap and leaves the hair *really clean.*"[29]

Advertisements assured women that beautiful skin was democratic: it was not a luxury reserved for the few, those with a "naturally" good complexion. On the contrary, *all* women harbored potential inner beauty that simply had to be coaxed into expressing itself outwardly. "Nature intended your skin to be flawless," announces a 1919 ad for Woodbury's soap, noting that "skin specialists are tracing fewer and fewer troubles to the blood." Instead, skin blemishes are the result of one "insidious and persistent enemy": bacteria and parasites smuggled into the pores via atmospheric dirt, soot, and grime.[30] It is up to the woman to keep a sharp watch over the proper evacuation of her pores.

But the true appeal of early twentieth-century soap advertisements lay not in their promise of glowing skin and gleaming hair, but in their suggestion that this "quickening" and "renewal" of the epidermis was but the precursor to a deeper, more existential transformation. Woodbury's caught the spirit of this symbolism best in its ads throughout the 1910s and '20s, which emphasized the skin as in a continual state of metamorphosis. "Your skin, like the rest of your body, is changing every day!" a 1915 ad announced. "As the *old* skin dies, *new* forms in its place."[31] "This," the ad goes on to suggest, "gives you your opportunity"—and only the foolish (sinful?) girl would fail to nab it. "How many girls despair of ever rousing a sallow, sluggish skin!" sighs another Woodbury ad in 1918. But the solution lies within every woman's grasp, with a proper cleansing regimen: "Have you ever thought that your skin *can* be changed?" The change you seek is within you—in fact, it is in the bar of soap you hold in your hand.[32] By drawing on centuries-old Protestant spiritual habits and narratives of conversion, soap manufacturers successfully marketed their product as a means of secular grace.

A 1919 advertisement for Resinol soap portrays two young women seated in a theater balcony, one gazing rapturously at the stage, the other taking a furtive sidelong glance at her companion, clearly trying to puzzle out the secret to her appeal. "You must have seen it—the clear unconscious smile of the girl with the fabulous complexion," the ad confides.[33] A clear complexion induces an "unconscious" inner confidence that ensures its lucky possessor "radiates magnetism," making her "a center of attraction among her friends." A clear skin is not an end in itself; it is merely the first step to a girl's eventual social and romantic apotheosis.

BBDO was representing Silver Dust Soap when the account came across Jean's desk in 1936. The company was doing a brisk business selling soap flakes to housewives for use with laundry and dishes with the tag line "Deeper Suds." "Richer, creamier, full bodied suds!" the advertising text promised, pledging that for "plenty of suds" and "depth of suds," housewives unanimously recommended Silver Dust. But Jean saw an untapped market: why not sell suds to clean the body as well as the dishes? "The wealth of B.O. and body daintiness advertising has laid the background for a need for super cleanliness in bathing," she suggested in a memo. "I think you might be able to interest Silver Dust in producing a flake soap for the bath— Fairy Foam, Bath Foam, Bath Suds, Foamy Flakes, Fairy Flakes, etc." Never one to shy away from her own products, Jean reported that she took an experimental bubble bath in Silver Dust flakes and found it "downright luscious." "It soaks out weariness," she informed her colleagues, "leaves your skin incredibly soft and smooth."[34] "Dishes sparkle, glassware glistens," the Silver Dust soap ads had pledged, and Jean understood intuitively that housewives' preference for "deep" and "creamy" suds in the dishpan could easily be transferred to the body. By combining the luxurious textual connotations of "cream" and "foam" with the breezy magic of mythical "fairies," Jean imbued Silver Dust bubble bath with a quasi-baptismal quality: a release from pedestrian worries, a penetrating "soak" that would wash "the weariness" clean out of a woman's tired body (and, perhaps, her soul as well).

Other soap brands were getting in on the act. In the same year Jean took on the Silver Dust account, Lux toilet soap ran an advertisement featuring starlet Carole Lombard on the glories of the bubble bath. "Often I come home from a long day in front of the camera thoroughly tired out," a slightly deflated and blurry Lombard confides in the "Before" photo. But the "After" photo features the starlet's face now delicately lit, its gentle white glow contrasting luxuriously with the black fringe of her lashes and black penciled arc of her eyebrows. A Lux Toilet Soap bath has done the trick, "pepping her up" with its "ACTIVE" deep-cleansing lather.[35]

The "wealth of B.O. and body daintiness" ads Jean noted referred to the surge of cleanliness-themed advertising following Listerine's astonishingly successful campaign to make "halitosis" a household word as well as a household worry, beginning in 1920. Developed in 1879 by Dr. Joseph Lawrence as a surgical antiseptic, and named after the father of sterilization science, Dr. Joseph Lister, it was originally marketed to dentists as a means of killing germs during oral surgery. It served a variety of off-label uses as well, including foot-cleaning, floor-swabbing, and gonorrhea treatment.[36] But by 1920, company president Gerard B. Lambert realized that Listerine's association with clinical cleanliness could be harnessed purely for its social cachet, rebranded as an agent of "personal oral hygiene." In collaboration with copy writer Milton Feasly, Lambert dusted off an ancient pseudomedical term, "halitosis," and leveraged it to prey on the social anxiety of Jazz Age youth. "What secret is your mirror holding back?" queried a 1923 ad featuring a lovely young girl staring wistfully into her boudoir mirror. "She *was* a beautiful girl and talented, too," the caption runs. "Yet in the one pursuit that stands foremost in the mind of every girl and woman—marriage—she was a failure." Unpleasant breath was, of course, the answer to the puzzle of why this young woman found herself "always a bridesmaid, never a bride."[37]

At about the same time Jean was working on the Silver Dust account, she was also brainstorming copy for Squibb toothpaste and working the "mouth freshness" angle so as to piggyback on Listerine's well-established name recognition. In a memo, Jean dashed off a dozen or so tag lines. "Is your mouth sweet enough to kiss?" queried one. "She has been kissed often . . . but always good-bye!" ran another, darker example of what was known as "scare copy." Jean suggested the ads should underscore that Squibb toothpaste contained "a mouthwash ingredient": promising girls they would be kiss-worthy round the clock gave added value to the ho-hum business of keeping teeth clean. "Any toothpaste that could advertise a mouthwash ingredient would immediately capitalize on all of the powers of Listerine, Lavoris, and other 'bad breath' advertising," she counseled.[38]

In her work for Wildroot Liquid Cream Shampoo, Jean helped the company zero in on its likeliest buyers: young women aged eighteen to twenty-five who washed their hair at home at least once a week, as opposed to their mothers who still had their hair "done" at the beauty parlor. "She wants her hair clean," Jean informed Wildroot executives of their target customer, "because, let's say it simply, she wants to get married more than anything else in the whole wide world."[39] "A girl wants two things from a shampoo—clean hair, and hair with a soft and alluring gleam," Jean schooled her clients. With this in mind, Jean and her copy team played with tag lines until they came up with a seller: "Gleams as it Cleans, Cleans as it Gleams." The phrase "So Clean, It Squeaks!" also tested well in Jean's research, so they developed a cartoon personality, Squeekie, who dispensed cosmetic advice to girls. The chipper red-haired spokesgirl was splashed, in colored comic strip form, across magazines and onto subway billboards. Each comic strip portrays Squeekie giving sympathetic counsel to "fuzzy-wuzzies," unkempt girls who had yet to discover the miraculous smoothing power of Wildroot.

Competing shampoo brands tried a variety of twists on the basic "clean" theme by offering shampoo "oils," "creams," and "liquids," each with its own mysterious advantage over the others. Wildroot hedged its bets by declaring its product a "liquid cream." "It's not just a liquid, not just a cream," the ads enthused, "but the *best of both*!" How this alchemical merger surpassed the merits of each formula is left to the reader's imagination.

Another sales genius discovered he could stir the pot of consumers' irrational fear of soap "scum"—among the oldest of soap fantasy/nightmares—then dash to the rescue with "soapless," scum-free shampoos. Here, too, Wildroot hedged its bets. While the eventual Squeekie ads proudly declared Wildroot to be soapless, a preliminary series of sketches for the campaign suggested, alternately, that its unique formula was (a) soapless, (b) "mildly soapy," or (c) some magical transcendence of the soap/soapless dichotomy altogether. "Better than Soap . . . Better than Soapless . . . It's Wildroot Shampoo!" read one.[40] Another version vaunted Wildroot's revolutionary "three-step" formula consisting of a mild "soapy base," plus a "water softener" to "cut soap and uncover hidden highlights," topped off with "processed lanolin" to prevent scalp dryness and dandruff. "Soapless Sudsy . . . Lanolin Lovely!" ran the almost nonsensical, yet sibilant and oddly hypnotic, jingle in the final ads.

The social suicide of dandruff was also a mainstay of shampoo "scare" advertising. Even before Listerine invented halitosis, the antiperspirant Odo-Ro-No had successfully introduced the shorthand "B.O." for "body odor" into the public lexicon. In Jean's work for Wildroot, the writers felt around for a catchy dandruff equivalent. "Can your scalp pass the 'fingernail' test?" asked one sketch.[41] In the male version of the Squeekie ads, men unlucky in love were asked whether their scalps could pass the "F.N." test and if not, to consider that this might be the source of their romantic problems. "If YOUR scalp can't pass the F.N. (finger nail) Test, you need Wildroot Cream Oil," announced the final caption.[42]

With scalp dandruff a recognizable "body daintiness" category, Jean sought to mobilize its dark, taboo power in her work for Lady Esther All-Purpose Face Cream by coining the concept of "face dandruff," or flaky, dry skin. "Face dandruff is a recognizable condition," Jean opined, insisting that Lady Esther could enlist "chemists, cosmetologists, and laboratory technicians" to vouch for the fact that "dry skin flakes off [your face] as dandruff just as it does in your hair," and that the condition could be "illustrated by microphotographs."[43] Lady Esther could capitalize on this fear by, predictably, suggesting social isolation if left untreated. "No man likes to kiss face dandruff," ran one line of reasoning. "If your skin is peeling, flaking off—LOOK OUT! You have face dandruff." Here again, Jean threw out a pseudoscientific quiz/test combined with a snappy acronym to market Lady Esther products: "S.A.—Skin Appeal." "Take this quick step to skin appeal," and "She has S.A—and plenty of it (it's really skin appeal)."[44]

The F.N. test and S.A. have been consigned to the ashbin of history. But the fact that B.O. is still alive and well in the American cultural unconscious as shorthand for social death proves that Jean had the right instinct; it was certainly worth a try. Jean's work on soap products and its cosmetic offshoots—shampoos, toothpaste, face creams—reveals nothing so much as advertising in thrall to a kind of frenetic dream-logic of contagion. Since any campaign that led to multiplied profits and products was an unquestioned good, the formula that worked for one body part or one product was immediately transferred to other body parts and products *ad infinitum*: replication gone mad.

In yet another defense of the advertising industry that she wrote for BBDO's *Wedge*, Jean again adopted the voice of an adman, this time one whose fourteen-year-old daughter Anne comes home from school to announce that—what else!—her teacher has warned students to be skeptical of advertising claims. In "You've Got to Watch Out for Advertising!," the narrator launches into a satirical riff on the dangers of shampoo and soap advertisements. "Yes, you've got to watch out for advertising, if you're a young and pretty girl like Anne," he warns. "Advertising might tell you about . . . a new shampoo to put a special gleam in those soft and shining curls," he teases. Or take soap: advertisements popularizing cleansers and detergents have resulted in the "dangerous" proliferation of cleaner, brighter students: girls clad in "sunny cottons," boys in crisp "white shirts."[45]

Jean's public endorsements of soap appear to have coincided with her own private appreciation for advertising's role in producing better-smelling, better-looking, more marriage-eligible women. Jean was, as we have seen, painfully frank about her own failures to meet the beauty standards of her day. She grabbed the first marriage proposal that came her way because, as a girl who was "short and fat," she feared she might never receive a second offer. Among the sparse private records retained in her archive are notebooks recording her daily weight and calorie counts, testimony to her lifelong struggle with body image. An early article she pitched to *New York Woman* magazine, "So You Want to Be Thin!," summed up the centrality of weight to a woman's self-image. "There are, after all, only two kinds of women," she opens authoritatively. "The fats, who want to get thin, and the thins, who want to stay thin!" Whether one classes oneself among the former or the latter, Jean sighs, one "sad fact" remains: "A woman carves her curves with her teeth!" Stick to the diet she proposes, Jean promises, and "you <u>can</u> become that sylph-like self that flits through your dreams."[46]

Despite her best efforts, for Jean dieting was mostly a losing battle. She occasionally turned the visible fact of her weight to humor in speeches and client pitches, especially on accounts dealing with food. Sometimes she referred to herself quite bluntly as "plump" or "fat"; other times, she drew joking, self-deprecating attention to her figure as sad proof of how tempting food could be.[47] The indulgent chuckles she elicited from the crowd no doubt put her, and her audience, at ease.

Jean made occasional reference to her daughter, Anne, in interviews, speeches, and even ad copy. (She referred, less frequently, to her son, John, as well.) The "Anne" named in Jean's *Wedge* article was, in fact, her own fourteen-year-old daughter (whether the anecdote of the skeptical teacher actually happened, we will never know). When Jean does refer to Anne in a professional or promotional context, it is usually—as here—to marvel at how "young and pretty" she is, to bask in the romantic attention and social success that advertising's beauty products have secured for her (and that, perhaps, Jean felt she had missed out on). Anne and her friends *like* feeling fresh and beautiful, Jean retorts to the naysaying teacher, and perhaps more to the point, "their boy friends seem to like their clean and shining hair" as well.

By all accounts, the young Anne imbibed her mother's lessons. In 1954, she compiled a scrapbook, entitled "Through the Looking Glass," outlining a complete health and beauty program for young women.[48] Divided into the twelve essential elements of beauty ("Your Hair," "Your Skin," "Your Figure," "Personal Daintiness"), the book offers helpful hints on how to achieve "that beautiful 'American Look,' today's ideal of glamor." The beautiful girl will pay attention not only to health and personal cleanliness, but above all to "ATTITUDE." "You may be clean and healthy and have good features, but still be ugly, if you let hate, envy, spite, tantrums, blues, worry, unkindness curdle your disposition," Anne warns. "Beauty begins within!"

By the end of "You've Got to Watch Out for Advertising!", it is not only dull skin and oily hair that is redeemed from dinginess by the hallowed industry. Advertising is, in fact, the secret to keeping the American economy and "distribution system" itself squeaky clean by winnowing out the "unsocial" capitalists, to quote Simon Patten, and ensuring that only the highest quality, lowest cost items flow through the system. "The little man around the corner" who peddles his product out of "a little hole in the wall," hidden away on a "dingy side street," will be utterly flushed out by advertising, Jean assures her readers. Instead, consumers will be educated to accept only the transparent, "strict and unvarying quality control" provided by nationally distributed standardized products. In Jean's parable, shampoo is much more than a product that will keep girls' hair lustrous and procure them marriage prospects. Soap becomes a metaphor for advertising itself, the force that will slough off any inefficiency clogging the industrial mechanism, bringing purified, smoothly flowing, richly alive capitalism to bear its glorious material and spiritual fruits.[49]

4

Of Makeovers and Movie Stars

In 1933, the Richard Hudnut company, an august Philadelphia *perfumier* attempting to branch out into cosmetics, hired BBDO to breathe new life into its makeup sales. It had stiff competition: Max Factor, Helena Rubenstein, Maybelline, and Elizabeth Arden, among others, were all hard at work carving out their pieces of the beauty market pie. Jean was assigned to the account.

Cosmetics began as a province of the "movie star" or professional actress only. The earliest makeup moguls were cosmeticians to the stars, with Max Factor perhaps the most famous.[1] Factor, at one time principal cosmetician to the imperial Russian Grand Opera and members of Czar Nicholas II's court, made his reputation in the nascent film industry by perfecting a stage makeup that wouldn't crack and sweat under the extreme heat of the camera lights. After developing a lightweight cream greasepaint in twelve precisely gradated shades—eventually expanded to thirty-two—that were adopted as standard by the industry, he followed up with a panoramic range of eleven shades of face powder.[2]

Off stage, heavy eye color, mascara, rouge, and lipstick were still considered marks of loose morals when used by the average woman. But by the 1920s, the appeal of "makeup" was beginning to expand well beyond Hollywood. Young women all over the country grew accustomed to seeing Theda Bara's thickly black lashes and rouged cheeks and admired Clara Bow's bee-stung lips. The figure of the flapper began to appear in the 1910s and '20s on magazine covers and in advertisements.[3] Newly emancipated from the shackles of trussed-up Victorian femininity, the flapper was shearing her hair, hiking her skirts, and painting her face with a youthful disregard for the dictates of bourgeois good taste. "Find Yourself!" beckoned one iconic 1929 cosmetic ad campaign, inviting women to experiment with a newly expanded palette, not only of shades of rouge but of intriguing new social and sexual identities.[4]

From its earliest days as a mass market product, cosmetics depended on its partnership with Hollywood stars and fan magazines to move merchandise. Max Factor stoked the demand for cosmetics by giving public demonstrations around Los Angeles, in department stores and theater lobbies, showing young women how to apply makeup tastefully. With the help of a marketing and distribution company called Sales Builders, Factor developed his Color Harmony Prescription Make-Up Chart to facilitate the sale of cosmetics in drug stores. The chart allowed women to check off boxes for their eye, hair, and skin color, and then directed them to "color harmonized" lipstick, powder, and rouge shades to match. In 1927, the system went into national distribution. Other cosmetic brands would follow suit.[5]

By the early 1930s, cosmetic manufacturers, the film industry, magazine publishers, and advertising agencies were engaged in an all-out campaign to fashion a new way of thinking about beauty and feminine identity that middle- and working-class white women would, quite literally, buy into. Tabloid and fan magazines rushed in to rival the more staid, mainstream ladies' journals as a leading source of cultural knowledge and norms, working hand in hand with the cinema in codifying a mass culture. As a result, it didn't really matter whether the woman who put her money down on the counter was exchanging it for a lipstick or an eye shadow, for a fan magazine or a movie ticket; all were interchangeable vehicles for the attainment of a much larger, more amorphous product: the dream of self-renewal and transformation. The purchase of one product was calculated to stimulate desire for the others, according to the cumulative, replicative logic of capital itself. Advertisers facilitated this consolidation whereby a wide range of products across multiple industries could profitably tap into a single desire. But entrance into the game required endorsements from movie stars—and this, as Jean noted in a memo on the Hudnut account, was largely the province of Max Factor. To "crack the Max Factor monopoly on Hollywood movie stars," then, was the task she set for herself.[6]

The fan magazines that enjoyed such a vogue in the 1920s and '30s — the most popular of which were *Motion Picture Magazine* and *Photoplay*—routinely followed a similar editorial formula.[7] Each issue contained a handful of in-depth interviews or profiles of stars, mixed in with regular features such as gossip pages, reader questions, beauty and fashion columns, and in some cases fiction (serial novels or short stories). And of course, sprinkled generously throughout, were advertisements, which ranged from full-page color ads to smaller, black-and-white text-box or half-page ads crowded toward the end of the issue. All of the advertisements, however, pertained in one way or another to beauty and daintiness products: body soaps and laundry soaps; feminine hygiene products; toothpastes, mouthwashes, and breath-freshening chewing gums; hair removal products; diet plans for "reducing" or gaining; and cosmetics. It was here that the cosmetic giants jockeyed for the readers' attention. The advertisements and features were often interconnected: in the most obvious case, through product endorsements, but more subtly and, ultimately, more seductively, by the fact that both advertisements and features drew from a common pool of themes, storylines, and vocabulary whose main goal was to convince readers to believe in the magic of self-transformation.

The fan magazines' most cherished and reliable narrative formula was the "makeover" story. No star entered Hollywood fully formed, like Venus rising in majesty out of the sea. Instead Hollywood took the dull and lumpy lead of the common girl and spun it into star-quality gold. The March 1932 issue of *Photoplay* magazine ran a feature on "It girl" Miriam Hopkins entitled "'Li'l Gawgia' Gets Glamour: The Startling Rise of Miriam Hopkins from a Scrawny Ingénue to a Girl Who's Got Everything." The author, Al Hughes, presents himself as a hard-boiled "old film hound" who, initially, would no more have predicted a movie star future for the "skinny blonde child mugging for the camera" than he would have for the Easter bunny. "Then, almost overnight, the moth turned into a butterfly," he reveals. "Miriam Hopkins suddenly, miraculously acquired glamour—that mysterious, magnificent quality that is vital to outstanding screen success."[8] Hughes suggests we put this prime specimen under a microscope to see whether we can wrest from her the secret of this transformation, but ultimately he finds no convincing answer. He chalks the change up to "snickering Fate," "one of the blinding, blistering miracles that life delights in committing, now and then," to the bafflement of mortals.

Another classic Cinderella tale was that of Olivia de Havilland, a California beauty who managed to rise from high school theater actress to movie star in a few short leaps. Olivia had already enrolled at a college to train for some pedestrian and no doubt nerdy profession, when Hollywood swept in and changed her fortunes. "She's one out of a million young girls, young movie fans, in small obscure towns all over this land who dream of the good fairy with the magic wand," the journalist enthuses—and for Olivia, those "glorious, impossible dreams of Hollywood [came] true—in the twinkling of a star."[9] So improbable is the change that Mills College was reportedly still holding open a scholarship for Olivia, should "this astounding bubble burst." At the end of the piece, the writer attends Olivia's nineteenth birthday party. When the doe-eyed beauty blows out the candles on her cake, she begins to tear up. "What's the matter?" her anxious friends ask. She replies wistfully she doesn't want to turn nineteen, because that means saying goodbye to eighteen—as if she fears the forward lurch of time might turn her coach back into a pumpkin.[10]

The scrawny little kid from Georgia and the hometown sweetheart were characters tailor-made for a Cinderella plot. But in fact, *all* the stars, from the faintest of emerging lights to the most established planets in the firmament, were subjected to this before-and-after plot device by fan magazines. In a 1937 article profiling Marlene Dietrich and the art of glamour, writer Jan Fisher draws the reader in with a classic narrative lure: "No matter how hard it may be for you to believe it now," she whispers conspiratorially, Marlene Dietrich was not always thus. "Some of us remember what she looked like when she first hit Hollywood," she writes: "a heavy (fat is such an ugly adjective), horribly dressed, overly made-up German girl."[11] The key to Marlene's success? She was not too proud to take a good, hard look at herself in the mirror, tally up her flaws, and set about changing them.

Similarly, a three-part exposé entitled "Joan Crawford, Starring in the Dramatic Rise of a Self-Made Star" narrates just how far Crawford—*née* Lucille LeSuer, the impoverished child of a single mother—has come, and how hard she has had to fight to get there. The profile opens with the standard before-and-after trope, with Crawford upset that a tabloid ran some old photos of her as a common chorus girl: a little too fat, a little too loud, a little too lipsticked. But, the writer pleads, "Don't you see that that's what makes you great—as the self-made men of the pioneer days were great? . . . You, alone and unaided, pulled yourself up by your bootstraps, . . . you dreamed better dreams, and you made them come true."[12] In contrast to the mysterious transformation of Miriam Hopkins, here the puzzle of stardom has a simple solution: brutal self-scrutiny, hard work, a passion for self-improvement.

Profiles of the stars thus pivoted between attributing a star's glamour to blind fortune or to hard work. In the first instance, the sheer mystery of glamour—whence it came, and how it worked its spell—was key to its allure. To peer too deeply into its secrets was not only fruitless but self-defeating; ratiocination was the natural enemy of charm. As the author of the Miriam Hopkins interview states, with a wry wink at the camera, "If we could find the answer, you and I and Maisie and Joe could rattle out to Hollywood in the old Ford and collect our million."[13] But at the same time, readers couldn't be left to think that glamour—or, at the very least, their own scaled-down version of it in the guise of romance, employability, popularity with peers—was *entirely* up to chance and "snickering fate." Hard work and effort had to count for something. In this version of the star narrative, glamour can also (perhaps!) be earned through sheer pluck and perseverance. These conflicting versions of the star narrative appear side by side in the fan magazines, unbothered by their incompatibility. In fact, the very contradiction guarantees the inexhaustibility of the formula: luck is key to success, but only if

combined with hard work; hard work will get results, but not without a dash of luck.

Like the star profiles, editorial content that addressed the readers
more intimately in the form of fashion, beauty, or relationship advice
also pivoted between describing "personality" as the effect of innate
personal magnetism *and* as a democratic prize that any girl could
win through hard work and self-discipline. In a feature entitled "A
World-Famous Psycho-Analyst Tells Just What Makes Them Click,"
Carl Vonnell examined what movie stars "have" that make them such
magnetic screen presences. He reports that Dr. Cecil Reynolds,
renowned professor in the "Science of psycho-analysis," attributes
Greta Garbo's charm to the "unreadability" and aloofness of her face.
It is the mystery of what lies concealed beneath that draws viewers to her like a magnet. Now, the reader might assume that such a
quality is a matter of chance—you either have it, or you don't. But,
the author rushes to assure us, backed by Dr. Reynolds's expert testimony, such is not the case. "You, yourself, have within you the same
things [Garbo has]—the only difference being that [she] knows how
to use it, and you don't." In other words, "this air of mystery can be
cultivated—by such as you, mind you!" All it takes is gaining "studied
control" over one's face, so as to "avoid putting everything you are
or feel in the show window." Know your own emotions—then hide
them from view, the great mind doctor counsels.[14]

Similarly, *Photoplay*'s Marlene Dietrich profile holds that any girl
who wants to be glamorous must imitate Dietrich's commitment
to self-improvement: "take an honest inventory" of your looks and
then "start working." Yes, certainly, Marlene Dietrich is alluring. Of
course. But just look how hard she works at it! Do *you* work that
hard, gentle reader? Such shaming tactics permeate the magazine's
voice. "Sylvia," billed as "Hollywood's foremost authority" on beauty
in her regular *Photoplay* advice column, crafts the persona of the
hard-nosed, no-nonsense task master who will tolerate no excuses
from her pupils. In a 1932 diet-and-exercise feature, she opens by
telling her readers that any girl, "with nerve and courage," can make
herself beautiful. But, she warns, only one in ten readers will profit
from the pearls of wisdom she is about to lay before them. "The

other nine of you may want to be beautiful, but you are too lazy" she chides. "I haven't any time to waste on lazy people."[15]

The fan magazines developed a highly codified, internally contradictory, and therefore supremely addictive recipe for self-realization. If you weren't a winner, the logic ran, it was because you lacked innate magnetism that was unequally parceled out by the fates. But right as the disfavored were ready to throw in the towel, the fan magazines whispered, "Maybe you just have to try harder." Then they played it on an infinite loop and watched it drive sales.

This content mimicked, in an explicitly feminine register, the advice popularized in the dozens of self-help manuals that flooded the market during the same period, aimed at a (primarily) white, male audience. Self-realization as cultural ideal was tweaked into masculine and feminine versions. A key early text in the self-help genre was titled *The Masterful Personality* (1921) by Oliver Swett Marden, whose nuggets of business wisdom had found their way into the Wade brothers' Pennsylvania Business School pamphlets. Orphaned at age seven and forced to work as a quasi–indentured servant to earn his keep, Marden eventually rose to earn a Harvard medical degree as well as a law degree from Boston University. *The Masterful Personality*, replete with such motivational chapters as "The Man You Could Be" and "You Can Compel People to Like You," explains that any man can succeed if he simply puts his mind to it.

Marden's vision of self-realization was rooted in Protestant theology. "One of the supreme tragedies of life is to fail to respond to the purpose of the Almighty, to answer for the talent He has given us. If we do our best in whatever situation we are placed, new power will be developed with every forward step we take."[16] "Supreme personality" was attainable only if we accepted that we were "co-creator[s] with God," "partak[ing] of all of His attributes and qualities."[17] Marden echoed Jean's father's uplift sermons, where he claimed the gift of Christ's grace has kindled a "new power" in us to become fully self-actualized, successful men. Marden similarly imagined what he called the "great Within" as the "powers, possibilities locked up within you," an expression of God's grace just waiting to be actualized.[18]

As in the fan magazines, 1920s and '30s self-help literature wavered between describing "magnetism" as an inexplicable gift of grace and a reward for hard work within any man's reach. "Personality," Marden asserts, is the mysterious *je-ne-sais-quoi* of successful selfhood, easy to spot but impossible to define. It is something "which eludes the biographer and evades the camera," "something which radiates from his presence, a real vital force" that draws others like a magnet to iron. Personality was innate: you either had it or you didn't. "We cannot radiate anything unlike ourselves," Marden contends.[19] In his chapter "Be Sincere! Be Genuine!" Marden urged readers, "Have the courage to be yourself!" "You cannot long conceal the truth about yourself," he warns. "When you try to give a false impression, you are living a lie, and sooner or later you will be exposed for what you are."[20]

But on the other hand, we were nothing apart from what we thought or imagined ourselves to be. "Most of us are the victims of wrong thinking," Marden briskly announces, prey to "error thoughts" or "disease thoughts" that needed to be driven out and replaced by "friend thoughts." Weakness and inferiority were only states of mind that, once banished from the brain, would cease to be our reality. "What you think you are," he informs readers, "you are day by day becoming. That is why the ideal you cherish, the mental picture you form of yourself, is so important in hastening . . . self discovery."[21]

The apex of the self-help genre was reached by Dale Carnegie, whose 1936 book, *How to Win Friends and Influence People,* went through seventeen editions in its first year. Both the self-help manuals and the fan magazines owed a debt to the expanding cultural currency of psychoanalysis, in particular William James's discovery of "subliminal selves" hidden beneath the conscious self. (The august Harvard professor, brother to novelist Henry James, was a more palatable figure in 1920s and '30s America than Sigmund Freud, whose New World vogue was yet to come.) The introduction to *How to Win Friends* quoted the famed psychologist's 1890 *The Principles of Psychology,* in which he observed that "compared to what we ought to be . . . we are only half awake. We are making use of only a small part of our physical and mental resources." Carnegie makes a solemn promise to his readers, all the while monetizing the "resource" metaphor in a vein familiar from Christian versions of the prosperity gospel: "The sole purpose of this book is to help you discover, develop, and profit by those dormant and unused assets."[22] Carnegie took Marden's self-help idiom, still rooted in the Puritan theology of election and salvation by signs, and updated it for a secular modern audience.

Forsaking the language of theology for the language of pop psychology, Carnegie was apt to see these subterranean psychic depths—Marden's "Great Within"—not as a theological mystery but as a set of mental "laws" governing all social interactions that simple scientific observation would help us uncover and exploit to our personal benefit. The person who followed the book's lessons and studied them well would, indeed, attain an almost Svengalian level of control over his fellows—but as a matter of scientific observation, not of theological grace.

"Gosh and gee whilikens, kids! If they only sold that stuff in drugstores," Al Hughes whistles mock-ruefully at the end of his Miriam Hopkins profile for *Photoplay*.[23] But of course, unlike the male audience addressed by success literature, the women who consumed fan magazines were encouraged to believe that they *did* sell that stuff in drugstores. At least, that's what the cosmetic industry and their hired guns, the advertising firms, were banking on.

The makeup advertisements that appeared in fan magazines and, increasingly, in mainstream ladies' magazines, borrowed tropes that the female audience would recognize from the world of cinema. The idea of Hollywood movie-star "type" was perhaps the most crucial of these devices.[24]

Hollywood, like any industry whose aim was to manufacture and sell a product, developed a "star factory" by which it hoped to rationalize or, at the very least, speed up production of star products. To guarantee legibility and buy-in with the audience, a star needed to conform to one of a limited menu of accepted cultural "types." For actresses, the types could range from All-American Girl to Vamp, from Exotic Beauty to Pixie, but once a star found her "type," it was difficult to break from. Because each star's type was assumed, in some way, to reflect her "real" or offscreen personality, consistency of character type across films was key to feeding the audience's fantasy of intimacy with the star. When fans saw their favorites' type confirmed on-screen, they could feel the pleasant rush of recognition. "Everything the audience knew about star 'types' they learned by accumulation, by going to movie after movie," suggests film historian Jeanne Basinger. "Roles were added up to create an unarticulated dialogue between fans and star on-screen." Fan magazines also played an essential role in fostering intimacy, deepening the star's association with type through their interviews and profiles.[25]

But of course, if the movie star had to be a recognizable type, at the same time she had to possess some essential trait that made her "unique" and irreplaceable. The mass-produced product had to be differentiated by subtle, small differences. A profile of Cesar Romero in a 1935 issue of *Motion Picture Magazine* was entitled "New Latin Lover Stirs Hollywood" and did a predictable job of introducing the star both as belonging to a familiar category (the Latin Lover) and departing from it in a way (the studios hoped) readers would find intriguing. The journalist confirmed that the standard trappings of the type were all there—smoldering dark eyes, mane of raven-colored hair, olive skin. The one off-note, however, was that this Latin Lover appeared bashful. "A bit of diffidence is all right for your Gary Coopers and Bing Crosbys," the journalist admitted, "even your Clark Gables in their lighter characterizations." But in a Latin type? Stuff and nonsense. As the journalist watched Romero defer to other stars on the set, however, he began to see that such an unexpected streak of timidity was a boon rather than a bane. He discovered that when Romero was filming his first scene with Marlene Dietrich, he had been so petrified as to be "literally shaking at the knees." The charm effect was complete. Like Clark Gable who was the He-Man type with a dash of "civilization," Cesar Romero was the Latin type with an endearing sprinkle of shy.[26]

The 1936 movie *A Star Is Born* was an adaptation of every fan magazine's favorite fairy tale: the transformation of small-town girl Esther Blodgett into screen star Vicki Lester. In a self-referential moment, the film shows a crowd exiting a movie theater where they have just seen the latest Vicki Lester movie. One woman chirps to her companion, "Ain't she cute? You know, I think she's the same type I am. Don't you?" Beyond its function on the screen, the paradigm of the Hollywood star "type" was made-to-order for the task of selling cosmetics and other products. Following Max Factor's Color Harmony Make-Up of 1927, other cosmetics firms scrambled to develop similar pseudoscientific makeup "systems" based on type. All sought to guide the bewildered consumer amid the flood of newly available makeup choices and shades as well as to ensure higher sales by packaging lipstick, rouge, and face powder as a set.

In a 1928 pamphlet, Max Factor warned women that failure to match makeup colors among themselves, and with one's overall complexion type, led inevitably to an "unnatural, grotesque effect." "Do You Know Your Type in Make-Up as the Screen Stars Do?" a 1929 Max Factor advertisement queried, offering complete lines of makeup in the categories of "blonde," "redhead," "brunette," and "brownette" to help steer women toward their best look.[27] Rival company Armand upped the ante that same year with the "Find Yourself" campaign, doubling Max Factor's palette to eight universal "beauty types" to which customers could match their coloring and personality by taking a fifteen-question quiz. Types were assigned according to a mystifying calculus that involved, among other things, cross-checking eye and hair color ("Are your eyebrows dark?") with sociability levels ("Does it make you nervous to enter a roomful of people?").[28]

But there was a problem at the core of the beauty "type" advertisements—the same problem, in fact, that confronted movie studios when they realized their mass-produced commodity (stars) had to be, at the same time, viewed as "one-in-a-million." While the appeal to quasi-scientific types and systems was meant to allay the fears of the laywoman, at the same time cosmetics promised to help each woman "stand out from the crowd" in individual splendor. Cosmetic advertising found itself in the rather tricky bind of having to persuade women that by matching themselves up with a type they were somehow, at the same time, *also* allowing their unique inner selves to shine through.

Tangee Make-Up essayed the most inventive, if perhaps the most scientifically bogus, tactic: the Color Change Principle. According to this claim, the one-size-fits-all Tangee lipstick, powder, and rouge would chemically transform on contact with skin to bring out the natural beauty of *your* coloring—and yours alone. "Your cheeks when rouged with Tangee are radiant with a delicate ruddiness that is *natural only to you*," the advertisements promised. "On your lips, Tangee changes to the blush rose Nature has hidden there."[29] Max Factor eschewed pseudoscientific alchemy, relying instead on sheer assertion backed by his Hollywood authority. "Screen stars, not wanting to look alike, asked Max Factor to create a makeup that would individualize their type," ran the advertisements. Now, Max Factor was putting this extraordinary cosmetic secret within reach of the average girl: powder, rouge, and lipstick that would "individualize [your] beauty, make you interesting, different!"[30] In the mad dash to "personalize" the Hollywood type, Jean saw an opening for Hudnut—and she took it.

Jean's most sustained work on cosmetics took place during the four years that, as she once quipped in a job letter, she "lived with the Richard Hudnut account" between 1935 and 1939. During this period, Jean had a hand in every step of her client product's journey from factory floor to drugstore aisle, including consumer research, copy writing, packaging and promotion, and sales. In her own recounting, she "rang doorbells, talked to clerks and demonstrators, took buyers to lunch, [and] waylaid factory women and office girls to know what they [thought] about makeup." She did more: she "tested cosmetic copy themes" and "tried makeup shades on human guinea pigs."[31] And ultimately, under Jean's direction, Hudnut launched a new line of products designed to give its competitors' various "personalized" makeup systems a run for their money. A 1936 Hudnut pamphlet

launched the new Marvelous Makeup line with a (no doubt apoc-
ryphal) anecdote: "A woman dropped her handbag . . . and that's
where it all began," the copy narrated. "Out tumbled one kind of face
powder, another brand of rouge, a lipstick that didn't match it—a
jumble of make-up." The pamphlet cast gentle doubt on the efficacy
of Factor's and Armand's typologies. Classifying girls as blondes or
brunettes was fine, as it went—but it "doesn't help girls with dark
hair and blonde skin," alas. The appeal to overall "beauty" types
seemed logical, but then, "so few women *know* their own type."[32]
What was a girl to do?

Jean had an answer as well as a new explanation for how mass-
produced makeup could yield individualized results. Latching on to
the talismanic power of the word "personality," she proposed that
this most intimate of all qualities was contained in the color of a
woman's eyes. Eye shades were limited in number, of course, but
as the proverbial "window to the soul," eyes could never be simply
reducible to a generic "type" in the same way skin or hair coloring
could. By matching one's total makeup palette to eye color—blue,
hazel, brown, or gray—a woman could guarantee her compliance
with universal beauty rules while at the same time facilitating the
expression of her unique "personality color." Yes, after years of careful laboratory research, Hudnut's beauty specialists discovered that
it was not hair color, not beauty type that paved the royal road to
harmonized, even "symphonic," makeup application, but *eye color*.
Hudnut's new Marvelous Eye-Matched Makeup was what American
women had been waiting for.

And the advertisements worked. In a BBDO memo in February
1939, Jean noted that since the launch of the "eye-matched make-up"
campaign in mid-1936, sales of Marvelous Makeup had more than
doubled. The campaign had been widely hailed within the industry
as "the first new idea in cosmetics in fifteen years." The increased
sales volume was paired with increased brand recognition; Jean
reported: "72 per cent of the women of the country became aware of
the [eye-matched] concept."[33]

But this success could not be chalked up simply to Jean's appeal
to the familiar Hollywood vocabulary of "type" nor to her ingenious

pushing of type while promising individuality. Marvelous Makeup's jump in market share must be attributed as well to Jean's success in poaching on territory previously occupied by Max Factor, and Max Factor alone: movie star endorsements. In the same 1939 memo, Jean noted with pride that "we were able to crack the Max Factor monopoly on Hollywood movie stars and signed up more than fifty important stars including Delores del Rio, Madeleine Carroll, Glenda Farrell, Miriam Hopkins, and others."[34] Delores del Rio, named "the most beautiful woman in Hollywood" by *Photoplay* magazine in 1936, was an especially big catch. While many advertisements for Marvelous Eye-Matched Makeup ran in black-and-white half-page format, del Rio was among a handful of Hudnut endorsers elevated to full-page, full-color status.[35]

Del Rio's association with "color" was no accident. The Mexican beauty was billed as an "exotic" type, a centuries-old category within the Western canon of feminine beauty, traditionally marked by "deep" or "vibrant" coloring in skin and hair. A mini-portrait of the star published in *Photoplay* in 1937 admired the "mellowed ivory beauty of this convent-bred Mexican," but noted that behind her "glowing black eyes" one could detect the "restless spirit of her Spanish ancestry."[36] Nor was del Rio's election to the empyrean title of Hollywood Beauty Queen in 1936 a mere quirk of fate: 1936 marked the debut of Hollywood's first full-length Technicolor films, *Dancing Pirate* and the *Trail of the Lonesome Pines*, both starring the "gypsy" imp Steffi Duna. While Technicolor technology had been around for years, it had only recently gained traction among film insiders. Industry giants' predictions that within a year or two black-and-white film would be completely *passé* caused a tremor of panic. The arrival of color threatened to disrupt decades-old Hollywood practices, from set design to narrative pacing to choice of actress type.

"Which Stars Are Doomed by Color?" ran the apocalyptic headline in *Motion Picture Magazine* in August 1936. "Color is demanding new faces," warned reporter James Reid. "Some of the most famous faces on the screen today will vanish. New faces will appear."[37] Natalie Kalmus, wife of Technicolor founder Herbert T. Kalmus and the official "color supervisor" on studio sets using the new film,

FIGURE 7. Jean's first notable copywriting success came when she worked on the Richard Hudnut Marvelous Makeup account in the mid-1930s, creating the campaign tagline, "Choose Your Makeup by the Color of Your Eyes." Jean signed more than a dozen Hollywood actresses to endorse the cosmetic line, including the "exotic" Mexican crossover star Delores del Rio, in this 1937 ad.

opined that stars who filmed best in Technicolor had "colorful complexions" with dark, rather than blonde, hair; a personality "vivid" enough to compete with newly brilliant settings; and a figure amenable to colorful, "picaresque" clothes. Such was Steffi Duna, subject of "Steffi is the Perfect Type for Color" in the same *Motion*

Picture issue. Duna was described as childlike, "small, black-eyed, as warmly vibrating as a rhapsody from her own native Hungary." And she knew instinctively that Technicolor was her golden ticket to fame. "Why shouldn't I like color?" she retorted brightly when the reporter asked her honest opinion of the new medium. "It gave me my face!"[38]

Perhaps the most pressing issue facing the industry, however, was that the makeup practices painstakingly developed for black-and-white film no longer worked in Technicolor. Technicolor film required higher levels of illumination, leading to the introduction of high-intensity arc lights on sets. The greasepaint that had ensured that actors' faces appeared smooth and flawless on black-and-white film became reflective when exposed to arc lights, so that faces now picked up color from the set, giving them a lurid, gaudy, and "unnatural" appearance. In Technicolor's early phase, some stars refused to be filmed in color at all, fearing the unpredictable skin shades might damage their brand. "Color goes a little screwy at times, and I'm just not sure I want to make a Technicolor picture," confessed Carole Lombard who, along with Greta Garbo and Joan Crawford, initially boycotted the new medium.[39]

But what truly disconcerted audiences and directors alike about Technicolor and its tendency to portray its objects in "unruly" and "uncontrollable" shades, as one Hollywood journalist euphemistically phrased it, was the way it scrambled received codes for what passed as "white" on-screen.[40] The birth of Technicolor in 1936 may have witnessed a burst of enthusiasm for all things exotic and picaresque, an apparent opening up of the silver screen, and the cosmetic industry that depended on it, to a range of non-Anglo shades and types. Yet on closer inspection, the del Ríos and Dunas can be seen to have served merely as test cases, carefully choreographed exceptions to prove the general rule of white supremacy in Hollywood.

Skimming through a January 1935 issue of *Modern Mechanix*, the reader falls on an arresting photograph. In the center we see the face and shoulders of a smiling woman, her head enclosed in a strappy, helmet-like metal contraption, a cross between a pincushion and an umpire mask. Behind her, Max Factor, dressed in a lab coat, spectacles, and rubber gloves, is gently adjusting screws on either side of the helmet. What looks like it would be at home on the set of *Bride of Frankenstein* (released the same year) turns out to be a Beauty Micrometer, also known as a Beauty Calibrator. Designed by Factor, the instrument "accurately registers the actors' facial measurements and discloses which features should be reduced or enhanced in the makeup process."[41] Facial flaws nearly invisible to the naked eye, the reporter confided, "become glaring distortions when thrown upon the screen in highly magnified images." Luckily, the Beauty Micrometer was able to catch such defects, so "an experienced operator" could apply corrective makeup. Corrections were made in accordance with a series of "ideal" beauty measurements: in the ideal face type, for instance, the length of the nose was equal to the height of the forehead and the eyes separated by the width of one eye.

The Beauty Calibrator presented a veneer of brisk clinical objectivity, in keeping with the makeup industry's embrace of systematization and pseudoscientific marketing campaigns. But the Beauty Calibrator was merely the latest change rung on a long American tradition of racialized anthropology, from phrenology and craniometry to endless racial taxonomies. Max Factor's contraption bears a sinister resemblance to nineteenth-century cranioscopic instruments designed to measure the skull structure and capacity of the different races.

Indeed, scientific racism and aesthetics were always natural allies. Joachim Winckelmann imported whiteness into the heart of the Western aesthetic ideal when, in his eighteenth-century art history treatise, he held up the white marble Roman statue known as the Belvedere Apollo as the prototype of European beauty. Declaring Chinese eyes "an offense against beauty" and the Siberian nose a deformity, Winckelmann canonized the Greek profile and facial proportions as universal standards for aesthetic judgement. Subsequent racial taxonomies that sought to classify races according to skin color and a complicated system of skull and "facial angle" measurements eagerly drew on classical Greek statuary to illustrate their points.[42]

But this Hollywood dust-up over color and facial "measurements" is, after all, hardly surprising. From its very inception, the business of

Hollywood had been inseparable from racial politics.[43] Whether they were inking up blackface minstrels, fashioning "swarthy" bandits and villains, or etherealizing lily-white leading ladies, makeup artists had to create clearly coded racial "types" that a general audience would instantly recognize. By the 1930s, American popular culture was saturated with visual cues and shorthand for signifying racial difference. Hollywood makeup artists, and mass market cosmetic companies in their wake, were able to tap into a well-established racial unconscious to reinforce white America's cherished vision of itself.[44]

One of Max Factor's most astonishing triumphs was transforming Rudolph Valentino, born Rodolfo Alfonzo Raffaelo Pierre Filibert Guglielmi di Valentina d'Antongoulla, from a swarthy villain into Hollywood's most in-demand leading man. "I was selected for villains because of my dark complexion and somewhat foreign aspect, I presume," Valentino once told an interviewer. This changed when he agreed to let Max take a crack at him. An initial assay with pink greasepaint translated on film into a ghastly white mask, so Max went back to grinding pigments and tried again. He finally settled on a dark yellow shade and made Valentino up for his second screen test. The director, Rex Ingram, balked when Valentino strolled onto the set: "Not THAT!," he reportedly objected. "Do you want him to look like the end man in a minstrel show? He's too dark as it is." But on film, he photographed perfectly: white enough, with just a dollop of darkness to give him exotic allure.[45]

Once Technicolor disrupted existing formulae for reliably reproducing "natural" skin tones on film, cosmetic manufacturers went head to head in what *Variety* magazine jokingly dubbed the "Hollywood Powder Puff War." If Factor ultimately won out, it was because his newly patented Pan-Cake Make-Up most successfully managed to conserve pre-color screen conventions for how "whiteness" should appear on film.[46] The cosmetic industry's manic quest to codify color and beauty types in the 1930s thus mirrored the film industry's scramble to adjust makeup regimens to Technicolor.[47]

Not to be outdone, Marvelous Makeup jumped on the bandwagon of coded racial eugenics. According to promotional pamphlets,

Richard Hudnut's scientists had toiled away in the laboratory for years, comparing girls and "[digging] deep into complications of racial strains and heredity," before discovering the principle of "Eye-Matched Make-Up." A woman's unique "personality color" was "related to skin and hair pigmentation, a color influenced by factors of heredity," and discernible through eye color.[48] It is no surprise that there were but four personality colors, all of them located squarely on the European continent. Blue eyes were classified as the Dresden type, brown as Parisian, hazel as Continental. Gray fell into a rather mysterious fourth category called Patrician—a kind of utopian geographical label unto itself, a magical land populated entirely by aristocrats.

Hudnut's typology—along with its bogus appeal to scientific heredity "specialists"—could have been pulled from zoologist Madison Grant's 1916 eugenics manifesto, *The Passing of the Great Race, or The Racial Basis of European History*. In it, Grant argues that while cranial measurements are important in determining race categorization, "eye color is of very great importance . . . because all blue, gray or green eyes in the world today came originally from the same source, namely the Nordic race of northern Europe" (although Grant concedes nose measurements, in a pinch, can also be useful, as "a bridgeless nose with wide, flaring nostrils [indicates] a very primitive character").[49]

This sleight-of-hand by which geographical or ethnic categories could be "elevated" by class associations was par for the course in Hollywood's historic efforts to pass off darker-skinned actors as white. Valentino's publicity agents, for instance, were scrupulous in specifying his characters were "Spanish" rather than Arab. The same went for Delores del Rio: though she was Mexican, and thus risked being tainted by "Indian" ethnicity, this risk was offset by constant references to her "aristocratic" Spanish heritage.

Jean experienced firsthand the selling power of pseudoscientific appeals to beauty type. "'Choose your makeup by the color of your eyes' . . . has been a proved money maker," she announced in 1939. The beauty type's reliance on coded references to racial purity was no doubt key to its success as well. "Loveliness is within every woman's grasp," the Hudnut pamphlet concluded confidently, and "it is every woman's responsibility never to neglect her beauty heritage."[50] Women didn't merely owe it to themselves to bring out their native loveliness; they owed it to white people as a whole. In the end, the film and cosmetic industries in the 1930s joined forces in promoting a single article of faith: whatever else it might be, the "typical" American face was a white face. And that, no amount of alchemy or magical thinking could change.

5

Community Is Correct

In an article she wrote for an advertising trade journal, "Main Street . . . and How to Find Your Way Back," Jean addressed the perennial worry among admen that, from their perch on Madison Avenue, they might not have their finger on the pulse of the average American. Giving them permission to move past these fears, Jean conjured a picture of a "little white house" on a tree-lined street, with a family inside, celebrating good days—"the birth of a kitten, four A's on a report card, a Boy Scout award"—as well knuckling through the tough times—"a layoff, a sudden illness, the girl who didn't get invited to the Prom." "Thing is," she coaxed them, "you *know* that house." Sure, the adman may live a citified life *now*. But Jean urged him to reach back to his own small-town childhood, nestled somewhere in the heartland. "It is a part of you, a far deeper part than dinner at 21 Club or a night in the Pump Room," she reminded him. "Main Street isn't as far away from any of us as we pretend."[1]

Let's suppose that the typical adman *didn't* have a white house with a picket fence—Jean's "little piece of heaven"—lodged in his American unconscious. Even then he would know about Main Street because his agency's tireless surveys and questionnaires and polls and panels guaranteed him a constant supply of information about the common man. In fact, Jean ventured, "I sometimes think Madison Avenue has earned the right to be called the Heartland of America. For we know a lot more about Main Street than the people who live on it." She proceeded to rattle off facts that she knew, for certain, about average Americans: the wife spent twenty-nine minutes preparing breakfast for her family. Seven out of ten ate dinner in the kitchen. The husband didn't like the taste of liver (he preferred turkey).[2]

And she was right. By 1940, an entire sprawling industry devoted to taking the collective pulse of the nation had emerged. Corporations and advertising firms who represented them, federal government agencies anxious to measure economic and political trends, and a newly minted professoriate of "social scientists" stood at the ready, prepared to poke and prod the common man to find out what made him tick. Jean, as a central member of the Women's Copy team for one of the nation's largest advertising firms, occupied a key position in this massive enterprise.

Efforts to give a face and a shape to the "average American" have a long history. John Hector Saint John de Crèvecoeur offered one of the first studied attempts to paint this mythical creature's portrait in his 1782 meditation *Letters from an American Farmer*. For him, the average American is of European descent and possesses a character marked by the "innovation" and "mobility" that freedom from the shackles of Old World prejudice makes gloriously possible. Alexis de Tocqueville undertook the charge again in his 1835 study, *Democracy in America*, where the typical American is a hearty descendant of "the English race" whose character is (again) marked by "the equality of social conditions" afforded in the New World. Both of these attempts chose to elide the messy reality of the American population—a mixture of African-born slaves, Native Americans, white European indentured servants, and white men and women—to enshrine the white, free-born, property-owning male as most "typical."[3]

Beyond such essayistic firsthand accounts, the statistical push to observe, measure, and quantify the American population had its earliest flowering as an adjunct to nineteenth-century reform movements. The Industrial Revolution brought in its wake an increasingly diverse, poor, and urban population whose "deviant" and possibly revolutionary potential needed to be managed. The poor, immigrants, African Americans, criminals, alcoholics, factory

workers—precisely those people absent from the profiles of Crèvecoeur and Tocqueville—all passed under the microscope of middle-
and upper-middle-class white reformers. While occasionally billed
as "scientific" studies, the central mission of these early sociological
forays, the majority of which were funded by private philanthropies,
remained prescriptive: to push for policy that would assimilate (or
at the very least neutralize) potentially disruptive social elements.
Indeed, the birth of the social sciences at the end of the nineteenth
century was part of a larger effort to replace the waning authority of religion with the more democratic, secular authority of social
"engineering."[4]

But as Americans became increasingly integrated into a "mass"
national culture both socially and economically, social data gatherers
shifted their focus from the margins to the center. The first of these
"main street" studies to be widely publicized was titled, appropri-
ately, *Middletown*. Published in 1929, the study of Muncie, Indiana,
was conducted by Robert Lynd and funded by the Rockefeller Foundation; it was designed to plumb the depths of Protestant religious
life in the modern heartland. Reformist like earlier studies were,
this survey was driven by Rockefeller's belief that a reanimation of
Christian values in an increasingly secularized age might salve the
wounds of social and economic strife brought about by industrialization (from which he had profited extravagantly). But unlike the
earlier studies, intended exclusively for experts tasked with devis-
ing policies to reform "deviant" populations, the studies canvassing
"typical" American communities were eagerly consumed by the very
subject of the studies themselves: the newspaper-reading and radio-
listening public. *Middletown* was an unexpected bestseller, and its
findings were hashed and rehashed on radio and in the press, sparking a nationwide conversation about who, exactly, Americans were.[5]

A number of factors in the 1930s produced this groundswell of
interest, at times bordering on panic, in pinning down who counted
as an "average American."[6] Demographically, the country was in
rapid transition. Between 1880 and 1930, twenty-seven million
immigrants, primarily from southern and eastern Europe, poured
into the country, bringing with them new religions, cultures, and

languages. Between 1915 and 1930, more than a million African Americans living in the rural south migrated northward and west, populating urban centers from New York to Chicago to Los Angeles.[7] These population shifts unsettled America's traditional vision of itself as white Anglo-Saxon and Protestant.

If America's traditional cultural and religious identity was open to question, so was its economic identity. The conviction that capitalism was a benign, progressive force evolving toward ever higher levels of productivity and abundance was, by the 1920s, one of the country's most widely held and unifying beliefs about itself. This faith in American capitalism as a natural social and economic equalizer was abruptly shattered by the market crash of 1929. The First Red Scare in the aftermath of the 1917 Bolshevik Revolution had spawned widespread conspiracy theories linking political radicalism to "alien" immigrant infiltrators, and the European political scene in the 1930s renewed these earlier suspicions. Stalin responded to the rise of Hitler and fascism in Germany by encouraging communists across Europe to join with socialists and progressives in forming an antifascist Popular Front.[8] Conservatives in the United States, including industrialists and their business allies, feared the spread of left-wing radicalism on their home soil and accused Roosevelt's New Deal measures of being a "collectivist" attack on Americans' traditional economic freedoms.

Not all signs of the times pointed to division. The country was increasingly knit together by an expansive network of mass media, nationally distributed magazines and newspapers in addition to the new medium of radio. Franklin D. Roosevelt's "fireside chats" united the country by bringing the president, quite literally, into the intimate parlor of each American home. And it was precisely by partnering with the expanding institutions of the national mass media that a man named George Gallup was able to take the country's free-floating quest for identity and give it a more concrete shape in the form of the national opinion poll.

In 1936 Gallup, along with a handful of other emerging pollsters, challenged the established presidential straw poll conducted in election years by the *Literary Digest*. Gallup employed a new model of "scientific sampling" and one-on-one interviews that allowed him to arrive at a correct prediction, using only a fraction of the *Digest*'s respondents and its laborious mail-in ballot method. The *Literary Digest* poll had the additional handicap of being wrong that year. Gallup's success in predicting the outcome of the presidential election gave him credibility as he expanded his polling subjects far beyond politics, digging into "virtually unexplored sectors of the public mind," as he described it. By 1940, Gallup had a syndicated triweekly column, *America Speaks!*, that gave eight million readers a "week-by-week picture of what Americans are thinking" on everything from FDR to labor unions, from the Neutrality Act to the best way to curb syphilis.[9] Opinion pollsters like Gallup and Elmo Roper moved quickly to professionalize, partnering with academic social scientists, writing for scholarly journals, and creating their own credentialing organization, the American Association of Public Opinion Research.[10]

Opinion pollsters like Gallup and Roper envisioned themselves as laboratory scientists, aligning themselves with a growing class of managerial "experts" who promised to lead the country forward in the turbulent post-Depression years. Yet Gallup and Roper were careful to highlight their difference from governmental managers. Far from being eggheaded technocrats, they billed themselves as pure conduits for the voice of the humble man in the street, broadcasting whatever he had on his mind and in his heart. Gallup credited the advent of mass communication networks—newspapers, radio, motion pictures, telephones—with expanding the scope of public opinion beyond a "small exclusive class" of politicians to "all classes and sections of the community." Even as these new organs were seized on by those in power to push their own agendas, he argued, modern research methods provided a "machinery for directly approaching the mass of the people and hearing what they have to say."[11]

In an atomized and bureaucratized world, Gallup promised that polling would reinvigorate American democracy, give power back to the people. "Shall the common people be free to express their basic needs and purposes, or shall they be dominated by a small ruling clique?" Gallup prodded his readers. "Shall the goal be the free expression of public opinion, or shall efforts be made to ensure its repression?"[12] Against the backdrop of the rise of Stalin and Hitler in Europe, public opinion polls were infused with symbolic meaning, elevated as tokens of America's commitment to freedom, openness, and democratic norms.[13]

Gallup's stirring defense of popular polling was part of a broader cultural movement by which "democracy" and "freedom" were increasingly enshrined as quasi-religious national values. This trend toward sacralizing democracy in what one sociologist later called a unique American "civil religion" had been under way at least since the country's entry into World War I, which Woodrow Wilson led under the crusade-like banner of making the world "safe for democracy." Wilson appointed George Creel head of the wartime Committee on Public Information, an agency tasked both with monitoring press access to sensitive government war information and creating pro-American propaganda abroad. Creel once confessed that democracy was "a religion with [him]," defining it as a "theory of spiritual progress."[14] Indeed, lest there be any doubt as to the evangelical cast of the democratic project, the title of Creel's 1920 memoir dispels it: *How We Advertised America: The First Telling of the Amazing Story of the Committee on Public Information That Carried the Gospel of Americanism to Every Corner of the Globe*. Gallup believed that by distilling the broadly democratic aggregate voice of the "common man" and bringing it into the halls of power, he was doing God-appointed work.[15]

One of Jean's signature achievements at BBDO was to found two in-house opinion panels, staffed by women: the Junior Council (aged twenty-two to twenty-eight) and the Homemaker's Council (aged over twenty-nine). The Junior Council, composed of 150 typists, secretaries, stenographers, and copywriters, was a key sounding board for Jean as well as for other account executives who wanted to test out campaign ideas. She made council members taste cakes and sip soups and wash their hair with competing shampoos. She made them flip through endless brand slogans and illustrations to

FIGURE 8. Jean founded two BBDO in-house research panels, the Junior Council and the Homemakers Council, to test client products and copy themes. Here Jean shows members of the Junior Council sample advertisements for Oneida Limited Community Plate.

find out what caught their eye and what didn't. She polled them ceaselessly about the minutiae of their domestic lives and their social lives, dug deep into their professional and romantic aspirations. She cross-checked their answers against national polls: Gallup, Starch Ratings, McCall's Reader Surveys. Then she took the results, her homegrown version of *America Speaks!*, to her corporate clients.

In step with Gallup and Roper's tendency to frame their quantitative data as the voice of "Americans" in the aggregate, Jean carefully pitched her findings as the tried-and-true voice of Everywoman. Jean often opened her speeches to clients with sociological mini-disquisitions on the "ordinariness" of her panel members, giving their bona fides as an accurate barometer of the client's target audience. In a representative 1946 speech to Oneida Silverware executives, Jean ran down some statistics that assured them that the Junior Council comprised "a pretty normal and typical sample of today's youth market." She rattled off a sampling of domestic facts about

"YOUR CUSTOMER, 1946"—she went to church ("63 say every week"), she liked to cook, she set the table when company came to dinner—before deducing from this data a plausible advertising strategy to get them to buy silverware.[16]

In 1940, Oneida Limited and its trademark Community Plate silver was one of a handful of national manufacturers battling it out for market share in an age when every middle-class American bride—as well as those working girls who aspired to that status—had to have a proper set of silverware for entertaining. Oneida had gotten on the advertising train early in the 1910s, hiring such iconic magazine illustrators as Maxwell Parrish and Coles Phillips to design full-page, sumptuously colored "pin-up girl" ads. But whoever was handling the Oneida account after its heyday in the Roaring '20s had obviously fallen asleep on the job. Oneida advertisements in the *Ladies' Home Journal* throughout the late '30s and the first half of 1940 were distinctly lackluster: a hodgepodge of anemically tinted elements thrown together into a half-page text box, without any single visual anchor to draw the viewer in. The slogan, "Leadership in Design Authority," struggled for attention—and authority—at the bottom of the page.

When BBDO landed the account in 1940, Jean rolled up her sleeves and got to work. While the previous ads had made half-hearted appeals to the bridal market, Jean designed an intensive, yearlong campaign for 1941 that would target this all-important population systematically. First, she contracted with four of America's most renowned clothing designers—Sally Milgrim, Hattie Carnegie, Orry-Kelly, and Vogue—to design bridal dresses inspired by Community Plate patterns. Jean explained the reasoning for this to Oneida's executives: with the fall of France in the early summer of 1940, "American fashion accounts hurried home from Paris"—and found, to their surprise, that American designers were ready and willing to take up the sartorial slack. "Fashion openings this year were just as crowded, just as important as ever before," she reported, "but in New York, not Paris." Department stores got into the spirit as well, featuring American designers rather than the European mainstays in their advertising. The USA was now the fashion center of the free world—and Oneida was poised to profit from it.[17]

The new advertisements dropped the washed-out palette in favor of richly textured, jewel-like color that popped off the page. The central image in each ad was a full-length photograph of a model in a signature white designer wedding dress, paired with a spoon of the matching Oneida pattern in all of its sumptuous silver glory. Carnegie's private clients included "the first names of stage, screen, and the social register," while Orry-Kelly was dressmaker to such august figures as Bette Davis and Mary Astor. "It's not a gown for Main Street," Jean admitted of Carnegie's luxurious confection, which featured a highly ornamental, nun-like headdress. But imitation by Main Street wasn't BBDO's aim. The point of the pairings, Jean was quick to point out, was to create dresses that would be "looked at . . . and talked about," that would fuel bridal fantasies (whether realized or not).[18]

Although she had significantly overhauled the visuals of Oneida's Community Plate ads, Jean wasn't satisfied with the campaign motto, "Leadership in Design Authority." Both the words "Leadership" and "Authority," she found through her in-house polling, were sounding a false note. When asked what the words meant to them, Junior Council women returned strange answers. "I know what leadership means, but I'm puzzled by that word authority," returned one girl. "Is it something like Port Authority?" queried another rather literal-minded respondent, referring to the intercommerce regulatory agency policing river traffic between New York and New Jersey. The logo was, decidedly, not meeting its mark.

Jean diagnosed the semantic stumble almost immediately. Appeals to authority could sell medicine and cosmetics. But when a bride-to-be buys a set of silverware, Jean guessed, she doesn't care what the experts say; she wants to know what her friends and neighbors will say. "Etiquette columns," Jean told Oneida executives in 1941, "are among the best-read sections of the newspaper," and etiquette books were topping bestseller lists. "This desire of men and women to know and to do the right thing is a serious one." Today's young woman, Jean suggested, is never sure of her taste, but "she wants—terribly—to be *right*."[19]

Jean was on to something. America's new brand of civil religion was also a religion of civility, centered on the values of tolerance, teamwork, and a scrupulous avoidance of "giving offense." The exercise of tact in all dealings with one's neighbor was the ultimate test of adhesion to America's consensus creed. Jean's brilliantly amended slogan for Oneida was "If It's Community, It's Correct." The adjective summoned up both an etiquette book and a Sunday sermon; it offered a handy tip on how to choose fish knives that doubled as a watered-down injunction to Love Thy Neighbor. It was the perfect distillation of the period obsession with averageness and agreement. One should strive to get along with one's peers, to fall in line, to be one of the gang: to agree with your chums on the most flattering cut of jacket or the proper table setting was not just polite; it was a sign of deep moral Judeo-Christian consensus. Jean knew instinctively that she could take this sentiment and make it sell silverware.

When Jean ran the copy by her test group this time, the slogan resonated. What does "Community Is Correct" mean to you? "It means Community is socially correct," offered one respondent. She could invite friends to dinner assured that she was executing her role as hostess properly. "It means it's correctly designed—correct implements and everything," offered another. She wouldn't be caught short—she wouldn't be missing dessert spoons, if such were required. But most important: "If you have Community, you know you are *right*" was the resounding answer.[20]

Jean's insight into the extraordinary selling power of peer acceptance was not limited to silverware. In notes for a speech before Betty Crocker executives, Jean focused on the talismanic magic of the word "homogenized" in marketing campaigns. Homogenized milk first caught on the United States in the 1920s; the altered fat globules would remain in suspension rather than rise to the top of the jug, producing a more consistently creamy, evenly textured product. But since that time, Jean observed, the word "homogenization" had surpassed its technical definition to become an adjective that had "extra selling strength—sometimes over and above and beyond its actual functions." It was an adjective that could be usefully tacked on to any "mixed" product, from cake to cosmetics, to boost sales.

And it was, in fact, a BBDO team that first struck on the idea of using it to market bread: Bond bread baked from previously "homogenized" or emulsified ingredients was touted as yielding a tastier product. Whether in face cream or bread, Jean suggested, "Always, even to women who could not explain it, [homogenized] has connoted something better, something richer, something good." When Jean tested the phrase "homogenized for moister, homemade taste" on cake mixes for baking housewives, the results came back resoundingly positive. Survey respondents identified the homogenized mix as likely to be "lighter, higher, fluffier, more surely successful" than the nonhomogenized competitor. They imagined it would be "more digestible" with "more thoroughly mixed ingredients."[21]

Such midcentury enthusiasm for homogenization—whether in cake batter or cultures—echoed the original Progressive Era faith in market standardization as the most efficient and "American" of social equalizers. The market left to its own devices would achieve on its own what Europeans sought to legislate through class-based politics and statist intervention. Simon Patten, that early Pollyanna of the corporate order, had praised expanding consumption and market standardization as the ticket to national harmony. Modern consumers, he insisted, were "generalists" who saw the world whole; they would eventually turn the tide against stick-in-the-mud provincials who clung stubbornly to "the tyranny of local conditions." "The standardized succeed," Patten lectured, while "the unstandardized leave town or drop into unmarked graves. . . . It is only the newer impulses and ideals which all have in common that serve as a basis of unity."[22]

Yet conveniently sidelined from these discussions was the fact that entire swathes of the population were blocked, on account of class and race, from transcending the "tyranny of local conditions" and entering the promised land of standardized equality.[23] In fact, the "homogenized" American as he appeared on the radio, in the movies, in the newspapers, and in Gallup polls in the 1930s and

'40s was anything but an empirically representative reflection of actual Americans. From the start, "everyman" studies were carefully curated to focus on native-born whites. In selecting a city for his *Middletown* study, proto-pollster Robert Lynd rejected South Bend, Indiana, in favor of Muncie precisely because of the former's cultural and religious heterogeneity. The completely atypical homogeneity of Muncie, lacking either a significant African American or an immigrant population, was chosen *for* its absence of "complicating factors," not in spite of them.[24] Given the iconic status Lynd's study eventually earned both in popular culture and in academic research, these sampling decisions had far-reaching consequences.

Gallup and his colleagues persistently sampled only native-born whites. They used the term "unreachables" for those who didn't respond to their inquiries by virtue of their class or racial distance from (and distrust of) the middle-class white pollsters knocking at their door. As a result, these voices were muted in the final tallies. There were also more intrinsic imbalances generated by a system that tied the larger and more rigorous polling to election results. By keying surveys to "likely voters," pollsters virtually guaranteed the results would be skewed in the direction of white, middle-class males.[25] Gallup's polls and those modeled on it were less democratic in fact than in theory.

That Jean knew full well the average American was, to some extent, a fiction is indicated by her detailed marketing plans, which address the diversity of her clients' target audience. When advertising firms like BBDO set about defining markets, they of course looked for lowest common denominators, something like a statistical "average" in the product's projected buying public that, if the client could tap into it, would stimulate sales. But as canny businessmen, they knew better than to put too much faith in—or money behind—the kind of generalized, aggregate American "averageness" featured on radio shows and in the columns of the *Saturday Evening Post*. Knowing "Where the People Stand" was fine, but it wasn't as good as knowing "Where Bride-Aged White Women Stand." Actual markets were crucially differentiated by such factors as gender, class, race, and education. It was important to hit all the targets, not just an airbrushed composite of the typical consumer.

Speaking to Oncida Limited's management in 1940, Jean broke down their prospective market into three slices of the American female population: bride-aged women, eighteen to twenty-nine, looking to buy silverware; married hostess-aged women, thirty to thirty-nine, whose "silver needs are expanding"; and women forty to forty-nine, mothers of the brides. But the advertising strategy had to dig deeper than gender and age, and segment more specifically by socioeconomic status. Beyond the *Saturday Evening Post* (the nation's most-read and widely circulated periodical), Oneida's Community Plate would also be advertised in the four most popular middle-class women's magazines—*Ladies' Home Journal, McCall's, Good Housekeeping,* and *Better Home and Gardens.* Finally, the working-class or "mass" market would be targeted as well, with ads in *True Story* and *Mademoiselle,* while the "class" market—"women of sufficient income and taste to want the best in fashion"—would be reached by ads in *Vogue* and *House and Garden.*

Corporate clients who paid for market and opinion poll research were thus privy to a level of heterogeneity in the American public that was systematically flattened when the same data was presented to "the public" itself as objective, poll-generated percentages on "What America Thinks" or "Where The People Stand."[26] For while Jean and Oneida were well aware of the considerable socioeconomic diversity within the American bridal market, the ad copy itself worked rigorously to efface such differences, to sell precisely the democratic "averageness" and social conformity that national opinion polls were enshrining in the popular consciousness. Middle-class whiteness was a useful fiction, an aspirational ideal masquerading as quantified, empirical fact. For marketing purposes, it functioned just as well—if not better—as an idealized composite than as a reality.

But the objectivity of national opinion polling was compromised by more than just design flaws and blind spots in the sampling methodology. Perhaps more insidious, because less obvious, was the ideological debt polling owed to the corporate, profit-driven mindset. All of the major early pollsters—Archibald Crossley, Elmo Roper, George Gallup—got their start in marketing research. Gallup's PhD in applied psychology, "An Objective Method for Determining

Reader Interest in the Content of a Newspaper," immediately got the attention of corporate behemoths such as Lever Brothers, General Foods, and the Hearst Sunday papers, who hired him as a consultant. The advertising agency Young and Rubicam brought him on as director of its research division in 1932. Given their training, early pollsters and communications researchers unsurprisingly modeled their social inquiries on the marketplace logic of consumer preference. They were market driven not only because their training was in market research and its noncritical stance toward its subject but because to reach the public, polls had to pass through the market logic of corporate-owned and sponsored news media, whether magazines, film, or radio. The market biases baked into the mass media shaped not only the form but also the content of the information that got air time.

Among Jean's papers is an undated typed manuscript she edited for the *Saturday Evening Post*, entitled "No Man Knows the Origin of the Marketplace." The short article rehearses an analogy long dear to political and economic liberalism: that just as economic competition in the free market allows superior products to rise to the top, so "free trade in ideas" in the public sphere and in the media helps democracies arrive at the "best" ideas. The mass media, in this construction, is a transparent, open forum where widely separated and widely diverse individuals exchange ideas and goods. While we don't know the origin and end destination of this one-page piece of promotional copy touting the value of the *Saturday Evening Post*, the rhetoric of the piece, and Jean's edits of it, shed light on the way idealized assumptions about "freedom" and "democracy" shaped the midcentury public's understanding of how markets—whether for goods and services or for news and information—worked.

The copy opens by imagining markets of yore, the "shifting, colorful, kaleidoscopic pageant" in which "the vendors' wares meet the buyers' needs in a harmony of fulfillment." Jean—or the author—anticipates the readers' objection: today's America is too big, too spread out, to make the fantasy of a single marketplace realistic. "Yet here you will be wrong," she cautions. The marketplace is no longer to be found in the literal public square but in the pages of national

newspapers and magazines: "Here men come, as they came to markets of old, to sharpen one mind against the whetstone of another."
"Here merchants spread their wares and shoppers explore—and
buyer and seller meet in a very real partnership."

The pages of the *Post* are, further, a radically democratic space,
its contents—from fiction to news to advertisements—shaped by the
desires of the people who read it. "Just as the buyers and sellers who
wear down the cobblestones ARE the marketplace, so . . . the readers
of the *Post* ARE the *Post*. It is they who have made it—in the image
of their own wants," the copy contends. In the "changing political
and social and economic pageant" of the news items, readers see
reflected the rich diversity of their world. And in the "ever changing
pageant of the advertisements," both buyer and seller will see writ
large the underlying desires and aspirations of the common man
for the "enrichment of his material life." The *Saturday Evening Post*
is "America's marketplace," an agora for the free and friendly and
democratic exchange of goods and ideas.[27]

Except that, as researchers in the nascent field of communication
studies increasingly noted, the widespread analogy of mass media to
a "free" market (itself a regulative fiction) was entirely misleading.
Mass media content was, from the get-go, shaped and constrained
by the material and institutional interests of its corporate owners and
sponsors, who paid for its circulation and diffusion. When the Social
Science Research Council drew up a 1948 report criticizing the most
prominent pollsters, including Gallup, for following "journalistic
rather than scientific demands" in their research, they were entirely
correct: the polls were funded by newspaper publishers, broadcasting companies, and other corporations, whose interests thus dictated
both their form and content. For instance, publishers who ran Gallup's *America Speaks!* column and radio studios weighed in on how
poll data should be presented, requiring "surveyors to encapsulate
complicated findings in an easily summarized chart or a fifteen-
minute broadcast" to avoid "perplexing" the reader or listener. The
obvious objective was, of course, to protect the network's ratings.[28]

A ratings- and market-based rationale shaped not only format-
ting decisions but also the content itself—particularly as reflected in

what *didn't* make it into print or onto the airwaves. The absence of "race issue" questions in Gallup's early polls was the result of his client newspapers being predominantly based in the South. NBC's radio programming in the 1930s and '40s prohibited the discussion on air of "labor questions," and NBC aired Roper's radio show precisely because it "avoid[ed] the partisanship that all too often means disgruntled customers."[29] When media analyst Leila Sussmann studied radio coverage of labor issues in 1944, she found that across major networks, a combination of editorial selection and presentation decisions led to labor being presented as "morally wrong five times as often as it was morally right."[30] The mass media provided a market for ideas that was "free" in theory—except when it threatened the popularity and profit of its shareholders; then, suddenly, it wasn't.

This development did not go unnoticed by sociologists and other influential academic researchers who worked side by side with nonacademic pollsters. Scholars in the nascent disciplines of sociology and communications studies sounded the alarm early on, pointing out that in their technocratic drive to generate data about populations—whether at the behest of government agencies or corporations—researchers tended to present those data in value-neutral terms, as scientific descriptions of natural facts, without calling attention to the deeper historical, political, and economic contexts shaping mass media and polling methods themselves.

Columbia University professor Paul Lazarsfeld flagged the problem in 1941, noting that "the technique of manipulating large masses of people is developed in the business world and from there permeates our whole culture," including the operation of mass media channels. Supposedly value-neutral content analyses or audience response polls failed to question the larger economic and social context in which mass media operated, leading to a dangerous species of "spurious objectivity," in the words of media analyst William Albig.[31] The political specter of his time, Lazarsfeld predicted, was that the mass media "public sphere" would lose its independence, henceforth operating solely within the "framework of commodity merchandising." What was worse, social science research, which helped to study, monitor, and guide mass media, was following suit: "more and more of this research is seen to succumb to the fate of mass media content itself in being implicitly tailored to the specifications of industrial and market operations."

Gallup's claim that opinion polls would wrest power out of the hands of the few—"powerful newspapers," "motion picture and radio executives"—belied the fact that it was those very vested powers that were, at least to some extent, the gatekeepers deciding what was fit (and profitable) to print and air. If the "public" that emerged from these polls and studies miraculously resembled precisely the kind of public a corporate order required to keep humming along, then, it was not a coincidence.

Jean didn't just rely on the data she collated from BBDO Junior Council questionnaires and national opinion, marketing, and readership polls. She also marshaled, in anecdotal form, the support of academic social scientists whose work illuminated cultural and social trends in America. Jean was fond of trotting out her gloss on David Riesman's 1950 *The Lonely Crowd*, a portrait of middle-class conformity in a nation transitioning from a producer to a consumer society. Riesman devised a neat, tripartite division of human history into three epochal social "types": the "tradition-directed" person of primitive society was supplanted by the "inner-directed" person of an industrial producer-society, now being ousted by the "other-directed" individual of modern democratic and consumer-driven culture. In Riesman's estimation, authority shifted away from its basis in tradition and family or class identity, as a standardized and democratized populace learned to look to their peers for validation and a sense of belonging.

In a speech at a United Fruit Cookbook Conference on the American family's changing eating patterns, Jean cited Riesman's concept of "other-direction," noting that she and her fellow advertisers were, precisely, the "others" currently setting the patterns. "It is a frightening thing, an awesome thing," she mused, "to know that we are holding in our hands not only the wellbeing of [an] individual can of soup or box of cake mix but we are serving as . . . an *other director* to a confused, driven, harried, helpless, crazy, mixed up world." Being an other director was a solemn responsibility, she concluded, one that demanded not only individual strength and bravery, but a dollop of divine assistance as well: "Have you *prayed* enough for that?" Jean finally queried of her gathered audience-cum-congregation.[32]

Jean's files are stuffed with clippings from social scientific studies that she thought might come in handy in promoting advertising as a profession, generally, and her individual client campaigns, in particular. In addition to using Riesman, her client pitches included snippets from anthropologist Margaret Mead's studies on gender roles and offhand references to William Whyte's portrait of midcentury white-collar culture in *Organization Man*. She was fond of referring to her Junior Council members as "100 Beautiful Guinea Pigs," a nod to a Depression-era bestselling book by consumer advocates Arthur Kallet and F. J. Schlink entitled *100,000,000 Guinea Pigs*.

Yet anyone who had actually digested these sociological studies knew their analyses of contemporary American culture were not intended as data-driven reports on "today's consumer," information to be put to work by advertisers and their corporate clients in the business of efficiently channeling consumer desire. These studies, like the *Middletown* study from which they drew inspiration, were imbued with critique at times bordering on undisguised horror at the scene they surveyed. They were intended as critical levers by which modern society could more clearly understand and thus improve itself.

Riesman, for instance, found in contemporary Americans' "other-directed" ethos a spooky abdication of anything like a coherent morality or value system. Instead, "approval itself, irrespective of content, becomes almost the only unequivocal good . . . : one makes good when one is approved of."[33] This heightened sensitivity to the ever-shifting "actions and wishes of others," rather than allegiance to a traditional external code of ethics, was the natural outcome of a culture increasingly driven by market logic. Even language, Riesman observed with some melancholy, had become a consumer good: "It is used neither . . . to relate the self to others in any really intimate way, nor to recall the past, nor yet as sheer word play. Rather it is used in the peer-groups today much as popular tunes seem to be used: as a set of counters" by which individuals establish their market viability.[34] The cultural phenomenon of "other direction," which in Riesman's eyes betokened an impoverishment of values, could be cheerfully repurposed to sell silverware.

The fact that Jean could strip Riesman's study of its critical thrust and use it to craft marketing strategies—all in perfectly good faith— was entirely characteristic of the midcentury advertising industry. As another example, *100,000,000 Guinea Pigs*, which was subtitled *Dangers in Everyday Foods, Drugs, and Cosmetics*, took aim at corporations, lax government regulators, and advertising agencies for "making profits by experimenting on [consumers] with poisons, irritants, harmful chemical preservatives, and dangerous drugs."[35] While the scientific accuracy of some of the book's claims were debated, it went through thirteen printings and served as a catalyst for the eventual passage of stricter consumer protections in the Federal Food, Drug and Cosmetic Act of 1938. The reference to guinea pigs was intended as a stiff critique of industry ethics. And yet Jean was able to strip away the value judgement and leverage the popular title for its sheer name recognition, giving BBDO an edge in competing for corporate clients. Such blithe dismissal of context and sloppy conceptual blurring was the very lifeblood of advertising, where context was considered "highbrow" and "jingles" didn't have to mean anything; they just had to stick.

Jean could speak with such confidence about Main Street, USA, not only because it was her business to study the average American consumer but because her own family so closely mirrored, at least on the surface, the idealized image she helped create: white, middle-class, suburban, Protestant. Jean's archive does not contain much personal material that would give insight into her private family life. For this, we must depend on the rare references Jean made to her husband and children in the interviews she gave and the articles she wrote. These allusions, of course, were carefully curated for public consumption. In a sponsored editorial that appeared in the *Daily News*, for example, Jean plugged Wildroot Shampoo by pledging her family's personal commitment to the product. The homey details she shared with her reader were calculated to establish her credibility as housewife and mother. "By day I sit at a desk and write ads," she began. But "by night I live in a house in the country with a husband and two children and a dog and a half dozen hamsters (by last count)."[36] Her teenage daughter Anne swears by Wildroot ("her hair's so thick and soft and young it kind of makes my heart skip [you know mothers!]"). Even her husband—"he's a little short of hair these days"—reaches for the bottle in the shower. All of Jean's references, from playful poke at her balding husband to mock despair at her children's ever-multiplying pet population, establish her as a stock maternal character: slightly harried, always loyal, ever loving wife and mother.

One place in the archive where Jean's work selling "average" American family values and her own private family life appear to intersect is around the celebration of Christmas. Jean was sometimes tasked with writing public relations holiday cards for clients to send out to their customers at Christmas. One series of "Season's Greetings" messages that she crafted for Oneida Limited drew on the kind of bland, sentimental well-wishing one might expect from a corporate Christmas card: "Good wishes Unlimited from Oneida Limited," ran one possible card insert. "Bless you . . . for being you, for being kind, for being a friend to be thankful for at Christmas!" ran another. A third option conjured up the cozy domestic atmosphere on which Oneida had built its brand: "Fragrant balsam . . . polished mahogany . . . glowing candles . . . gleaming silver. . . . All these are part of Christmas! May yours be deeply content."[37]

But these corporate greetings are almost indistinguishable from a series of Christmas-themed meditations filed in a folder marked "Personal—Inspiration." On a scrap of bright pink paper appears a poem by Christian inspirational poet Grace Noll Crowell: a prayer for clarity and peace at Christmastime amid the "breathless rushing" of "hurried, flurried women" caught up in the tempest of gift buying and tree trimming. Another typed snippet, with the heading "Busy! Busy! Busy!," takes up the same theme but is pure Jean. It paints a picture of a couple collapsing in post-Christmas exhaustion, after the turkey has been eaten and the gifts opened and the kids packed off to bed. They realize with a sudden pang that the Christmas cards they sent out that year had been filled with apologies for having been so busy, not having had time to connect, for being absent in their friends' lives. "This year, please God, we hope to change the pattern," murmurs the speaker. "Because . . . what better time could there be to share a fragment of the peace that passeth understanding than with every note you send with a Christmas card."[38] The format of the page, with its formal title, makes it seem as though it might have been a piece of advertising copy, a homespun vignette to be used as an inset for a Christmas ad.

But it is just as likely that Jean could have cribbed a line or two of the copy to include in her own personal Christmas cards. Photographs in Jean's archive include custom-made Christmas greeting cards: one series, circa 1937, feature a photo of Jean and Willard's toddler son, John, superimposed on a reindeer-drawn sled; in another, John beams at the camera, a silhouette of Santa and his pack of toys looming in the background. "Merry Christmas from Willard, Jean and John," reads the cheery script. Later Christmas photographs from the early '40s feature both John and his younger sister, Anne, grinning in front of a stocking-draped fireplace. It is difficult, looking at these overlapping files, to say where Jean's public persona ends and her private one begins.

The question for the biographer is not, ultimately, to what extent the "real Jean" coincided with her public performances of white middle-class suburban motherhood. This is a question to which the surviving documents can, in any case, supply no real answer. Rather, the more interesting point to note is how difficult it is, in poring over Jean's archive, to detect any difference between scripted and unscripted selves, between the average housewife she wrote ads for and the housewife she privately aimed to be, between "real" maternal sentiment and its commodified, mass-marketed signifiers. It gives us a measure of how powerful a social force this fictional composite of an "averaged American," shaped and then endlessly amplified through mass media, was at midcentury.

6

Back Home for Keeps

In the spring and early summer of 1940, as Hitler's armies smashed through village after village on a blitzkrieg that would end in the fall of France, a grim but steady Franklin D. Roosevelt took to the airwaves to prepare Americans for the eventuality of war. The country's largest manufacturers scaled back the production of consumer goods to convert their plants to war materiel, soon churning out the armaments, planes, and tanks that would likely be required. Consumers were encouraged to conserve in-demand materials such as rubber, metal, and gasoline. Magazine advertisements began to reflect, both in tone and iconography, the general surge of patriotic feeling and preparedness sweeping the country. BBDO's ads for Community Plate were no exception. After Jean's initial 1940 campaign pairing designer bridal gowns with silver patterns, a new set of ads appeared striking a more somber tone: white-clad brides stood arm in arm with handsome husbands-servicemen, whose stiff military uniforms aimed to make the reader stand at attention.

Within a few months of Pearl Harbor, American consumer good production had dropped by a full 29 percent. The wartime economy not only removed vast quantities of consumer goods from the market but discouraged consumption more generally. This, understandably, put the advertising industry in a bit of a bind. "During the war we advertisers found ourselves with a problem," Jean once reminisced: "No product." This was an understatement: advertisers stood to lose up to 80 percent of their business over the course of the war if they couldn't figure out a way to remain relevant.[1]

But they were at a distinct disadvantage. Advertisers and their corporate allies had taken a public relations hit during the Depression. The New Deal was seen in many quarters as a heroic regulatory corrective to corporate capitalism's excesses. In accepting the Democratic Party's renomination for the 1936 presidential race, and speaking before a crowd of more than one hundred thousand cheering fans, Roosevelt affirmed his commitment to what he called Americans' right to "political *and* economic freedoms." The amazing world ushered in by industrialization and the modern market was indeed a "new civilization," Roosevelt conceded. But it had also created a new caste system of economic "royalists" who, while they were happy to have the government guarantee political freedom, had "maintained that economic slavery was nobody's business."[2] Roosevelt and fellow New Dealers held that political equality in the face of economic inequality was meaningless, and they pushed through Congress an unprecedented suite of activist legislation that sought to equalize access to economic opportunity, from the Social Security Act to the Wagner Act guaranteeing workers' rights to organize and bargain collectively.

Corporate leaders and industry trade organizations struck back, coordinating their own massive public relations campaign to convince consumers that economic prosperity was best guaranteed by private business, not a meddling federal government.[3] In opposition to Roosevelt's emphasis on economic freedom as a collective and state-sponsored national enterprise, they coined the more individualist term "free enterprise" as the beating heart of American capitalism. Free individuals acting freely in the market, not shackled by government interference, was the only truly "American Way."[4]

But businessmen faced uphill work. In 1938, Congress had established a Temporary National Economic Committee (TNEC) with a mandate to investigate the "concentration of economic power in American industry and the effect of that concentration upon the decline of competition." President Roosevelt expressed hope that the committee's investigations might ultimately lead to "a more equitable distribution of income and earnings among American people."[5] First up on its agenda: studying whether corporate reliance on intensive advertising campaigns to establish brand dominance violated antimonopoly law. The outbreak of war only sharpened the squeeze on advertisers. Rumors flew that Congress might introduce a bill striking out a time-honored provision of the tax code rendering advertising expenses tax exempt. If passed, corporate federal taxes would nearly double, and their advertising budgets would plummet. The advertising industry had to come up with a response.[6]

They riposted by claiming that the government's bid to curtail advertising amounted to an attack on Americans' basic freedoms. In response to the TNEC hearings on the monopolistic effects of branding, the *Chicago Tribune* accused the Justice Department of trying to "repeal the First Amendment." Senator Robert A. Taft, Republican from Ohio, suggested that once the government was granted power to control what appeared in advertising columns, it was but a short step before it began telling "every newspaper what it shall put in its news and editorial columns."[7]

Others went further. An industry-commissioned study conducted with Harvard Business School, *The Economic Effects of Advertising*, concluded ominously that the anti-advertising forces afoot were "moving in on the advertising process in a manner not unlike that of the Hitler strategy of divide and rule."[8] The implied analogy between fascist and communist repressions abroad and repression at home proved a popular rhetorical trope during wartime, and advertisers were quick to compare any attempt by the federal government to regulate their industry to the "general attack on individual freedom throughout the world" at the time.[9]

If New Dealers insisted that political freedom was moot without economic freedom, the opposing camp charged that any attempts to meddle with economic freedoms risked encroaching on the sacrosanct domain of political and religious freedoms. In a 1940 speech to members of the National Association of Manufacturers, president H. W. Prentiss laid out what he called America's unique "tripod of freedom": representative democracy; civil and religious liberties; and economic freedom, or "the institution of private enterprise." "Throughout the ages, these institutions have gone together," he lectured his audience. "They are inseparable. When one goes, all go," he concluded ominously.[10]

Given these tensions, advertising industry leaders could hardly believe their luck when, mere days after the Japanese attack on Pearl Harbor, the government's newly created Office of Price Administration reached out for help in creating public support for the war and facilitating access to the mass media. One industry insider, understandably pleased, predicted that "the advertising office's greatest skeleton, fear of federal interference, will crumble into dust with Uncle Sam himself turning to advertising to gain defense program results."[11] The result of this entente was the creation of the War Advertising Council, a panel of representatives from advertising agencies and the print and radio industries, charged with helping the government to implement its wartime information strategy.

In addition to advising advertising agencies on how to create appropriate war-themed content for their clients, the Ad Council served as a clearing house of sorts, matching up government agencies in need of publicity campaigns with creative and media partners in the private sector. Government campaigns promoting everything from the sale of war bonds to the planting of victory gardens partnered with the relevant industries—soap manufacturers, for instance, in the drive to conserve fats and grease. The resulting advertisements managed to neatly harmonize private sales objectives with national campaign goals.

Jean collaborated on a number of such war-themed ads. She did a series of advertisements for the Continental Can Company in partnership with the National Nutrition Program, a federal campaign encouraging women to increase their household consumption of fruits and vegetables. "Americans should eat more vegetables," pronounced a stern and gray-templed surgeon general, leaning out from behind his desk. The ad promised that eating canned greens would "build a nation of people more fit, vigorous, competent . . . than the world has ever seen." "Better nutrition for all—that's a defense program in which we can ALL take part" ran the closing sentence of a similar Continental Can plug for fruit juices.[12] Another long-term client Jean helped through the war years was Eat-Mor Cranberries. She oversaw the design of a chummy cartoon character, the Cranberry Corporal, who barked out friendly orders to housewives to make "sugar-saving" cranberry sauce or cranberry-orange relish.

The ads also featured recipes, all tested in the BBDO kitchens, to help housewives stretch their sugar rations.[13]

Nor was the government's effort to win hearts and minds limited to advertisements. June 1942 saw the creation of the Magazine Bureau, designed to serve as a liaison between women's magazines and the Office of War Information (OWI), and charged specifically with promoting editorial content and fiction tailored to the war effort.[14] Since a sizable portion of women's magazine content was traditionally devoted to such rigorously nonmartial topics as fashion, cooking, and interior design, editors were occasionally hard pressed to weave war themes into their pages. In some cases, fashion and makeup features were rebranded to make them look less like frivolous feminine pursuits and more like active efforts to boost soldier morale. According to this strategy, women on the home front could best support their men by keeping themselves beautiful. A style feature in the March 1942 issue of *Ladies' Home Journal*, "Keep Them Easy on the Eyes!," showed snapshots of grinning servicemen juxtaposed with chic feminine silhouettes decked out in the latest designer dresses. A woman's effort to remain fit and fashionable, far from being vain, was its own kind of war work, the editors pledged.

Yet "keeping a polish on their dispositions," as one chipper ad for Modess feminine napkins urged, wasn't going to turn the tides of war. That would depend on women taking up the manufacturing factory jobs left vacant by men away at the front. Traditionally male industries—the metal trades, ammunition assembly, and aircraft and automobile manufacturing—suffered severe labor shortages.[15] In short—it wasn't simply as patriotic consumers and fashion plates that women had to step up; they had to enlist as producers as well. The Magazine Bureau would play a crucial role in publicizing these "womanpower" campaigns.[16]

Under the direction of Dorothy Ducas, in July 1942 the Magazine Bureau began publication of a bimonthly *Magazine War Guide*. Among other items, the guide collected information from the War Manpower Commission and the OWI Bureau of Campaigns on where women workers were needed. Magazine publishers and editors, in turn, used the guidelines to solicit appropriate fiction and news articles that would encourage women, in ways both overt and subtle, to enter the labor force. In the fall of 1942, Ducas produced a booklet entitled *War Jobs for Women* in response to complaints by the War Manpower Commission that the magazines were not representing women's war work effectively. They were emphasizing nonessential and more traditionally feminine fields, such as modeling, rather than the industries in need of labor.[17]

To lure women into traditionally masculine industries, the government writers suggested, ladies' magazines should represent modern women as heirs to the pioneering frontier women who "fought rustlers, highwaymen, and bandits beside their men." Pulp fiction's modern-day heroines needed, similarly, to be portrayed "*not* as weak sisters but as coming through in manly style."[18] Illustrative of this new style is a 1943 *Ladies' Home Journal* ad for Kotex. The first image shows a downcast young woman in pajamas seated in an overstuffed chair with her head in her hands. "I was an Absentee 3 Days a Month," the caption reads, forced into passivity by her menstrual cycle. After reading up on nutrition and exercise tips in a pamphlet from Kotex, however, this young war worker was back on the job. "I'm taking a man's place," declared the lovely girl at her drill press, "and from now on I'm going to be a round-the-month worker!"

The *Magazine War Guide* was quick to point out, however, that women's patriotic duty to take up men's work did not free them from their domestic responsibilities. War work, far from making women "like" men, should increase opportunities for romance and a path to deepening the traditionally self-sacrificing virtues of the female sex. In magazine fiction and advertisements, the patriotic female war worker, ever selfless, met with the reward of male approval and romance.

An ad for Woodbury soap in *Ladies' Home Journal* in 1943 featured a photograph of one Marguerite Kirshner, lipsticked and svelte, deftly wiring an airplane panel at the Boeing plant in Seattle. "She turned her back on the Social Scene and is Finding Romance at Work!" read the exuberant caption. "My job is worth every broken fingernail and dirty oil smudge a million times over!" Marguerite confided. She may be sacrificing the superficial tokens of feminine beauty, but Marguerite had "thrown in her lot for Victory" and gained inner beauty as a result. Besides, thanks to Woodbury facial products, her complexion was as fresh as ever, making her a perfect picture of feminine health and strength holding the line on the home front. "Busier lives—but beauty as usual," the advertisement concluded.

By contrast, girls who denied their country's call to duty or clung to prewar models of frilly, vain femininity lost at love, as did girls who became self-absorbed or career-obsessed in their new roles, seeing their work as "empowering them personally" or otherwise failing to "subordinate ego to a cause more important than self."[19] Undertaken in the right spirit, "man's work" was not at odds with domestic virtues; it was a young woman's best path toward embodying those traditional qualities most fully. The rhetoric aimed at mobilizing women as war workers reprised the turn-of-the-century calls for white-collar office women to find professional fulfillment through "service" to a male boss or to a larger company as institutional *pater familias*.

A 1943 *Ladies' Home Journal* poll of active GIs returned these same ambiguous directives for American women on the home front. In "Orders for the Girls at Home," the informal poll reported that only 8 percent of soldiers disapproved of the idea of their girlfriends working in an office or war plant while they were away. But there was vociferous insistence that these girls maintain their femininity, "a positive shout against mannish hair and the discarding of make-up and nail polish." And a full 81 percent of GIs polled said they expected their women to "immediately" vacate their jobs at the war's end.[20]

Had the same questionnaire been directed at working women, the numbers would have been flipped: a 1944 survey of women in the war production sectors found that 75 to 80 percent of them planned to remain in the labor force after victory.[21] In crafting its job recruitment campaigns, the government had misjudged its demographic. While it predicted the vacant jobs would attract middle-class homemakers eager to "pitch in" during the war and return home promptly at war's end, the majority of women war workers in fact came from the working class. A full 50 percent of these "new" recruits had at least five years of prewar work experience already.[22] The war offered these women an unexpected economic boon: sudden access to unionized, high-wage jobs in the durable goods sector that had previously been off limits to them.

This financial independence was not something they were eager to give up at war's end. Yet by and large, give it up they did—aided, in no small part, by advertising agencies like BBDO. Having once collaborated on getting women into the workforce, the same firms toiled just as busily at getting them out of it and back into the domestic sphere. BBDO, where Jean's wartime work for Oneida silverware would offer a perfect example, was no exception.

"For four years or more," Jean wrote in a 1943 BBDO report entitled "War vs. Non-War: A Study in Consumer Attitudes," "American magazine advertising pages have crackled with pictures of planes and tanks and guns." "Some advertisers had good reason to use such pictures," she noted. "Some had no reason but liked the look of them." Whatever the initial reasoning, it was more or less certain that "the public will at some time tire of these pictures." Was it possible that that time was "RIGHT NOW," Jean wondered?[23]

Her anecdotal probing suggested that it might be. According to surveys, war-themed advertisements got high reader ratings—but the best-read ads were consistently those that contained "inspirational" rather than military messages. Jean cited a *McCall's* study of women's magazine fiction for the first six months of 1943. Of 116 short stories and novels, 60 were non–war themed and 56 war-themed. On the face of it, an even split. "But look beneath the surface," Jean coaxed. The best-read nonwar stories featured such titles as "First Kiss," "Oh My Darling," and "You Belong to Me." Among war-themed stories, those featuring men at the front were the most poorly read; those featuring love-and-kisses titles like "Every Man Needs a Girl" and "The Roses Were for Her" scored highest. "War stories. Yes, perhaps. The man was in uniform," Jean observed. "But he was not in action. They were not combat stories. He was at home—and he was in love."[24]

Jean was quite frank in her assessment of what motivated consumers. While high-sounding political ideals and patriotism were fine as far as they went, they could not compete with the more immediate, day-to-day concerns of the average American. "Men and women in their personal lives are selfish and self-interested," she reasoned. "There is very little that appeals to that personal self-interest in a carload of planes and tanks and guns." "Perhaps it is time to come a little nearer to home—to build up a warmer, friendlier desire for [the advertiser's] postwar product," she suggested in conclusion. In short, "to make Jim and Mary remember and look forward to the cars and refrigerators and stoves and watches they will have a chance to buy tomorrow."[25]

One of BBDO's long-standing clients, Hamilton watches, had hopped on the planes-and-tanks-and-guns bandwagon early. "Marines! They Get There by HAMILTON Time," claimed one spread, featuring a sketch of helmeted marines standing at the ready atop a landing craft. "Marine landing attacks are timed to the second—by a Hamilton wrist watch made especially for the Marine Corps." But another set of ads that appeared, among other places, in the 1942 Christmas edition of the *Saturday Evening Post* struck a loftier, more philosophical tone— and garnered high praise for it. In lieu of military iconography, this ad featured an image of the Statue of Liberty, torch held triumphantly high against a stormy gray sky, with the caption, "We Shall Ride This Storm Through!" "These things, too, shall pass away," the ad said soothingly. As if promising a return to normalcy and the angels of our better natures, beneath the Statue of Liberty was tucked an image of a uniformed serviceman receiving a kiss from his beautiful wife, with his-and-her Hamilton watches laid tenderly side by side at the bottom of the page.

In a typed manuscript titled "Excerpts from Letters to the Hamilton Watch Company About Christmas Advertisement," Jean recorded snippets of reader testimony to the power of such "inspirational" copy. "The ad is simple and yet it reaches something that is first in people's minds today. We need to be reminded that there will sometime again be peace," wrote one respondent. "We liked the broad scope it included—the past, the present, and the future of the problems confronting the world today," confessed another letter writer. "For aren't we all hoping for 'the golden hour of peace'?"[26]

Having tested the waters, in 1943 Jean decided that Oneida Limited's Community Plate advertising was due for an overhaul—and that it, too, would begin to move away from the war itself and back into the home. Early in the war the Community Is Correct campaign had been given a dash of wartime flavor by portraying brides in white and grooms in uniform cooing over wedding silver. These ads even incorporated a bit of levity, picturing the bride turning away from her husband to take one last longing glance at the silver. "This IS something to have and to hold!" remarked one bride, caressing a shiny silver fork. But these images of domesticity, while quippy and cute, no longer hit quite the right note. With its built-in associations with domesticity, nurture, and comfort, Jean judged, silverware was a perfect candidate for ad copy that would "come a little nearer to home."

The result was a sweeping new campaign for Oneida called Back Home for Keeps. Each ad featured a close-up portrait of an all-American beauty engaged in a kiss with a uniformed soldier, presumably just returned from the war. "The day is coming!" announced the accompanying text. "You'll laugh, you'll love, you'll live . . . when he comes back home for keeps." And on that day, "crystal will gleam and silver will sparkle on a table set for two." The artist Jean hired was Jon Whitcomb, a New York magazine illustrator whose close-up gouache pictures of pretty girls were so popular in the 1940s that the term "Whitcomb girl" became publishing shorthand for "cover girl."[27] Whitcomb's images bodied forth idealized portraits of heartbreakingly beautiful white girls, at once chaste and alluring.[28] Whitcomb's success can be attributed not only to his artistic skill but also to his canny ability to predict public tastes to accommodate the time lag between his creation of an image and its appearance in the magazines. "My crystal ball must aim for four to six months ahead, when the ad will appear," he once observed.[29] Together, Cassandra-like, Whitcomb and Jean gave their audience the image of themselves they wanted to see, even before they quite knew that they wanted to see it.

The Back Home for Keeps campaign launched in *Life* and *Ladies' Home Journal* in September 1943 and continued beyond the end

FIGURE 9. During World War II, Jean helped BBDO shift its tone away from military themes to more sentimental, domestic settings. Her most successful campaign in this genre was the "Back Home for Keeps" series for Oneida Limited Community Plate silverware, which ran in national magazines from 1943 through the end of the war.

of the war, until December 1945. Oneida and BBDO knew the ad campaign would be popular but not how popular; they were overwhelmed by more than half a million written requests for their posters. The May 14, 1945, issue of *Life* magazine ran a column devoted to the "pin-up craze" sparked by the campaign, with posters plastering the walls of military housewives' homes, girls' college dormitories, and the barracks "of those servicemen who have wearied of the anatomical pin-up."

In a triumphal speech to Oneida executives in December 1944, Jean offered them a "dip into the mailbag," quoting from the more than 100,000 fan letters BBDO had received. "'My fiancé is in France and each of your pictures makes me visualize his homecoming,'" gushed one young woman. "I have picked out my pattern in Community for our long-dreamed-of postwar home.'" Even soldiers, it seemed, were ready for a whiff of sentimentality in their visions of postwar domestic fulfillment. In a letter to Oneida Limited dated December 3, 1944, section sergeant William E. Miller wrote of the "world of enthusiasm" evoked in his paratroopers by the company's ads. "The girls remind us of our own," he confessed wistfully, "the ones we've left on the campuses of Vanderbilt, Northwestern, and Ohio State." If the company would be kind enough to send the soldiers full-color reproductions of the posters, "you don't know how appreciative the men in this little room across from an English moor would be."[30]

Whitcomb and Jean's crystal ball had, indeed, been prescient: "Your advertisements fit the times more than any others I have seen," allowed another fan.[31] American women—and men—recognized themselves in the ads and saw there images that fit their ideas about who, after the turbulence and confusion of war, they wanted to be. The only thing a manufacturer in wartime could hope for, Jean once noted to Oneida executives, was to emerge in peacetime with "a name in good condition and people waiting to buy his product." This, Jean had roundly delivered.

One housewife writing in praise of the Back Home for Keeps campaign recounted that she had sent her fiancé a copy of an ad, which he carried in his shirt pocket as a sort of talisman through two years of fighting in the South Pacific. "We are together in our home [now] and would like very much to have the series framed in maple to match our living room," she concluded. If this sudden shift from the drama of combat to the comfort of fabric swatches may appear abrupt, it had, in fact, been well prepared by the OWI. As difficult as the experience of war was, the booming war economy translated into higher wages and more purchasing power for more Americans, a welcome relief after the lean Depression years. Fears of a slowdown once war production stopped led to active efforts to stoke investment—psychic as well as material—in a postwar expansion economy, a utopia of abundance where toasters and washers, cars and suburban homes would be available to all.

An issue of the *Wedge* that Jean wrote during this period, entitled "Days of Decision," opened with a paean to the lofty decision-making that statesmen, policy planners, and economists would undertake as they built a postwar world. "In the year or years following the war, there will be many things to decide," she opened gravely. "Statesmen, generals, politicians will make decisions; economic planners will make decisions." Yet she quickly pivoted to zero in on "Joe and Mary," and how their consumer decisions—about everything from cake mixes to vacuum cleaners—would make or break a postwar business's bottom line.[32] By tying humble domestic purchasing decisions to the decision-making of world leaders, Jean underscored the new global order as one where democracy and mass consumption, political and economic freedoms, would work hand in hand.

If the Depression had posed a temporary setback to Progressive Era faith in capitalism, the postwar boom heralded a return to confidence in "free enterprise." This was true even among tried-and-true political liberals, who after the war tacked sharply toward the center (if not to the right) on questions of class and economic inequality. Key to establishing this bipartisan entente was the emergence of John Maynard Keynes as spokesman for the essentially progressive thrust of government-funded mass consumption. According to Keynes and his followers, consumption on a grand scale would reboot the economy and help guide the nation on its tricky postwar path between revolution (communism) and reaction (fascism).[33] Such a consumer-based path to democratic ends was attractive to liberals and conservatives alike, promising, as it did, "the socially progressive end of economic equality without requiring politically progressive means of redistributing existing wealth."[34] It offered, to

borrow the title of historian Arthur Schlesinger's 1949 political manifesto, a "vital center" around which the nation could come together.

During the war, the War Advertising Council had built a sturdy
foundation of goodwill, both with the federal government and with
the public, for their selfless efforts to rally the nation together around
victory. But when the government dissolved its Office of War Information at war's end, the Council was loath to follow suit. "Should
business likewise scrap its information leadership," the Council
warned, "there would then exist no coordinated method for informing and inspiring the people, or securing public action."[35] Dropping
the "War" in its title, the Advertising Council reorganized itself as a
private nonprofit foundation dedicated to "public service" advertising. And it would go on to play a major role in the postwar project
of selling a new-and-improved, expansive, democratic capitalism—
what they called "a people's capitalism"—to the public.

The Advertising Council couldn't have played this role without
the support of the federal government and the major mass media
outlets—and it was successful in garnering both. During the war,
liaisons between the government and the Ad Council were housed
in the Office of War Information. When that body was dissolved,
President Truman moved its functions into the White House itself,
eager to maintain an open channel of communication with the public. But in this new arrangement, the government was demoted to
second-in-command when it came to deciding which public service
campaigns should be funded. Whereas during the war the Council
worked at the behest of the federal agencies and accepted all of their
requests for information campaigns automatically, at war's end the
Council reserved the right to accept or reject requests as it saw fit.

In addition to now having a literal space in the White House as a
semiprivatized government mouthpiece, the Advertising Council
also secured the support of all the major American media corporations, from newspaper empires like the *Washington Post* to national
broadcasting networks NBC, ABC, and CBS, in helping to promote
and disseminate their pet "public service" campaigns.[36] Among the
largest of these campaigns was an educational drive, launched in
November 1948, devoted to "improv[ing] public understanding of

our economic system," or what they christened "The American Economic System."[37]

Council-sponsored advertisements from this campaign emphasized America's extraordinary capacity for mass production as both the product of the country's founding "tripod" of freedoms, as well as that freedom's best guarantee. Take away economic freedom, the logic ran, and the other pillars of the American way—religious and political freedom—would surely follow. Teamwork in the service of expanding productivity not only led to higher living standards and higher wages for all, but helped demolish godless communism into the bargain. "Is World War 3 Inevitable?" queried one promotional poster showing a priest standing in the ruins of a bombed-out church. Not if Americans could learn to pull together, put their backs into boosting production, and "swing the balance for freedom and peace."[38]

By 1950, ads from this series had appeared in hundreds of popular magazines and newspapers, on thousands of billboards, and in tens of thousands of posters plastered on trains, subways, and buses nationwide. When Ad Council president T. S. Repplier returned from a six-month global stint studying communist propaganda methods abroad, he brought home with him a novel public relations tactic. To establish goodwill toward business, the United States should explain that having "outgrown" the exploitative excesses of early corporate capitalism, the nation had now entered a new and final phase of completely evolved "capitalism of, by and for the people." A People's Capitalism exhibit that opened in Washington, D.C., in 1956 stressed that as a result of the country's freedom-driven productivity, America was fast "becoming classless," and that "almost everybody [was] a capitalist" now.[39] In a postwar political climate marked by increasing anticommunist sentiment, American liberals had to scramble to redeem their earlier dalliances with socialism and renew their political credibility. Lending support to the Ad Council's vision of an expansive, fully evolved, progressive "people's capitalism" was one way liberals could prove their patriotic bona fides.

The feminine domestic ideal inherited from the nineteenth century was invested with renewed psychic and political energy in the postwar period. Women, it was held, would make themselves most useful not by usurping the public producer role of their husbands but by orchestrating efficient consumption from the privacy of the domestic interior—just as Christine Frederick had originally imagined. As the postwar reality of a world split into a communist East and a capitalist West sunk in, Frederick's rigidly gendered prescription for political and economic behavior was about to get a massive, geopolitically charged shot in the arm.

The rush to matrimony, homemaking, and an enthusiastic embrace of the traditional patriarchal family was fueled by enormous incentives that were built not only into the structure of the postwar economy and its tax codes, but into the nation's new infrastructure: an explosion of suburban single-family homes and a network of national highways to facilitate access to them.[40] The GI Bill sought to jumpstart the economy by providing returning servicemen with a trio of economic subsidies: unemployment pay while they searched for a job, tuition remission for further education or job training, and low-interest loans to buy homes or start businesses. While women veterans were, in theory, included under the bill, a combination of outright discrimination and peer pressure to renounce their "soldier" status on returning to civilian life resulted in a very small percentage of female veterans actually claiming benefits. White male veterans, on the other hand, were given a massive boost up the social ladder in both earning power and prestige.

Jean was quick to recognize that the postwar economy and its domestic tendencies represented a bonanza for corporate advertising, and she was just as quick to act on it. All of the advertising campaigns she devised in the year following the war underscored the soaring bridal and homemaking markets as a chance of a lifetime. Her speeches to current and prospective clients in 1945 featured robust data on what she referred to as "YOUR CUSTOMER, 1946"—and this customer was a woman decidedly homeward-bound and inward-looking.

The war was long over by the summer of 1946, but Jean told Oneida executives that the domestic themes they had tapped into during the war were still alive and well. Citing extensive polling of her Junior Council members that she had then cross-checked against national polling to ensure that it was "a pretty normal and typical sample" of America's young women, Jean claimed they all had homemaking on their minds. When asked whether they wanted a successful career, a happy marriage, or both, the resounding answer was wedded bliss: "They want what their mothers wanted—84 girls want a happy marriage. Only two give a darn about a career. And 14 think they could swing both." "Dearest, dearest, dearest dreams," Jean resumed mistily. "Age-old dreams, most of them. A man of my own, a home of our own, children. That's looking inside your customer, 1946."[41]

But Jean went further, digging into their reading habits, their leisure activities, their day-to-day worries. What do they fret about? Losing weight; finding a husband; caring for a sick parent. "You probably don't need much more evidence that women are emotional creatures," Jean concluded. "Not a job worry in a carload. Not a political worry. My man. My home. My mother. My children—these are the things on your customer's mind." Magazine and newspaper readership surveys returned similar results. Women read local deaths and births and the Hollywood gossip columns; men read sports, politics, and the stock market pages. "When you get outside the sharp focus of a woman's own interest, of all the people near and dear to her," cautioned Jean, "you lose her attention."[42] Oneida would be wise to remember that the domestic yearnings it reignited in the hearts of America's young women were still very much alive. Oneida may be tempted to experiment with new techniques or new approaches. But, Jean warned, "I hope you will never go so far away that you will lose the key to a women's heart—because it is YOUR PRODUCT, the home-stuff, the dream-stuff you call Community that puts you there. And it is because a woman recognizes that you belong . . . that she lets you stay."

Judging by Oneida's ad campaigns throughout the rest of the decade and into the 1950s, the company took Jean's advice. "Let's Make It for Keeps!" ran the amended tag line for Community Plate silver, now featuring ecstatic civilian couples exchanging wedding rings. "Girls with love in their hearts have homes on their minds," prompted another period ad, cajoling young men to pick up a set of silverware for their sweethearts. Other ads pushed even further in

FIGURES 10 AND 11. The theme of domestic wedded bliss was so popular that Oneida continued it into the postwar period, targeting the booming bridal market with these 1948 and 1953 advertisements.

portraying women either as childlike primitives, dazzled by shiny things, or as charming manipulators using their wiles to loop head-over-heels husbands into buying them. "She's in love . . . and she loves Community!" gushed one variation on this theme.

If Jean's work during the war taught her one thing, it was that "a little bit of love," as she phrased it in her 1945 Dupont speech,

FIGURES 10 AND 11. (*continued*)

worked marvels in marketing. "People don't change," she philoso-
phized. "They want to love, they want to be loved; the things that
matter most in their lives are the little warm, human, intimate and
personal things."[43] What worked was "simple and genuine," something with "a bit of a heart-tug in it." Jean had hit on a way of marketing to women that was perfectly suited to postwar America: a
culture where political quietism and containment was the order of

the day, a retreat from history into the timeless, sentimental verities of the heart.

Jean's work for Oneida marked a turning point in her career. In 1944, she was appointed BBDO's first woman vice president; in 1954, she became the first woman elected to the firm's board of directors. In between, she gained national distinction when the Advertising Federation of America (AFA) named her "Advertising Woman of the Year." In the letters of congratulation that came pouring in after each new accolade, Jean's male colleagues often couldn't resist ribbing her for having secured such traditionally male rewards. "Congratulations! They couldn't have done it to a nicer guy," joked one on her AFA nomination; "Congratulations to a swell 'guy'!" wrote another.[44]

Yet during her decade-long professional ascent, and across the dozens of profiles and interviews that appeared in media outlets from the *New York Times* to the trade journal *Printer's Ink*, Jean was most often lauded as a shining example of how a woman might succeed in the corporate world without ever sacrificing her domestic duties as wife and mother. "Mother Named Advertising Woman of Year," ran one headline.[45] "Ad Woman of the Year Successfully Manages Career and Family," beamed *Printer's Ink*.[46] And in an editorial Jean wrote herself, she took a mock-confessional tone: "My Name is Jean Rindlaub and I Live a Double Life."[47]

Jean's interviews from the period are all marked by a ritual deflection away from herself and toward the service of others. "She is quick to point out that whatever success she's had has been due to others," noted one reporter, while another observed, "Mrs. Rindlaub seldom says 'I.' It is consistently 'we.'"[48] As if seeking to match the aura of maternal expansiveness that Jean attached to her work, interviewers regularly described her as soft and approachable: she "laughs easily" and "talks rapidly but softly," wrote the *New York Times*.[49] A *Houston Post* writer noted she was "mild-appearing," with a "quick smile" and a "comfortably padded figure," carrying a jumbled handbag stuffed with pictures of her family.[50] "Petite, dark-eyed," ran another column, again downsizing her physical presence.[51] This was a self, the interviewers appeared to agree, who excelled in folding the "I" into the "we," the apotheosis of feminine self-sacrifice.

On her end, and in keeping with her interviewers' narrative framing, Jean was careful to emphasize the essentially amateur nature of her advertising work. It was a "job," she stressed; not a career. When asked how she felt about being named Advertising Woman of the Year, she quipped, "'I'm scared to death.'" That was because, explained a reporter, "she doesn't think of herself as a career woman at all." "In her own estimation she's just another woman who has combined her job with being a wife and raising a family."[52] In her acceptance speech at the awards ceremony in June 1951, Jean predictably folded this professional honor seamlessly into her humble daily rounds as an average American wife and mother. Everyone has their years, she opened philosophically, both the good and the bad. "The year you get the job you want. The year you marry the man who matters. . . . The year your son is born." And then, every once in a blue moon, and in no way outshining your domestic pursuits, "the year someone names you Advertising Woman of the Year."[53]

7

Believe in Betty Crocker

In 1952, Jean wrote an issue of BBDO's *Wedge* entitled "All the Rest of Your Natural Life." This advertising parable opened with the portrait of a sleep-deprived young father of a newborn son asking the narrator, "Tell me . . . how long does this keep up?" When the narrator presses him to specify, he returns, "Oh, you know . . . this losing sleep and getting up to look at the baby and wondering if he's covered and walking the floor." To which the seasoned friend replies, philosophically, that "*this*"—"the greatness and the goodness and the terror and the trial" of being human and caring for other humans—"keeps up all the rest of your natural life." The piece went on to pledge that BBDO knew how to tap into "the emotional tides that ebb and flow in the hearts of men"—and promised to bring its selling power to bear on any client's product.[1]

When the issue crossed the desk of the vice president of U.S. Steel, a longtime BBDO client, he admired it so much he sent a letter to his friend Bruce Barton, a founding partner and chairman of the board at the Madison Avenue giant. "My compliments to the fellow who did the job," he wrote, hinting that Barton himself might be the author. "I agree with you one thousand percent," Barton responded, explaining that the "fellow" was none other than Jean Rindlaub. He added that she was so precious an asset to the firm that "we lock her up in the safe every night so that U.S. Steel or some other big corporation can't steal her."[2] The executive's mistake was understandable. Barton had made his name writing public relations copy for such corporate behemoths as General Motors and General Electric, spearheading what would become a standard style of institutional "service" advertising during the 1920s. And "All the Rest of Your Natural Life" seemed like vintage Barton.

There were many avenues by which corporations could project an image of themselves as public servants concerned with the welfare of their larger communities.[3] But the strategy on which Barton built his reputation was that of imbuing big business with a folksy "human touch," using what historian Roland Marchand called "a homespun yet expansive language of service."[4] In his work for General Motors, Barton realized that size was the firm's biggest weakness, opening it up to perennial charges of being a greedy monopoly or a soulless, bureaucratic machine. His advertising sought to counter these charges by forging an associative link between greatness and benevolence: GM, the ads promised, was large and capacious enough to gather the whole nation under its wing, bringing prosperity and better living to all. In a complementary move, Barton humanized GM's line of cars as a "family of vehicles," introduced to the public in all their lovable particularity: the august Cadillac, paterfamilias; the more modest Oldsmobile, the family "pioneer"; and finally the Chevrolet, humble but reliable foot solider in the "unfinished task of making the nation a neighborhood."[5]

Barton's work for General Electric aimed even higher in its claims for the corporation's benevolent, millennial mission as bringer of light. He recommended the company create a series of ads illustrating "what electricity is doing for human life," highlighting the myriad ways that its main customers—central power stations, the railroads—were increasing the health and comfort of average Americans. Vaulting, "big picture" images of generators and combines were juxtaposed with close portraits of humble American family life by lamplight, illustrated by Norman Rockwell.[6]

These analogies, by which people were trained to see their own family circle as a microcosm of the nation and globe, all united in one big Family of Man, had been key to the sentimental appeal of Barton's advertising style, as they were to Jean's. More important, this rhetorical mode was perfectly suited to advancing the national narrative that was steadily gaining ground in the 1950s: that the free, untrammeled consumption of goods in the pursuit of private happiness was the lever by which the public good—and the equitable distribution of goods—would be attained.

An article Barton wrote for a 1955 issue of *Reader's Digest*, "Advertising: Its Contribution to the American Way of Life," has been preserved in Jean's files, carefully clipped. In it, Barton rehearses the familiar paean to free-market capitalism as an agent of moral and material progress, guarantor not only of a vaguely formulated Christian righteousness but also the purest form of democracy. He explained advertising as the facilitator of modern mass production and mass economies, exerting a downward pressure on prices until "the luxury of the rich became the possession of every family that was willing to work." Free-market competition not only worked as a leveling force, creating equality of access to the fruits of the earth and toppling "elites," but was an essential arm of the democratic process itself. Every day, customers voted with their pocketbooks and thus kept each manufacturer striving "through continuous research to improve his product" and earn the public confidence. In totalitarian societies, Barton noted, advertising doesn't exist—for allowing a people to choose consumer goods in the marketplace could easily tip over into allowing them to choose leaders at the ballot box. As a force that wields the power to move markets and change lives, Barton concluded, advertising "needs to be handled carefully, truthfully, sometimes even prayerfully."[7]

Barton, a minister's son, had been reared on the very same Prosperity Gospel staples as Jean, and he developed a signature style that one GE official dubbed "business sermonettes."[8] It was a style that dovetailed perfectly with Barton's most famous extracurricular endeavor: chronicling the life of Jesus as an exemplary "servant leader" and the most successful adman in history in a 1925 bestselling biography, *The Man Nobody Knows*. "Whosoever will be chief among you, let him be your servant. Even as the Son of Man came not to be ministered unto, but to minister, and to give his life a ransom for many" (Matthew 20:27–28). Barton's New Testament–inspired concept of the business-servant leader was to have a long afterlife in the intertwined worlds of American free enterprise and evangelical

Christianity.[9] It is not surprising, then, that Barton's advertising carried an aura of head-bowing prayerfulness, a firm faith that in making ads, he was following the Gospel's call to be about his Father's business. Jean would continue that ministry.

Jean's own work in the field of institutional advertising for General Mills in the late 1940s and '50s bore the unmistakable stamp of Barton's style. In a series of projected service advertisements, Jean worked to soften the "big" in "big business," both by painting General Mills as a "big sister" to the average American housewife and by linking its size not to big money but to largeness of spirit. "Something called the profit system has been taking quite a beating at the hands of America's critics of late," the copy opened ruefully. "People are supposed to be half-apologetic when they talk about making a profit." But that system was the "secret of all successful business"—indeed, of a successful America. General Mill's Four-Square profits meant the farmers who grew the grain, the workers who milled it, the stockholders who funded it, and the people who ate it all enjoyed greater wealth and health, basking in "the highest living standard of any people on the face of the earth." The next time someone was to suggest a "substitute for the profit system," the copy closed, one should ask: "How's it doing at showing its people a PROFIT?" A companion ad was entitled "This Little Miller," projected to feature a "fanciful, Disney-ish" cartoon of a miller at the head, and undoubtedly intended to put a human face on "big business." "What is big business?," the ad queried. "Time after time, you know it yourself, it is a little business that had the courage, the faith, the purpose, the spirit, to grow big." Under the "American system," big business doesn't just mean big plants, number of employees, volume of goods; big business is "first of all big in *spirit*."[10]

Another parallel series of ads specifically portrayed housewives as "partners" with General Mills. One ad, "Me and My Partner—General Mills!" was slated to feature an image of a newlywed couple, the wife feeding her husband a spoonful of pie at the kitchen table. "Yes, for quite a while now—years—General Mills has been operating a little cooking partnership with the women of America," the copy opened. Housewives put up the cash and the cooking skill; GM put up "all that sun and wind and rain and knowledge of soils and farming skills can do for grain, all that careful, honest testing can do to guarantee quality, all that helpful big-sisterly advice and counsel . . . can do" to help make women better cooks. In another ad from the same series, "It was only a book about cookies," the narrator gave a series of homey snapshots of American families and cookies—mothers baking them, grinning kids pulling them from the jar—before reminding the reader that "we're not really talking about that." General Mills' sponsored series of cookbooks was just one illustration of the fact that "'big business' though it may be, it's a warm and friendly and woman-minded business, a neighborly, responsible cooking-partnership with the women of America, when its name is General Mills."[11]

That Jean firmly believed her own copy is beyond doubt. In a memo she sent to higher-ups in BBDO dated November 23, 1948, she vented her frustration at the current fad for advertisements that hooked themselves to specific social causes. "Advertising has always been a social force," she insisted, simply by serving the smooth functioning of a free-market economy. "The social consequences of mill shutdowns, layoffs, pay cuts and other grim results of failure to market the things a manufacturer makes are very real," she warned.[12] In the shadow of the totalitarian horrors of war-ravaged Europe, Jean—like Barton—was adamant that the "American business model" provided the only way forward. To free-market naysayers, she had a ready riposte: "Up to now nothing else has ever come along that has done so much in the way of material things for the comfort and happiness of its people," was her standard reply. "And I have yet to have too positive a demonstration that an underfed, underprivileged, over-dominated people are spiritually happier than a free and privileged people."[13]

In this, Jean was giving new shape to the old utopian Christian capitalism first formulated by the Social Gospelers in the early part of the century and tweaked, by Barton, into a powerful means of promoting the corporation as a "service" institution working in the public interest. Managing producer supply and consumer demand, and bringing the two into harmony, was a sacred role without which

God's kingdom of peace and goodwill would never be realized. In her ad series for General Mills, Jean expanded the word "profit" to include not only the cash profits going into corporate pockets but the more incalculable profit in emotional and material well-being created by the corporate machine: not only "the highest standard of living in history of any country on earth," but also emotional dividends of "healthier, happier" families.

The conceptual blurring and deliberate imprecision in the words used to rally the public around free-market values at midcentury was key to heading off any real political challenge to the status quo. When Barton breezily equated consumer choice with political choice, he was performing a sleight-of-hand that diverted political energy toward private consumption. Similarly, what Jean called "love-and-kisses" or "heart-tug" copy worked through the rigorous flattening-out of difference, shearing away historical context to bask in universal human experience: "the greatness and the goodness and the terror and the trial," as she writes in "All the Rest of Your Natural Life," of simply being human. When Jean challenged the General Mills customer to ask how good any alternative economic system was at "making its people a PROFIT," the question was thoroughly rhetorical. So completely had she collapsed her public into the egalitarian catchall of "the people," so thoroughly had she blurred the concept of "profit" to refer to capital and to amber waves of grain and to maternal love, all at the same time, that the question lost all sense. It might be easier, the copy seems to nudge, to stop worrying and just bake a cake.

Jean's most successful copy relied on precisely such facile shifts of scale, collapsing the personal, the familial, the national, and the global into a sentimental vision of shared "human interest." In no campaign of her career was she able to do this work so consistently and effectively as in her advertising for Betty Crocker cake mixes—an account she was handed in 1952, on the strength of her wartime "heart-tug" copy for Community Plate.

The fictional character of Betty Crocker had been a mainstay of General Mills' sales strategy since before its founding, invented as a name and signature in 1921 by General Mills's parent company,

Washburn-Crosby Flour. Betty Crocker rode the rising tide of demand for female home economics and "domestic science" experts in
the first decades of the new century. In 1924, Washburn-Crosby purchased one of the nation's first radio stations, WCCO, and launched
The Betty Crocker Cooking School, with the part of Betty voiced by
Blanche Ingersoll. The show's popularity spread, and soon there
were at least thirteen "Betty Crockers" nationwide on the airwaves,
all delivering copy prepared by (now) General Mills' in-house copy
writer, Marjorie Husted.[14]

But it was Jeanette Kelly who in 1944 really consolidated the
operation and the Betty Crocker concept by proposing that Betty
Crocker should be housed in a "test kitchen" at General Mills headquarters, a laboratory from which she would disseminate recipes as
well as cooking "standards" by which home bakers might measure
their own culinary efforts.[15] The idea, according to advertising vice
president Samuel C. Gale, was "to sell results rather than products."[16]

Betty Crocker made the leap to television in 1950 when radio personality Adelaide Hawley was hired to represent her in a cooking
show on CBS, *The Betty Crocker Hour*. The following year General
Mills changed tack and cast Hawley in a talk-show/entertainment
vehicle for ABC, *The Betty Crocker Star Matinee*, in which America's favorite homemaker interviewed Hollywood notables. Hawley,
blonde and smiling, didn't in the least resemble the sterner, dark-
haired matron who had been the face of Betty Crocker since 1936,
when General Mills had hired an artist to paint "a perfect composite of the twentieth-century American woman."[17] This inconsistency
didn't appear, however, to dent her character's believability or her
following.

By 1952, General Mills felt it needed to rethink the Betty Crocker
strategy yet again, to breathe fresh life into her character as an
emblem for the entire portfolio of products (which included, among
others, Gold Medal flour, Bisquick, Wheaties, Cheerios, and a pano-
ply of Betty Crocker baking mixes). In the burgeoning field of cake
mixes, in particular, General Mills was now lagging behind Duncan
Hines and Pillsbury. BBDO, along with a handful of other ad agencies, was invited out to company headquarters in Minneapolis to

present ideas on how—and if—General Mills should continue with
Betty Crocker as a branding device.

Jean saw immediately the immense value of Betty Crocker's trusted
name, if properly deployed. Betty Crocker, she argued, was "a valuable piece of property" who "shouldn't be shut up in a museum" and
"shouldn't talk like a stuffed shirt." Instead, it was time to reinvigorate her as a "warm and friendly and believable personality, someone
women turn to in a crisis."[18] Betty Crocker, in short, should come
across as "a woman who would understand and share the problems
and perplexities of General Mills' best customer, today's American housewife."[19] It was on the force of Jean's feeling for the Betty
Crocker "character" and how to mobilize her that BBDO won the
account.[20]

The cake mix advertising campaign Jean designed and presented
to General Mills executives in March 1953 was "simplicity itself,"
she assured them. In her own in-house polling matched against
national surveys, Jean discovered the secret to the American housewife's reluctance to bake cakes. It was not that baking cakes took
too much money, or too much trouble, or too much time. Rather,
quite simply, "Women are scared to make a cake." This fear of failure, she pronounced grimly, "holds back more women from baking
cakes than any other thing we can find."[21] All the other factors that
surveys had tested to measure cake-baking attitudes—should a mix
use dried eggs or fresh? milk or water?—were beside the point: a
woman wanted a cake that looked and tasted mouth watering, and
would buy the one she trusted to turn out that way. General Mills
needed to meet that fear head on, she proposed, and combat it with
a "fighting promise," directly from the mouth of Betty Crocker: "I
guarantee you a perfect cake, every time you bake . . . cake after cake
after cake after cake." The "Betty Crocker Guarantee," combined
with big, colorful pictures that look "good enough to eat," was Jean's
secret to winning the cake wars.

General Mills wavered, initially, on including a guarantee with
their cakes. "They think guarantee is a little strong for that nice ladylike character Betty Crocker," Jean explained to colleagues on the
account.[22] But Jean was adamant that the old-fashioned prejudice

that "nice ladies don't sell" simply didn't hold up in this context. In a gingerly worded memo to the advertising czar at General Mills, Jean explained that allowing Betty Crocker to issue a sales guarantee would in no way tarnish her reputation. Across platforms, from radio to magazine to television station identifications, "a great deal of space and a great deal of time and a great deal of money is being devoted to the development of the character and personality of Betty Crocker," she argued, to make her "the warm, believable, understanding character" that the American housewife yearned for. Jean assured them that the apparent vulgarity of selling would disappear into this larger background of service. "It is our point of view that when Betty Crocker promises a young bride or a weary cook that she can remove the fear of failure that has made cake-making an ordeal, then that is service, in its finest form." When the voice of Betty Crocker gave a guarantee, it was not a "sales message," Jean qualified; "it is actually rather cake-insurance, cake-ASSURANCE, cake-baking REASSURANCE."[23] Eventually, Jean's logic won the day.

In late August 1953, General Mills vice president Walter Barry wrote BBDO's Ben Duffy of the company's general enthusiasm for the new Betty Crocker cake mix double-page spread ads, just appearing in women's magazines. "Not that one swallow makes a summer," he temporized, but "we sense a determination on the part of everybody at BBDO to really go to town on this exciting challenge."[24] The Betty Crocker print and television campaign went into full effect on September 2, 1953. By the end of the month, the Market Research Corporation report on cake mixes showed Betty Crocker had narrowed the gap with Pillsbury by four percentage points, putting them effectively neck and neck. "Congratulations!" Jean's colleague and BBDO vice president Charlie Brower scribbled on the bottom of a memo he passed on to her. "I never knew advertising to work this fast."[25]

By the time Jean went to Minneapolis to give the General Mills execs their yearly campaign wrap-up for 1955, Betty Crocker was outpacing her competitors in the cake mix market. It had been a "red-letter year" according to all the major readership and opinion polling, Jean touted, with "one of the all-round best seen, all around best Starch [ratings], all around best Gallup campaigns of the food year." Among *Ladies' Home Journal* ads—the ones Walter Barry had tentatively praised—Betty Crocker now ranked as best read and best seen; Pillsbury came in a distant sixteenth. Moving into 1956, Betty Crocker was going to continue to capitalize on these advertising strategies: the soul-soothing Betty Crocker guarantee, joined with "service" in the form of timely, newsy, baking ideas for every season.[26] But on top of that, she was going to "blossom forth with a new kind of cake mix advertising," "the first advertising ever in cake mix history to take full advantage of the tremendous emotional importance a woman attaches to baking a cake."[27]

The sample copy for these advertisements singled out "heart-tug" family moments: a cake to mark a child's first birthday or to welcome Daddy home from a long day at the office; a "kiss-n-make-up" cake to end a silly quarrel. In the eventual "kiss-n-make-up" ad, a young wife and husband touched foreheads, smiling contritely, and held hands over a voluptuously white-frosted cake with "I'M SORRY" scrolled in pink across the top. "Who knows who began it? Who cares . . . really?" asked the copy beneath the image. "The thing to do now is to end it." And the good housewife knew just how: "Steak. Thick, no-respect-for-the-budget steak. And French fries. And a splendiferous, enormous, I-love-you-truly magic of a cake." They would remember this night, Jean promised—this night, and "the love that rings it 'round for a long, long, two-hearts-forever time."[28]

Another ad in the print series, "Daddy's Cake," pictured a little girl carrying a giant chocolate cake to the dining room table. "It took a long time to light the candles on Daddy's cake," mused the copy. "Such a small candle-lighter. Such a lot of candles." But it would take much longer for Mommy and Daddy to forget this "tremendous moment of family oneness," when "the sparks from a pair of soft brown eyes afire with the glow of candles carry a cosmic charge strong enough to weld a gay young mother and a strong young father and a small young daughter into a single whole. And time stands still." And just as the homemaker flipping through her *Ladies' Home Journal* suddenly felt a lump in her throat, the ad copy prompted her: "Baking an *eternity* cake? A cake that matters . . . forever? No lesser mixes for this job."

Cake: Betty Crocker White Cake Mix. *Frosting:* new Betty Crocker Fluffy White Frosting Mix, tinted pink

All the rest of your natural life

The first birthday. And the first step. And the first word. And the first day of school. And the first mumps. And the first bumps too big to kiss away. And the first date and the first dance and the first roses and first love and the joys and terrors and triumphs of the days that lie between. They're all here . . . in a single moment, in a single family, lost in the wonder of the first baby . . . and this first birthday.

Don't go away. It's a moment to remember. A moment to mark with a very special cake . . . one that's nothing less than perfect. A cake you just know must be made from Betty Crocker Cake Mix.

For Betty Crocker guarantees the perfect cake . . . for the perfect moment . . . cake after cake. Don't pin *your* faith on something less. Ask your store for that mix that bakes a cake that's homemade light and homemade good and easy!

But don't wait for a big moment! Why not celebrate a *little* moment—this very special little night?

"I guarantee a perfect* cake— cake...after cake...after cake!"
Betty Crocker of General Mills

PERFECT! Yes, all our Betty Crocker Mixes—Cake, Frosting, Date Bars, Brownies, Pie Crust, Answer Cake —are guaranteed to come out perfect or send the box top to Betty Crocker, Box 200, Minneapolis, Minn., and General Mills will send your money back.

FIGURES 12 AND 13. Jean was appointed to oversee the rebranding of Betty Crocker for General Mills in 1953. This 1956 series of advertisements relied on marketing sentimental family "moments," from celebrating baby's birthday to mending newlywed quarrels.

The "emotional copy" of the magazine advertisements was echoed on television, where Betty Crocker now made regular guest appearances on such family-friendly variety programs as *The Bob Crosby Show* and *The Garry Moore Show*. In 1950, eight million American homes had television sets; that number more than quintupled, to

Cake: Betty Crocker Chocolate Devils Food Cake Mix. Frosting: new Betty Crocker Fluffy White Frosting Mix, with coconut.

Kiss 'n' make up!

Who knows who began it? Who cares ... really? The thing to do now is to end it. And our gal is making a valiant try. Steak ... thick, no-respect-for-the-budget steak. And French fries. And a splendiferous, enormous, I-love-you-truly magic of a cake —a cake that whispers two words so potent he'll leap right out of his chair.

Can you count on that? Certain-sure. Just as sure as that someday they'll disagree again. This is a *family!* But they'll

remember this night and the love that rings it 'round for a long, long two-hearts-forever time.

Of course you know how to get a cake that tastes and looks as great as that. This day ... of all days ... you make certain-sure to buy the mix that comes out perfect every time. It has Betty Crocker's name on the package. And you might want to bake it for the man you love ... even if he didn't go away mad!

"I guarantee a perfect* cake— cake...after cake...after cake!"

Betty Crocker of *General Mills*

*Yes, all our Betty Crocker Mixes—Cake, Frosting, Date Bars, Brownies, Pie Crust, Answer Cake —are guaranteed to come out perfect or send the box top to Betty Crocker, Box 200, Minneapolis, Minn., and General Mills will send your money back.

FIGURES 12 AND 13. (*continued*)

forty-one million, by 1958.[29] In 1956, corporate sponsors were still scrambling to figure out how best to use television to push sales. Adelaide Hawley's early Betty Crocker vehicles from 1950 to 1952 had yielded disappointing results. As a reporter for the trade magazine *Sponsor* noted, the medium "presents curious problems for the further development of the Betty Crocker idea."[30] Entertainment shows rather than "service" shows seemed to be the way television was heading, yet "the entertainment format violated the basic service concept of Betty Crocker." "None of the General Mills agencies

has up to now been able to come up with an answer" to this conun-
drum, *Sponsor* concluded.

While in her 1956 General Mills briefing Jean admitted that the jury
was still out on how best to use television, "one way that has a sound
record of sales success is through the use of trusted, believable, recognizable, real personalities." And that, Jean suggested, was precisely
what BBDO was banking on by integrating Betty Crocker's warm,
friendly personality into the warm, friendly setting of TV talk shows
with "trusted" personalities like Crosby and Moore. The "relaxed, easy-
going, story-telling, personal involvement" quality of the walk-ons
seamlessly blended entertainment and sales pitch, so that the viewer
was hard pressed to tell where one stopped and the other started.[31]

This was especially true when Betty Crocker moved out of the
morning slots and into evening prime time, with a series of regular
appearances on *The George Burns and Gracie Allen Show* from 1955
through 1958.[32] One of the half-hour show's central conceits was to
blur the boundary between real life and fiction: while the plot lines
were pure invention, the establishing shot often panned to Burns
and Allen's actual house. The couple's adult children made walk-
on appearances—sometimes as actors playing a role, sometimes as
themselves. Burns also routinely broke the "fourth wall" when, at
the end of each show, he could be seen watching episodes of *The
George Burns and Gracie Allen Show* on the television in his study.

Such a tongue-in-cheek nod to theatricality, and to the blurred
line between real-life personality and television "personality," was
a perfect vehicle for Betty Crocker. "Oh George, you'll never guess
what kind of cake I baked today," chirped Allen to Burns in one episode. "Well, what do we have here?" he responded, taking a plate
of cake from his wife. "Well, it's a Calico Cake." ("A Calico Cake!"
whistled her bemused husband, turning to the camera.) "Yeah! Betty
Crocker taught me how to make it!" Viewers may have suspected
that Adelaide Hawley was a hired actress and that Betty Crocker was
a fantasy, but it didn't matter in the context of personality-driven
television, where entertainment trumped verisimilitude every time.

The discovery that personality was a tried-and-true seller on television quickly expanded beyond live actors to invest inanimate

objects as well: each of Betty Crocker's cakes was imagined as a "personality" in its own right. The Calico Cake was not the Marble Cake was not the Devil's Food Cake; each had its own distinct character and niche, and had to be marketed as such. "In print, and in television, every mix in the Betty Crocker family has advertising that reflects its own personality," Jean assured General Mills executives, "advertising [that] answers its special problems, and builds it, independently, toward the top-of-the-market spot it deserves."[33]

Much like Bruce Barton's ingenious marketing of the General Motors "family" of vehicles, Jean solidified General Mills as the ultimate "family" brand. She did this not only by gathering all of General Mills' products into a single Betty Crocker "family"—the crazy, fun-loving Calico Cake; the homespun Ginger Cake; the elegant Angel Cake—but by associating Betty Crocker with one of America's best-loved fictional families: Burns and Allen. Toward the end of her General Mills address, Jean congratulated her executive audience on their recent media coup: "You rode into good night time with big night names—Burns and Allen—and you moved right in and integrated these two well-known personalities right into the Betty Crocker family," she affirmed. "It is our firm opinion at BBDO that you could see its results in your sales."[34]

Betty Crocker's promise seeped into the American unconscious, saturating the radio waves, popping off the pages of the *Ladies' Home Journal*, smiling out from the family television. A January 1955 episode of *The Bob Crosby Show* offered a case in point. The host read aloud a letter he'd received from a fan recounting that her young son had come to her recently and asked that she bake an "after cake." Perplexed, she told him she wasn't quite sure what kind of cake that was. "You know," the boy pressed. "The kind Betty Crocker promises come out perfect: cake *after cake after cake*."[35] In the end, General Mills' fear that the "Betty Crocker Guarantee" would tarnish her reputation by turning her into a salesgirl was unfounded. Betty Crocker was selling peace of mind and the fantasy, if not the reality, of family togetherness. It was a product for which American housewives were happy to pay.

Jean's Betty Crocker campaign, launched in 1953, reached its peak in the half decade following 1955. Her sentimental appeals to family—with a devoted wife and mother at its center, dispensing love with every cookie or cake—was welcome balm to a generation of new families eager to turn the page on war and settle down to the ease and abundance of peacetime. But this turn inward to the pleasures of private consumption took shape against the backdrop of the Cold War. Looming on the horizon was the specter of communism on the move, a force to be contained abroad and ferreted out and destroyed at home. The arms race and the atom bomb cast a long shadow, threatening that America's postwar abundance could go up, at any moment, in a giant mushroom cloud.

A newspaper clipping in Jean's papers, a 1957 opinion column by Anita Colby entitled "Leave it to the Girls to Blast the Bomb!," captured the period anxiety well. Colby records a general sense of helplessness among postwar women who "are sitting around listening to . . . man talk," "terrified" at his predictions for the future. After shuddering through Orwell's bleak prognosis in *1984*, now women must reckon with Nevil Shute's recent bestselling novel *On the Beach*, a postapocalyptic account of a group of atom bomb survivors. Shute is such a compelling storyteller, Colby quipped, that "by the time that last page is finished you are convinced you're finished, too."[36]

Enter Jean: Colby recorded that, just as her faith in the future had been all but destroyed, she decided to consult her friend Jean Rindlaub. From Jean she heard a different, woman-centered version of the "boom" to come: not nuclear Armageddon but a baby boom, and a consequent boom in living standards and "general well-being." "While the men have been seeing nothing but disaster ahead, women have been serenely planning for a bigger and brighter future," Jean assured her. The families that women had started, uncertainly, in wartime were now almost grown up, "all set to keep the cycle of family and home going" into the future. The population explosion would fuel an expanding economy, leading to a level of prosperity yet undreamed of. Colby closed out her column by urging readers to rub the "nuclear dust" out of their eyes and "take a look at the other side of the prognosticating business—the woman's side." For her, women's only choice for wresting the future away from disaster rested, predictably, in the private sphere of reproduction and consumption. It was not through politics but "serenely," quietly, through domestic investment and by wielding their dollars wisely that women would bring about the long-awaited Kingdom of Peace.

Jean's Betty Crocker guarantee was aimed, initially, at easing the modest fear of failing to bake an edible cake. Yet the guarantee also worked to keep larger global and political anxieties at bay, suggesting that women could best contribute to world peace through the small, humble, homey act of baking a cake. In her series of "emotional copy" cake ads, Jean suggested a "Cake for Every Birthday" advertisement. The copy assured women, rather incredibly, that a home in which every child's birthday was celebrated with a Betty Crocker confection was a home immune to the dangers of teenage delinquency. "You can quote me," Jean imagined a Family Relations Court judge pronouncing. "You rarely find a juvenile delinquent in a house where there's a birthday cake for every birthday." The copy went on to pledge, "When LOVE FLIES in the window, crime—or the things that breed it—walk quietly out the door."[37]

Jean's advertisements from the mid-1950s are permeated by her "love-and-kisses" copy, appeals that posit maternal love as the healing balm that can help make bearable a crazy, mixed-up masculine world of striving and struggle. In a talk to prospective clients in 1954, "We Love LOVE!," Jean pressed this idea home. "You could think of a cake—or a pie—or a tray of R.C. colas—as a contribution to family living—a shared social experience for the family," she urged. "And there are people who would tell you that it is good experiences shared that deepen and enrich the family's living and that deeper family living is the beginning of better community living and better community living might be the answer to such social problems as juvenile delinquency and adult inadequacy."[38]

In another proposed campaign, Jean suggested the Betty Crocker guarantee should be explicitly identified as the lowly housewife's contribution to world peace—one properly contained within the feminine domestic sphere. "I can't change the headlines, but I've got to do something," sighed one troubled woman. "So I've gone back to baking bread." "I can't make the world over," another mother testified. "So I keep the cookie jar full. And the house full of children. With crumbs left over for the birds." A woman could do worse, Betty Crocker suggested, squaring her shoulders in the face of chaos. Baking was "one small way to start re-making the whole wide world."[39]

Jean was convinced that by privately consuming "love and kisses" in the form of a cake or a cola, American families were furthering the cause of global peace and social harmony. Her files are filled with tidbits clipped and copied from social scientists whose work backed up her theory. "Lack of love and understanding toward others is attacked by a scientist who sees humanity doomed unless new human values are adopted," ran the headline of an article by Dr. M. F. Ashley Montagu that Jean typed out for her files. "Men who do not love one another are sick," proclaimed the medical anthropologist, as "love and cooperation among men . . . have a support in the findings of biological science."[40] A memo Jean received from a colleague included a newspaper clipping entitled "Psychiatrist Says Man Needs Love in His Diet to Make Him Happy." "Man is not fed by calories alone," argued Dr. Richard McGraw. "In home cooking, approbation, affection, love are mixed in with the batter." Jean's friend quipped: "Aren't you glad the psychiatrists are catching on to what you've been saying all along?"[41]

Jean taught women how to think of consumption as an act of love; she tutored them in the sentimental language of capitalism and offered them a script that helped them square feminine virtue with the cold, masculine logic of the market. And when housewives felt the world outside their doors was too big and out of control, Jean gave them a soothing, private language of hope that was vastly more attractive than the hard language of reality.[42]

8

The "New Togetherness," or How Adwomen Learned to Man Up

Jean's copy for Betty Crocker and Community Plate paints a picture of midcentury American women as docile, domestic-minded creatures, universally in thrall to the ideal of starting and nurturing a family. While the charge of sexual desire binding husband and wife was faintly hinted at in the "Back Home for Keeps" ads, American codes of prudery kept the images from depicting anything more intimate than a kiss. As illustrator Jon Whitcomb said of American magazines, "love . . . is never pictured as going very far beyond courtship." As an illustrator it was imperative, he noted, "to learn where this invisible line of taste is located and to stay on the conservative side of it." In one "Back Home for Keeps" mock-up, Whitcomb included a bedroom in the background behind the embracing couple; it never made the final cut. "So, for the duration of the series, returning warriors were pictured entering the gate, on the front steps, in the hall and all over the living room," he reminisced, "but not in the boudoir." Jean's Betty Crocker cake mix ads toed the same invisible line. While fronted by an exquisitely coiffed and attractive Adelaide Hawley, the Betty Crocker persona still endorsed the *mythos* of housewife as, first and foremost, maternal nurturer.[1]

And yet alternative sexualities and gender roles were hardly absent from popular culture in the 1950s. On the contrary, in an epoch when "proper" gender roles were delineated with an interest bordering on panic, sex was omnipresent, and "deviant" sex open for discussion—if only to more rigorously circumscribe what counted as "normal" sex.[2] One need only read the excerpt from Margaret

Mead's 1949 anthropological study, *Male and Female*, in the stolidly middle-class *Ladies' Home Journal*, to see that sex was a topic of open conversation. Mead's article is preceded by an anxiety-producing header: "Are American boys and girls being educated toward—or away from—happier, more successful years as husbands and wives?" Happily, Mead's fieldwork among seven Pacific Islander tribes could give an answer. Mead opened by noting the generally repressive atmosphere surrounding sex in the United States: Americans were used to "covering up" their bodies, she said, "referring to them in slang terms or with borrowed language, to hiding even infants' sex membership behind blue and pink ribbons." Studying the South Sea cultures, which were still unabashedly in touch with the naked biology of sex, might help us understand the ways in which American bodies "have learned how to be male, how to be female."[3]

Mead's article offered a window onto the diversity and exoticism of human sexual behavior. Yet *Ladies' Home Journal* readers were absolved from any charge of crass voyeurism by Mead's clinical, matter-of-fact tone. These titillating details of sex abroad were being aired, she reassured them, only in the interest of creating happier, healthy families at home. Mead could thus skip lightly from discussing the "heated, orgiastic pleasure" of infant masturbation, to detailing the "angry, eager avidity" of sex within the headhunting Mundugumor tribe (among whom "biting and scratching are important parts of foreplay"), all without alienating her audience.[4]

As in many anthropological studies of sex during this period, Mead largely framed sex roles as social constructions: in Simone de Beauvoir's famous formulation, one was not born, but became, a woman. Mead vehemently disputed one psychologist's assertion, for instance, that women who chose not to have children suffered long-term psychological damage. The pain they experience stemmed not from a biological destiny left unfulfilled but from the psychic pain of a perceived failure to inhabit her culture's feminine ideal. "Human society has a great accumulated store of ways of teaching human beings what they should do," she commented. "and a corresponding battery of punishments, externally and internally imposed, for those who fail to do what they have learned."[5]

But in fact, the middle-class housewife didn't have to go to the bush of New Guinea for her weekly quota of risqué sex. Alfred Kinsey's 1948 bombshell, *Sexual Behavior in the Human Male*, had already made headlines the previous year and blasted wide open Americans' assumptions about what their neighbors were doing in the bedroom. According to Kinsey's study, American men routinely violated the culture's codes of white middle-class sexual respectability, with fewer than half of reported male orgasms occurring within the "normal" context of marital intercourse (masturbation, extramarital affairs, and homosexual sex accounted for the other 50 percent).[6] Yet even a study as nominally liberating as Kinsey's was a product of the period's excessive investment in studying, measuring, and normalizing predictable codes for feminine and masculine behavior. People scanned it not to receive carte blanche for deviation, but to allay sexual anxiety by locating themselves on a scale approaching "normal." The fact that Mead and Kinsey framed gender roles as social constructs, not biological facts, in no way reduced the imperative that men and women align with one side or the other.

Jean's archive, perhaps not surprisingly, contains no hint as to how she felt about (or performed in private) her own gender identity and sexuality. The closest we get is in the semiautobiographical articles and advice columns she wrote for mainstream magazines. In her anonymous article "Marry the Man!" Jean champions traditional marriage as a woman's only true path to happiness and emotional fulfillment. In her articles schooling stay-at-home wives on how to be good spouses, she enjoins them to be quiet, respectful, and supportive; to anticipate their husbands' needs, from emotional support to a well-lit reading chair to sex, and cheerfully provide for them.

But in her professional life, Jean was an expert at code switching, performing feminine or masculine roles with equal agility. She could write ad copy that warmed the cockles of her target housewife's sentimental heart, then flip into the folksy-yet-authoritative tone required to appeal to the male white-collar readers of BBDO's *Wedge*. The advertising industry at midcentury sold rough-and-tumble competitive capitalism as masculine sport whose ultimate payout was millennial maternal abundance for all. Jean's intuitive knack for gender morphing made her an ideal candidate for the job.

Readers of Jean's advertising copy, if they weren't tipped off otherwise, often assumed she was a man. At least one contemporary colleague felt compelled to mention her masculine appearance, describing her as "dumpy" and hirsute. Jean no doubt found that impersonating a man in voice, character, and even, perhaps, in physical bearing made working in a man's world a bit easier. Margaret Mead's observation that professional American women perceived as "unattractive" or masculine were accepted in the workplace, whereas "attractive" or female-coding women were given much less leeway by male colleagues, would certainly substantiate this.[7]

Predictably, her advice to women trying to climb the corporate ladder urged them to avoid falling into such dead-end feminine traps as being frigid, shrill, or bitter. Better to join in the joke, roll with the punches to get ahead in business. In her pitch for a weekly advice column, "To Girls on the Way Up," Jean proposed a piece addressing how to deal with sexual advances in the workplace. "But he tried to KISS me!" Jean imagined an office girl shrieking. "What of it?" she tossed back. "Would you go into hysterics because a boy tried to kiss you on a date—or would you laugh him out of it?" Taking such advances in stride, "casually," was the best way of defusing them, she insisted. And anyway, she queried, could you be *sure* he tried to kiss you? She proposed ending the column with the cautionary tale of "a girl who lost her job because she mistook casual office courtesies" for sexual advances.[8] She dispensed similar advice to the girl who questioned whether she was being paid less than her male colleagues. Jean suggested that, often as not, there was a legitimate reason for the discrepancy: "Women don't take chances, don't work with a man's sense of responsibility," she argued. "When they do, they are paid as well."[9]

In a standard speech Jean gave to women's professional groups, "Life Behind the Petticoat Curtain," she challenged working women to take a square look at themselves in the mirror before complaining about bias in the workplace. "Are [your petticoats] too starched?," Jean queried, "Are you too quick to take offense? . . . Do you go around saying, 'Oh, men!'?" Such shrill sisters never get ahead, she warned. And then there was "the gal who packs a pair of pistols in her petticoats," the "she-male who believes in fighting her way to the top." The Amazonian routine doesn't work either, she informed her audience. Rather, the most successful women were those who had learned to take life's ups and downs in gender-neutral stride. "Minority groups are inclined to press," she warned. "The mature woman has learned to relax." The mature working woman, in other words, had learned to be nice. She had learned to reach deep inside herself to find the cheerful resilience that turns every professional setback into an advantage, that transforms "every bump into a bounce," Jean concluded brightly.[10]

While many early advertising firms prized their female copywriters for their supposed oracular insight into the "woman's point of view," an alternative school of thought declared sex irrelevant to good copy. Jean's colleague and cowriter Charlie Brower was firm in his belief that "there are only two kinds of writers—good ones and bad ones," and that "there is no basic writing secret possessed by one sex and denied the other." In a memo to Alex Osborn, vice president and founding member of BBDO, Brower affirmed that when training women copywriters, both he and Jean "try to make women into good ad makers first of all, and let them be women second."[11]

At times, Jean found it professionally useful to play up "la petite difference" that separated her, as a woman, from her male colleagues—especially in speeches to potential clients.[12] When asked to speak on a panel of male social scientists and nutritionists at a 1954 United Fruit cookbook conference, she opened by feigning intimidation at her co-panelists' intellectual caliber. "The first thing I did was to call up Pat Partridge and say, 'Look here, what am I doing up there among all those brains?'" To which Partridge, head of advertising at United Fruit, replied, "'We put you in there to represent the common woman."[13] She confessed she found that to be a "tremendous responsibility," but as a common woman herself, with her simple, humble, common troubles, she vowed to do her best to be a faithful spokesperson.

Slipping into the voice of Mrs. Middle Majority, Jean described being assaulted by an endless barrage of health dos and don'ts thrown about by doctors, food manufacturers, and advertisers: "I've seen the common woman muddle through Fletcherism, the Hay diet, the Hollywood diet, Gaylord Hauser, high colonics, low colonics, Yogi, deep breathing, carrots to curl your hair, rain water for your complexion, raisins for iron," she listed. "Here I am, my common woman, your common woman, and I need help," she pled.[14] Jean literally stumbled over her pronouns, situating herself as both ethnographer and subject, help giver and help seeker, at one and the same time.

But this was pure performance. Behind the scenes, Jean knew that her ability to funnel the average housewife's dollars into her clients' pockets had nothing to do with being biologically female and that she was far from a "common" specimen of her sex. The fact that she was a woman working a corporate job in a big city was precisely what most disqualified her from speaking for "the woman's point of view." In a 1944 talk to fellow advertisers, Jean made this very point while lecturing on the folly of thinking that having women on staff somehow put them in touch with their female consumer base. "By the sheer fact that she is in a big city, by the much more significant fact that she has a job, that she gets a sizeable paycheck," Jean warned of the typical adwoman, "your girl Friday has ceased to have a normal woman's point of view."[15]

Unlike the stay-at-home wife raising a passel of children and keeping house for her husband, the adwoman is someone who had been "turn[ed] loose on the streets of New York," who went "home at five or six to a Sutton Place apartment or a Greenwich Village hideout," "clutter[ed] up her nights with casual to serious drinking, her days with flip to frantic thinking." "We've got to admit, fellow females," Jean went on to admonish her colleagues, "our women's viewpoint is cockeyed, undependable, abnormal."[16]

The adwoman couldn't speak *as* a "normal" woman. But she could speak *to* and *for* them. Any agency worth its salt, then, would send its girls out to the provinces, to farm and factory and suburban playground, so they could then report back on what "real" women had to say about their hopes and needs. Like amateur anthropologists, these women could take their field notes and spin them into ad copy. They "see your product as it looks to Mrs. America," Jean explained to clients. "They talk about it in words from her own lips. They can make her want it, for they know *why* she wants it." These brainy, fast-talking, independent creatures could "pass" for normal women—mingle with them unobserved, draw them out, and bring back the scoop. Jean's ad ladies are not themselves "real women," but they are expert at ventriloquizing real women—providing agencies with material well worth the subterfuge required to mine it.

Jean described ad women as "abnormal" specimens, a species of intersex creatures who felt right at home in the hectic, hard-driving city life normally reserved for men. Jean's own identification with men is revealed in her proposal for a series of articles for *New York Woman* on negotiating the complexities of modern marriage. In an article with the conspiratorial title "I Know Things About Your Husband," Jean gave housebound women readers a glimpse into the secret work world of men to help them understand their spouses. "Your husband is *tired*!," she launched as her opening gambit. She let women in on the average working man's secret griefs: his diminished sense of self-worth, "kicked around by the men above him, plagued and pestered by men below"; his grim acceptance that "there isn't any let-up in that ceaseless grind to get the bills paid."[17]

The good wife would understand his pain—and seek to provide balm, not heap more worry on his head. "Fill up the cookie jar," she suggested in another article listing tips on "How to Keep a Husband Happy." Or again: "The lord of the manor has lost a lot of his just desserts; spare him a few privileges!" The good wife would do well to make sure his chair was comfortable, she counseled, "his light is strong and well-placed," "his table equipped with convenient ash-trays."[18] Jean anticipated her reader's curiosity as to the source of her insight: how could she know what men are like on the job? "Because day after day I work with your husband—in his office or his shop, his store or his factory," she retorted. "I've had a tough day at the office too!"[19] Jean knew, in short, because she was a "husband" herself, the proverbial man in the gray flannel suit.

Perhaps because she identified so strongly with men, Jean could be vicious when it came to nonworking women who refused to do the domestic labor that she considered intrinsic to the marriage compact. Her unpublished essay "Wife—or Parasite?" was a screed against the shirking housewife—selfish, wasteful, lazy—who failed to make the domestic space a physical and emotional haven for her beleaguered husband. In between the "she-male" career woman, who was really a man masquerading as a woman, and the overly effeminate parasite wife, Jean held up the "two-job wife" as the perfect representative of true womanhood.

The two-job woman was a hybrid creature, combining a masculine work ethic and pragmatism with a feminine instinct for nurture. She was canny and cool; she smoked to unwind after a hard day's work. In an article saucily entitled "Stay at Home Wives Need a Spanking!" Jean channeled the voice of a fictional two-job wife excoriating the rest of her sex for failing their menfolk. In this vignette, the narrator leans back and lights a cigarette before suggesting that these lazeabouts could use a "downright sizzling session with the hairbrush."[20] Part of the problem, she muses, is that these women have "not the vaguest mental picture of the tension and nerve strain and the ceaseless bang bang bang of a man's day." Because they worked, two-job women knew the value of a dollar; because they worked, they knew of their husbands' exhaustion and met them at home with cheer, not selfish complaints. And what did a parasite wife give her husband in return for "his name and the better part of his paycheck?"[21] Too often, she drawls, not enough. While the parasite wife whined about the miseries of housework and even felt entitled to withhold sex from her love-starved husband, the woman who worked "[took] her job casually in her stride as she takes her major job of being a good wife seriously."[22]

Jean, of course, was a "two-job woman." As she rose up the ranks at BBDO, Jean was often singled out in the press as a shining example of how to combine a career and family. Yet as she told one reporter, "she doesn't think of herself as a career woman at all"; rather, "in her own estimation she's just another woman who has combined her job with being a wife and raising a family."[23] Her belief that the career woman could maintain her femininity only if her motives for work remained properly domestic both within and outside of the home—to serve, to help, to spread goodwill and peace—was evident in the talks she gave to girls and women's groups. Ambition, whether intellectual or financial, was the poorest of motives for working women, she warned. She winced at feminist catchphrases or at groups who asked her to speak on such subjects as "Woman, Our Decision Makers." Yes, women make decisions, Jean quipped: "They decide to marry men. After that, most decisions become a family affair."[24]

Jean was always uncomfortable with the idea of women seeking power for personal prestige or attention. Rather, any decision-making power they might wield was a path to further the well-being of their husbands, families, or extended community. The real woman who stepped into the public sphere did so only to expand the scope of her primary domestic responsibility, to do the "community housekeeping" that naturally fell to the second sex.

In a speech to Wildroot Shampoo executives capping a week-long workshop on their account, Jean addressed the men in the room with the facts and figures she had gathered on their target female customer. Rattling off survey results and campaign highlights, Jean proved that when it came to researching and marketing, she was "one of the boys." But at the end of the speech she turned to the women in the room—executive wives who had been summoned in their capacity as "ethnographic subjects" who might give added insight into the mysterious purchasing processes of the female brain. "And now I'd like to use my closing minutes for something else—just girl talk to just girls." She complimented the wives on how earnestly they had been scribbling notes during the workshop, "asking questions, helping their husbands." "I have watched women this week being helpmates—being friendly, being patient, being affectionate, being loyal, being admiring, building their men." And she assured them that the white-collar girls—like herself—sitting across the podium were, in fact, no different: "The women on the Wildroot advertising team have just the same goal—we, like you, are just trying to be HELPMATES. Working together, we can build a good life for all of us—as well as healthy sales charts for Wildroot Liquid Cream Shampoo."[25] Jean's intuitive ability to inhabit male and female perspectives alternately (or simultaneously) was a hallmark of her career—and, arguably, the secret to her spectacular success.

"Sentimentalism," Ann Douglas writes of the nineteenth-century sanctification of the feminine virtues of home and hearth, "provides a way to protest against a power to which one has already in part capitulated." The mythic, sentimentalized figure of the maternal "angel in the house" gained such traction in nineteenth-century America because it provided a counterweight to the moral misdeeds of market society. Women who advocated for domestic virtues, like the Beecher sisters, were thus "in the position of contestants in a fixed fight: they had agreed to put on a convincing show, and to lose. The fakery involved," Douglas concludes grimly, "was finally crippling for all concerned."[26]

Jean would not have described the face-off between the spheres as a fixed fight and would firmly have denied the charge of fakery. That there were losers in this arrangement, Jean knew. Her research taught her that the role of housewife, despite its rewards, also felt like a trap to many women. In her talk to Oneida executives in 1946, she convinced them that the modern young woman, aged eighteen to twenty-six, wanted nothing more than to get married, to have a home of her own. Yet Jean's polling uncovered a puzzle: "What do they hate to do most? . . . [They] hate to stick to a budget, to bake and mend and sew and dust and mop and hang curtains. Do you notice how many of these things they hate are things they do at home—and yet, in spite of it all, they're tumbling over themselves to get in one."[27] Having noted this contradiction, Jean said nothing more about it. Perhaps she dropped it in to emphasize the sacrifices women were willing to make to get their man. Perhaps—given that her audience was all men—it was a humorous jab at that oh-so-contradictory yet ultimately lovable creature, Woman.

Again and again, the housewives she interviewed confessed boredom; anxiety; a dimly felt desire to "make a difference" in the larger world, with no clear path to do so. In summarizing a study of women's magazine readership in 1949, Jean noted the key features of "Mrs. Middle Majority": "She is a housewife," Jean started off the list, "with limited experience because her life is limited to a familiar, narrow routine and she lacks the background which would lead her to seek wider interests." "She is fairly unimaginative," Jean specified, "because her way of life does not call for any originality or imagination; instead, discourages it." And finally, most damningly, but noted with the cool neutrality befitting the tone of an office memo, "she has a sense of futility because her life is pretty drab and monotonous."[28]

But Jean's responsibility as an advertiser was not to spring women from their trap. It was to make the trap more comfortable. Advertising was a kind of ministry by which she could help wives and mothers "adjust," to use the therapeutic vocabulary of the age, to their prescribed roles. And while she gently acknowledged that these roles could chafe, she never seriously questioned them. Her job was to provide balm.

In 1961, husband-and-wife psychologists Richard E. and Kathryn K. Gordon published *The Split-Level Trap*, a series of case studies from suburbia. Their five-year study of upwardly mobile white suburban families in Bergen County, New Jersey, revealed a darker underside to the dream of postwar abundance (or, as *Good Housekeeping* hyped in an excerpt from the book, "the hidden, intimate— and shocking—story of life as it is lived behind the slick façade of modern suburbia").[29] One "Alice Hager" found herself prey to paralyzing panic attacks in the supermarket and often retreated to bed with a migraine when faced with the tireless "clunk-clunk of the washing machine, the yowl of the vacuum cleaner, and the shrill voices of the children."[30]

Nor was suburban life particularly kind to men. Take the case of Fred Bright—midlevel salesman, desperately climbing his way up the company ladder to keep one step ahead of the monthly mortgage and car payments. Haunted by the specter of financial failure, Fred developed a peptic ulcer. "When a man is gripped by anger or fear," the psychologists explained, "his body automatically makes ready for violent physical action—fighting, running, climbing a tree." But

in the suburban jungle, this instinct "has no provision to accommodate itself." As his fight instinct turned inward, Fred's stomach quite
literally began to digest itself.

Alice eventually recovered from her nervous breakdown, and
Fred eventually sought medical attention and learned to relax. But
the tragedy of it, the Doctors Gordon averred, was that "all the pain
and all the struggle were unnecessary." Alice and Fred could have
avoided unhappiness had they only better prepared themselves for
the psychic stresses peculiar to life in the suburbs by following a
course of "Nine Proved Ways to Make Your Life Easier and Happier,"
heading off nervous breakdowns at the pass. With proper training
and a dose of "do-it-yourself" psychotherapy, the doctor team suggests, all could navigate toward "happy, adjusted, successful living."[31]

Jean, ever alert to pop psychology trends, caught wind of *The
Split-Level Trap* and immediately got to work with a plan for how
advertising might respond to it. Is it true, she wondered, "that
today's women . . . feel frustrated, foiled, baffled, unhappy?" If the
trap indeed existed, "what can advertising do . . . to make it bearable?" And, finally, "What effect is it having on buying decisions?"[32]
Jean suggested BBDO fund a grassroots investigation into the question of how to salve this epidemic of feminine discontent, while at
the same time monetizing it.

Jean updated the rhetoric of sentimental domesticity to fit the
twentieth century's global ideological battle between capitalism and
communism, between West and East. The American home and family was a crucial symbolic feature of this rhetoric. The compromises
of the arrangement—the middle-class housewife's sense of entrap-
ment, the white-collar husband's sense of anonymity and futility—
took on a tragic nobility when framed as the necessary sacrifice that
Americans made to uphold the democratic values of economic and
political liberty. In this context, it could be admitted that men were
losers, too. Their gray-flannel jobs clipped their wings, cooped them
up, shut down imagination. Where her women ancestors put up
resistance—however toothless—to market values, Jean accepted the
terms of the fight and sought to frame the capitulation to capitalism
and its distribution of gender roles as a necessary sacrifice, a kind

of stoic acceptance—by both men *and* women—of a flawed reality that nevertheless was the best of all possible worlds. The Cold War and the specter of communism helped enormously in making this compromise palatable. Communism was a useful rhetorical tool that Jean brandished whenever the "American business system" came under fire. No, the "American way" might not perfect, she conceded. But it was better than the alternative.

But Jean didn't limit herself to proffering "adjustment" advice to women; she was just as apt at providing it to men. When writing for the *Wedge*, aimed at fellow admen and potential corporate clients, she invariably adopted the voice of the genial, folksy, white businessman who was her principal audience. In "My Brother Has an Account in his Pocket," Jean channeled an adman imagining how he might talk to his brother Jim about choosing the right ad agency to grow his small business. "We'd be out in the kitchen, I think, mixing a couple of tall ones," she opened the column. "He'd be sitting on the kitchen table, swinging his long legs. I'd hand him a glass and straddle a kitchen chair." With man-to-man intimacy established, the narrator launches into a pitch to "his" brother on how BBDO would be the right choice for him.[33] Jean was sure to signal right away that this decision wasn't about money but about family stability and "togetherness." "'Every cent I've got in the world is tied up in this thing,'" Jim worries. "'I don't know what Madge and the kid will do if anything goes wrong.'"[34] The narrator can sympathize, of course: he's a family man, too. He recalls fondly "how we walked the floor together, Jim and I, the night [his son] took so long to be born." He "think[s] about Madge and what a good scout she's been" before answering that, yes, Jim can trust BBDO.

He goes on to disabuse his brother of any notion that this Madison Avenue agency is snobby or out of touch with "the common man" and his hard-working values. BBDO isn't manned by stuffed shirts, not by a long shot. Jim will need a team who "are going to care a lot" about his business, "worry if something isn't right," and BBDO has them: "We've got some damned good worriers," he assures his brother. "We're short on the smart boys, the guys who know all the answers. But we've got a lot of hard-working people who have an itch to find out." No fancy-pants eggheads here; just regular fellows who will do their job humbly, earnestly, honestly.

The narrator knows there are no easy answers in this day and age. "It doesn't take much brains today to know we're in a funny world," he muses, a world where people cut corners and steal a march on their fellows to get ahead, "like that gang down in Washington." People will always try to game the system (especially those suspicious "big government" types). But BBDO doesn't have any truck with those people. "We don't go around in shining armor," the narrator admits. "But you get to talking to anybody who matters around the place and you find a guy who genuinely believes that when the world comes up with anything better for the majority of the people than the American business system then that's the time to get excited about it." In the meantime, BBDO boys are doing the only honorable thing possible: they're "in there with their sleeves rolled up working away at it."[35]

Jean's advertisements sanctified the image of the white middle-class family as holding the line against communism creep, upholding the American commitment to freedom, individuality, and choice. The average man wasn't a knight in shining armor; he spent his time wrestling with the usual pedestrian worries: keeping ahead of the bills, pacing the halls while his wife is in labor, enjoying a nerve-steadying "tall one" with a buddy. In the end, Jean knew so intimately the politics and economics of the gender ecosystem within which she was selling, and on whose delicate balance successful selling depended, that she could switch seamlessly back and forth between male and female roles without even blinking.

Jean could undertake these gender-switching high jinks with impunity; her ultimate goal was to reinforce the very boundaries that, paradoxically, her performance revealed to be a fiction. Others who sought to stray outside the strictly policed borders of well-adjusted white heterosexual gender identities in the "normal" 1950s, however, were not treated so leniently. The emergence of a postwar American foreign policy centered on communist "containment" would eventually be used to turn matters of private sexual identity into

public affairs of state. Sex "deviants" were framed as national security risks.[36]

George Kennan's infamous "Long Telegram," dispatched home
from Russia in February 1946, depicted Soviet leaders as a "self-
hypnotized" and "neurotic" cadre of despots disconnected from
any objective sense of reality, steeped in "an atmosphere of oriental
secretiveness and conspiracy . . . [where] possibilities for distort-
ing or poisoning sources and currents of information are infinite."
This duplicitous world force would stop at nothing in its attempts
to "penetrate" and convert the West to its beliefs, infiltrating "labor
unions, youth leagues, women's organizations, racial societies,
religious societies, social organizations, cultural groups, liberal
magazines, publishing houses, etc." From the very outset, the Red
Scare—the epic battle between East and West, between a feminine,
oriental, neurotic collectivism and virile, clear-eyed individualism—
was framed as a battle over sex.

It was but a step from here to identifying Communists—with their
soft, effeminate, "oriental" ways—with the sexual deviance represented by homosexuals. Americans stood in danger of losing their
masculinity and needed to "firm up" to face the Soviet menace both
abroad and, more insidiously, at home. Historian Arthur Schlesinger
captured the period tone in his 1949 manifesto, *The Vital Center*,
in which he warned that America needed to man up in its foreign
policy toward the Soviets.

Communists, Schlesinger warned, were suspiciously like homosexuals: they could "pass" in public but would always be able to recognize each other—and carry out their clandestine plots—by means
of secret signs. Government policy planners framed homosexuals
and other sexual "perverts" as security risks, weak links through
which the enemy could easily penetrate. In a report written by a
Senate committee in 1950 and entitled *Employment of Homosexuals
and Other Sex Perverts in Government*, homosexuals were specifically
portrayed as a contagion. "One homosexual can pollute a government office," warned the report; the authors went on to note that "it
is almost inevitable that he will attempt to place other homosexuals

in Government jobs."[37] Panicked fears sparked the "Lavender Scare," where gay men and women were hunted down and hounded out of government jobs.

Indeed, the male narrators of Jean's 1950s *Wedge* articles—all hard-working family men—mimicked for a more popular audience the "voice" of postwar political realism, the ideological shift by which New Deal liberals tacked right to meet conservatives in what Schlesinger called "the vital center" of a new, manly, clear-eyed American politics. Liberals who had flirted with left-wing ideas, from Popular Front socialism to the more domesticated New Deal, found themselves scrambling to reassert their political relevance in the increasingly polarized Cold War climate of the 1950s. Schlesinger's essay was a game plan for postwar liberals, urging them to leave behind the dreamy, feminized, utopian hopes of their nineteenth-century reformist forerunners and confront the "hard" realities of the Soviet menace.[38] Jean's narrator in "My Brother Has an Account in his Pocket" misses none of these politically gendered cues. The speaker is a devoted family man, domestic without being feminized. Being a simple man himself, he has a healthy suspicion of "that gang down in Washington." And he trusts that the American business system, while not perfect, is the best we've got. He's ready to roll up his sleeves and get to work.

Jean's description of "abnormal" adwomen—girls who drank highballs in smoky bars every bit like men, teetering home late to Greenwich Village "hideouts"—gestured toward New York's bohemian counterculture, a space where those disenchanted with white suburbia retreated to explore alternative gender, race, and class identities. It was a place where African American culture, particularly jazz, could appear unadulterated rather than "whitened" for popular mass consumption. It was a place where gay men and lesbians felt they could pass under the radar or, even, find a community of their peers. It was a place where outliers and the marginalized felt at home. Its inhabitants, if they were skilled at passing, could work in advertising, selling the white suburban dream to an American mass market. But they had to keep their real identities under wraps.[39]

Midcentury anthropologists like Margaret Mead and Alfred Kinsey were, in different ways, looking to break open stifling psychoanalytical assumptions about biology and destiny: that women were programmed for domesticity; that there was one, prescriptive, "normal" way to have sex. Yet when their research made it into mainstream culture, it did so only to reassert the very sexual orthodoxies it set out to question. It was common practice among advertisers to cite social science research to give their marketing plans an aura of data-driven accuracy or, more broadly, to lend institutional gravitas to the enterprise of selling itself. Not surprisingly, when Jean sought to make a compelling case to clients about how to deploy gender in their marketing plans, she turned to Mead.

In a 1954 essay she wrote for the *Christian Herald* entitled "The New Togetherness," Jean quoted Mead's general observation that for every society, "the most important problem is the division of labor— who is to catch the fish, collect the refuse, climb the coconut trees, tend the fire."[40] But where Mead held a critical lens up to the ways in which modern American gender roles were painfully constraining, Jean used the quote to lend authority to the archetype of family-as-team, a trend touted by mass circulation lifestyle magazines in the 1950s. The "New Togetherness" offered a pseudoliberated vision of family life, in which traditionally gendered activities like cooking (feminine) and wood working (masculine) were now becoming family affairs, with men donning kitchen aprons and women pulling up a stool at the workbench. This loosening of stereotypes around domestic chores and leisure pursuits had arisen in part, Jean suggests, as a result of the increasing numbers of women working outside the home. "Our society has been radically revising its point of view on many of these problems," Jean commented in her article. "Women today are helping to 'catch the fish'—and men are often helping to clean and cook them!"[41]

Indeed, despite the overwhelming postwar cultural narrative pushing women toward domestic pursuits, the period actually saw a steep increase in wives and mothers entering the workplace: by 1955, one in three American "housewives" held a job outside the home. The fad for family "togetherness" at mid-decade can thus be seen, in part, as a cultural strategy to soften this "radical revision" of traditionally gendered public and private spheres. The playful role swapping described as the New Togetherness served to reinforce existing gender inequalities, defanging the potentially disruptive social effects of the uptick in "two-job women" by containing gender-role experimentation within the solid four walls of the nuclear family home. The trap inherent in the split-level suburban home wasn't sprung; instead, it was made more bearable, leavened with a bit of (closely contained) screwball-comedy fun.[42]

Much of Jean's food advertising in the 1950s focused on adding "fun" to the monotony of suburban eating, spicing things up with crazy new ideas for how to serve soup, for example, or how to jazz up a can of tuna fish. "Fun is something our research people tell us you want these days," Jean revealed in a 1957 talk to New Jersey homemakers. "Serve things in new ways, at new times, in new places—don't be forever sticking into the same old rut," she urged in a piece of domestic advice that might have been as applicable to the bedroom as the kitchen.[43] This marketing tactic was particularly successful in Jean's work for Campbell's Soup. Canned soup at midcentury was perceived as boring, run of the mill, ho-hum—thus stalling sales. Jean brainstormed a dozen ways to inject soup with new energy, including one campaign pushing soup for breakfast and another with the catchy slogan "New Soups from Two Soups"—combining cream of mushroom with tomato, say, for added zing. "Soup on the rocks," or cold canned soup served over ice in a zany twist on the five-o-clock cocktail hour, was surely one of Jean's strangest suggestions for mealtime fun (and one which, happily, has not withstood the test of time).

"Togetherness—it's an 'everyone' thing!" Jean assured her audience. When the lady of the house got tired of vacuuming the den, she could always mix things up by tending to her suburban lawn. Nowadays, "even the power lawn mowers seem to be chugged around by women often as not," Jean chuckled indulgently.[44] Women could ride power mowers and men could wear aprons with abandon—as long as they did so within the confines of the white picket fence.

9

The Liking of Ike

Television, Anticommunism, and Magical Thinking

In her address to General Mills executives in 1956, Jean confided that although television was still in its infancy, and one could "argue for a long time" about the best way to use the new medium for advertising, one method with a "sound record of sales success" was the use of "trusted, believable, recognizable, real personalities"—like Betty Crocker. By combining her with talk-show hosts Garry Moore and Bob Crosby, General Mills had managed to seamlessly integrate cake commercials into the "relaxed, easy-going, story-telling, personal involvement" content of the shows themselves.[1] It hadn't been easy, Jean averred, and there was still much to learn. But General Mills and BBDO were committed to exploring the deep value of "personality selling," "constantly striving to learn how to make the most of this factor of personal involvement which has so much to do with the customer's choice of brands."[2]

If in 1956 Jean knew something about the power of television and the peculiar feeling of intimacy it created, she had learned much of it in 1952 when the Republican National Committee (RNC) and the Citizens for Eisenhower hired BBDO to work on Dwight D. Eisenhower's presidential campaign. For there, the agency deployed the power of "personality selling" via mass media in order, for the first time in history, to propel a product-candidate directly into the White House. Political reporter Edward Folliard, following Ike on the campaign trail, was struck by the power of the general's "personal attraction" to the exclusion of any substantial political debate. When Folliard asked an older man at a rally to explain the phenomenon, he reportedly replied, "'Well, I don't know. I'd like to have old Ike cook me a steak.'"[3] Likeability wasn't a serendipitous add-on to Ike's political platform; it *was* his political platform. And BBDO knew it could sell it.

Jean's mentor Bruce Barton was not only a top-flight advertiser; he was also a lifelong counselor to the Republican Party and Republican candidates, in addition to serving a term in the US House of Representatives himself. His first political advisory role—albeit an informal one—was for fellow Amherst College alumnus Calvin Coolidge, in his 1924 bid for president. In 1936, the RNC tapped Barton to head its publicity campaign for Alf Landon's presidential run. In 1948, Barton's previously off-the-record mentorship of New York governor Thomas E. Dewey was formalized when the RNC hired BBDO for Dewey's presidential campaign.[4] When former Allied commander, NATO head, and all-around-national hero Dwight D. Eisenhower became the frontrunner for the Republican presidential nomination in 1952, the RNC again came knocking at BBDO's doors.

Even as early as his days advising Coolidge, Barton understood how the incipient mass media of radio and television were going to change the nature of American political campaigns—and, eventually, the nature of American politics itself. "The radio audience is very different from the assembled crowd," Barton advised Coolidge. "The radio audience tires quickly and can walk out on you without your knowing it."[5] The solution was to keep speeches short and simple; find a catchy, emotional message and hammer it home. While traditional party politics assumed the electorate was composed of competing interest groups, each of which needed to be appeased, Barton's work in national advertising had trained him to view the public as a homogeneous unit. His sense was that politicians would do well to see the electorate in similar terms: not as a public of competing constituents but as a mass of consumers who could be persuaded using simplified slogans.

In advising Dewey during his second bid for the presidency, Barton warned him to steer clear of his usual crew of Albany policy wonks in developing themes for his speeches. "Albany doesn't think about the United States," he counseled his friend, "It thinks about Jews and Catholics, and the CIO and the AF of L, and of . . . God knows what." "Forget about all the racial and economic groups to whom platforms make their separate appeals," he urged. Instead, Dewey should aim to reach "the unorganized mass of folks who don't belong to anything."[6] Politicians should appeal not to politics but to humanizing, timeless verities of the heart: fear and love, disgust and pride.

In the end, Dewey didn't listen to Barton's advice and lost the presidency to Truman. Four years later, however, Eisenhower offered a perfect specimen to test out Barton's theories. Eisenhower was not a politician and thus had no team of party-machine "managers" attached to him. Indeed, he had not even publicly declared his party affiliation until right before the primary campaign.[7] In the nation's eyes, he was simply "the General": the man who had led the Allied troops to victory. Even after adopting the mantle of the Republican Party and officially becoming a politician, he would frequently punctuate his speeches with the phrase "I'm no politician"—without, apparently, sensing any contradiction. In the words of contemporary political commentator William Lee Miller, Eisenhower was "the good man above politics"—and that was precisely what the culture, at that particular moment, was yearning for.[8]

Both the Republican National Convention and the grassroots booster organization Citizens for Eisenhower-Nixon tapped BBDO to spearhead Eisenhower's 1952 bid. BBDO was placed in charge of radio and television, while two other firms were also brought in: Kudner for print media and the Ted Bates Company to produce a series of television "spots" titled "Eisenhower Answers America."[9] Television was in its incipient stages—in 1952, only 30 percent of American households owned a TV—but the advertising industry already sensed its untapped capacity. Barton gave Eisenhower some tips on how to come across to best advantage on TV: use notes instead of reading from a prepared speech to give the impression of "talking to people, as one frank, unassuming American to his fellow Americans."[10]

As an example, Barton cited the popular television show *Life Is Worth Living*, hosted by Bishop Fulton J. Sheen. Set against a stage backdrop that strove to split the difference between knowledge-steeped library (walls lined with books) and the spectator's own humble living room (plush sofas clustered casually around a coffee table), the impressively be-robed bishop lectured a live audience on how to live their best Christian life, scribbling on a blackboard for emphasis and sprinkling his commentary with the occasional home-spun joke. (So popular was the bishop that he gave Milton Berle's talk show, slotted opposite his on NBC, a run for his money; Berle, when asked about his competitor's success, reportedly quipped, "He's got better writers—Matthew, Mark, Luke and John.") In September leading up to the election, Barton dashed off a letter to BBDO president Ben Duffy suggesting that Eisenhower go on television with a question-and-answer style program. Barton believed that a broadcast staging a cast of recognizable American "types" quizzing the general on their everyday concerns and questions would lend "human interest" punch to Ike's candidacy, while simplifying the issues for voters.[11]

It is unclear whether Barton's suggestion for a staged Q&A town forum was ever realized. Ultimately it was an up-and-coming adman at the Ted Bates Company, Rosser Reeves, who developed and saw to fruition Eisenhower's most significant television campaign. The Bates agency had been an early industry trailblazer in "penetration" studies, or experiments set up to measure the number of viewers/listeners who actually remembered a commercial message. They established a "copy laboratory" in their offices, subjecting panels of guinea-pig viewers to television commercials and quizzing them afterwards.[12] Reeves understood that, in general, getting maximum "penetration" was hard to achieve. This was particularly true of political speeches, the majority of which, in his opinion, "stank." Interviewing a sizable sampling of people who had heard a standard Eisenhower campaign speech, Reeves discovered that an abysmally low number of respondents—between 1 and 2 percent—were able to recall anything he said.[13] Political speeches were by definition low "penetration," but Ike seemed to be remarkably forgettable.

This presented a particular danger in the age of mass media. Reeves had an idea for how to get the general "across" to the electorate. Major corporations typically sponsored one-hour radio and television programs at enormous expense—with the payoff that they cornered an equally enormous audience for their product. The Bates agency was known for its pioneering work taking advantage of station break time slots, "spots" each totaling a minute or less, that would air between shows. Spot advertising gave clients key—albeit brief—exposure to a massive built-in audience, at a fraction of the cost of sponsoring an entire show.[14] In August 1952, Reeves approached the national chairman of Citizens for Eisenhower with the idea of doing a spot campaign for Ike. By stripping his message down into a series of pithy, twenty- or sixty-second sound bites and repeating them on a loop, Eisenhower would gain what hours of uninterrupted speechifying couldn't deliver: audience penetration.

Eisenhower and his advisors were initially skeptical. The feared a spot campaign on the model of a Lever Brothers ad or a General Mills plug would cheapen his candidacy. Reeves reportedly delivered a classic *reductio* argument in response. "The essence of democracy is that the people be informed on the issues. Is there anything wrong with a twenty-minute speech? No. . . . Then what's wrong with a one-minute speech or a fifteen-second speech?" Nothing, was the presumed answer. In any case, Eisenhower acquiesced.[15]

Filming with Eisenhower began on September 11, in the Transfilm Studio in Manhattan.[16] Reeves was particular about the presentation, insisting that Ike remove his glasses, hiring makeup and lighting men to touch up the general's face for the cameras, and coaching him on "the appropriate level of enthusiasm" in the delivery of his lines. The question part of the spots were filmed later, with performances provided by tourists—carefully curated to represent a "cross section of ethnic and regional types"—pulled from Radio City Music Hall. They were filmed reading questions off of cue cards, which were later spliced together with Eisenhower's responses.[17] The final campaign consisted of twenty-eight twenty-second Q&A spots and three one-minute spots. And so, on October 12, began an advertising blitz that, in the words of one commentator, featured "Dwight D. Eisenhower responding to the questions of individuals whom he had never seen in words written for him by an advertising man."[18]

Barton had earlier predicted that hand-in-hand and face-to-face electioneering would soon come to an end, and 1952 sealed the prophecy. As Alan Taranton, who collaborated on Reeves's spot ads, opined the night before the campaign aired: "Anything that General Eisenhower . . . will say [in person] on the subject of high prices, taxes, and corruption will represent a marginal supplementa-tion to these short . . . almost 'on-the-hour-every-hour' Eisenhower broadcasts."[19]

As part of his effort to convince Eisenhower and his team that brevity did not betoken a cheapening of the issues, Reeves report-edly cited Lincoln's Gettysburg address as a masterpiece in the genre, coming in at under 272 words. Whatever value the spot ads might have had, the Gettysburg address they were not. One one-minute spot ad zeroed in on what Reeves, in consultation with George Gal-lup, had determined to be a major source of popular discontent with the Democratic administration: a spike in graft and corruption among politicians. A cranky citizen appeals to Ike with a newspaper in his hand. "'Graft. Corruption. High Prices.'—headlines like that make me fighting mad, General!," he grumbles. To which the presi-dentially stern Ike responds: "Yes, and the cold facts behind them would make you even madder. But we're going to put an end to these national scandals. There's going to be a change next January."[20]

William Lee Miller, in a 1953 article commenting on Eisenhower's use of public relations men in his campaign, had stern words for the practice. "A public relations man may defend his new role in politics by saying that he just takes good political ideas that haven't gone across and makes them go across," Miller observed. But advertising is "not simply neutral," and "public relations men in politics seem spectacularly unaware . . . that the media over which you say some-thing and the devices by which you say it alter what you say."[21] But, of course, this was precisely what the public relations men *did* under-stand. Political content had become irrelevant—or in any case, bore no necessary relationship to actual policy and follow-through. The adman, Miller went on to lament, coached politicians to craft their speeches using examples that were "memorable, whether or not they are illuminating or representative." When a "man in the crowd" on one of Ike's spot ads asked how bad waste in Washington was, Ike responded: "How bad? Recently, just one government bureau actually lost four hundred million dollars and not even the FBI can find it. It's *really* time for a change!" The example had no content beyond shock and entertainment value: not an argument, but a punchline.

Rather than fitting "his actions to a reality that already existed," Miller observed, the politician-turned-adman now "create[d] situations of reality."[22] As Reeves commented after Ike's inauguration, "We did a tremendous amount of work and worry on how to 'package' the General" for the television spot campaign. "We changed the lights. We threw away the glasses. We put him in different clothes. We made him look vigorous, and dynamic—which he actually is."[23] That image and reality should coincide might add value to the package. But it wasn't required for the sale.[24]

In Jean's file is a script, typed on BBDO letterhead, of a planned television "Eisenhower Broadcast to Mothers" set to air on the eve of the election, November 3 1952. From Ben Duffy's scribble on the cover page, it appears that "due to the time factor," the show was ultimately scrapped in favor of a simple Q&A segment. But, Duffy noted, the transcript was "so good" that he wanted to pass a final copy along to her for safekeeping. The speech and staging of the piece were Jean at her heart-tugging best. But the themes that the script covered, however casual and spontaneous they appeared in Eisenhower's homespun delivery, unfolded in lockstep with the three issues Gallup had identified as of pressing importance to voters: Korea, corruption, and communism.[25]

The script's stage instructions indicated Ike and his family settled comfortably in a studio "living room," over which the camera would slowly pan: "Camera comes in on Eisenhower, seated in a family circle. He looks up." "Good morning, friends," Ike addresses the camera. "Come right in. I want you to meet the family." He introduces his first, "best" girl—his wife Mamie—before the camera passes to daughter-in-law Barbara Jean (his son John was off fighting in Korea) and their three children. He announces that he is determined to "talk sense" to the mothers of America, as the women in his life have always been "sensible women, wise women, strong women." He knows, he says, that Korea must be first and foremost in all mothers' minds. He pledges to make it his first priority if elected—because he, too, knows what it feels like to see your boy board a plane "in the chilly gray dawn," not knowing when or whether he will be back.

The script then shifts to a pledge to "clean up" corrupt politicians. "I believe it is America's women who have been quickest to resent the lack of integrity, the shameful misuse of public office, the mink coats, the freezers, the wasteful tossing away of our hard-earned tax money . . . the sorry picture that Washington presents today to the children of America." He harks back to his own mother's values: a good country woman who believed in God, in hard work, and thrift. But all too often, her values and those of her forebears are not seen in government. "There has been no serious effort, no evidence of genuine intent to cut our expenses" among the Democrats in power, Eisenhower laments. Well, "every good housekeeper knows" that costs in the home can be cut. "I believe in Government GOOD HOUSEKEEPING—and I pledge you, the good housekeepers of America, to live up to that belief."

He closes out by reminding his viewers that this has been "family day" in the Eisenhower household—but that if they vote for him, "every day will be family day in the White House"—not only because the halls will ring with the laughter of his grandchildren but because "in the heart of your President, will be a deep-grained feeling that the welfare of the American family should be the first consideration in making any major decision." (At the heart of this promise as well lies his uncompromising opposition to any "socialized medicine" nonsense.) His mother used to say his family was "a little short of ready cash but extra rich in love and loyalty, in the things that make it pleasant for brethren to dwell together in unity." And that is what he pledges to bring to America: that "privilege beyond all privilege," summed up in one "short but all-embracing word . . . PEACE."[26]

Jean wrote a political advertisement following precisely the same recipe she used to write a Betty Crocker segment: scan the polls;

find out what consumers want to hear; then embed it in a heart-tugging storyline that makes people believe that women, from their humble station in the kitchen, are in fact the behind-the-scenes moral backbone of the nation. She'd used the formula to sell cake; it worked just as well to sell a president.

Eisenhower won by a landslide. While it isn't clear to what extent the spot ad campaign boosted his numbers, what is certain is that he took the admen with him to the White House. Eisenhower found himself faced with a divided Republican Party in Congress: what he called "loud talking conservatives" pitted against the more ecumenical brand "Ike" represented. The party infighting got more press coverage than his own policy goals, and he and his advisors found themselves casting about for a means to "present his message over the head of Congress directly to the people in a way that cannot be criticized, and would help prepare public opinion," in the words of Oval Office–cabinet liaison Maxwell Rabb.[27]

On November 23, 1953, Eisenhower circulated a memo to White House staff comparing his situation to that of the "advertising and sales activity of a great industrial organization" with a good product to sell. What was needed, he said, was "an effective and persuasive way of informing the public of the excellence of the product."[28] The solution was a series of live telecasts, direct reports from the capital, scheduled to air on all TV networks and radio simultaneously. The date selected for the inaugural telecast was Christmas Eve, 1953.

The producer Eisenhower selected was someone with on-camera experience aplenty: Hollywood celebrity Robert Montgomery. Montgomery, who began his career as a cinema darling and earned an Oscar nomination for his leading role in *Night Must Fall*, had gone on to direct before finally finding his niche as host of NBC's 1950 television series, *Robert Montgomery Presents*.[29] Montgomery introduced and frequently acted in the hour-long shows, which were abridgements of Hollywood films. As an early import to television, Montgomery played a key role in legitimating the new medium among his fellow stars. Montgomery had already appeared with Eisenhower on the campaign trail and was happy now to step up and take on the direction of a Christmas Eve broadcast.

Arriving at the White House in December, Montgomery went to work helping to craft the president's speech, explaining his vision for the broadcast as a kind of "television version of Franklin Roosevelt's 'fireside chat.'" The filming took place on the south lawn, amid lighted candles and the twinkling of holiday decorations. Eisenhower invited the nation to join him in thanksgiving and prayer for the recently achieved peace (the Korean War Armistice Agreement had been signed in July) and the prospect of a bright and prosperous future, before the ceremonial lighting of a Christmas tree.

The broadcast was a success, and Montgomery—now the president's full-time TV consultant—got busy planning others. A March 15, 1954, telecast went less well; Eisenhower had yet to master the teleprompter and appeared stiff and scripted behind a lectern. As a result, Montgomery coached the president to ad lib the next broadcast, encouraging him to be freer in his gestures and even giving him carte blanche to indulge his trademark tic—folding and unfolding his arms—a habit previous counselors had told him was "distracting." In the April 5 broadcast, Eisenhower not only didn't remain behind his desk, he strolled out in front of it and perched himself casually on its corner. The appearance was praised by *Life* magazine as Eisenhower's "most professional television performance to date"—an assessment that Eisenhower found gratifying. "That's what I've been telling you boys for a long time," Ike expostulated. "Just let me get up and talk to the people. I can get through to them that way."[30]

The Christmas Eve broadcast was noteworthy in yet another respect: Eisenhower's emphasis on Christian faith as the core of American identity and the nation's secret weapon in the mounting crusade against communism. Alluding to the cessation of hostilities in Korea, Eisenhower referred to the tree-lighting ceremony as part of Americans' "traditional celebration of the birth, almost 2,000 years ago, of the Prince of Peace." The world might still stand divided into "two antagonistic parts"—Communists versus the Free World—but America had a special weapon in reserve that would, one day, guarantee victory: "sincere and earnest prayer." "More precisely than in any other way, prayer places freedom and communism in opposition, one to the other," he suggested. For, "the Communist can find no reserve of strength in prayer because his doctrine of materialism and statism denies the dignity of man and . . . the existence of God."[31]

In his personal life, Eisenhower was not a particularly religious man. He attended church only sporadically. But he almost instinctively crafted his message to dovetail with a general trend of religious revivalism sweeping America at midcentury, what one contemporary critic called a "surge of piety" that was sending Americans back to church.[32] In a stroke of marketing genius, Eisenhower had kicked off his campaign for president by calling it a "great crusade," leaving open who, precisely, the Infidel was and what was the prize to be wrested from him.[33]

Jean played her own small part in this national back-to-church movement. An active member of Christ Church in Teaneck, New Jersey, in 1950 she and her husband led a Bible discussion group, spurred on by the parishioners' collective sense that "the use of the Bible in the home had declined" and that "people don't know this greatest of all books as well as they once did."[34] To gauge her audience's day-to-day familiarity with the Bible, she opened the discussion by asking them whether they ever noticed people reading the good Book "in a bus or on the subway or on a train or plane or anywhere else in public except in church." "Would you yourself have the courage," she probed further, "to take out a Pocket Testament or Bible and read it on a bus or subway?"[35]

Jean's suggestion that it would require courage to read the Bible in public echoed sociologist John Murray Cuddihy's assessment of American religious culture at midcentury. In a country where "pluralism is the de facto 'established' religion," Cuddihy argued, Americans were schooled to "wear the pious smile of sociability" and keep their political and religious commitments politely to themselves.[36] To speak of religion in public was a breach of etiquette, something akin to airing details of one's sex life. It was, quite simply, "not correct," in the terms of the successful catchphrase Jean had once formulated for Community Silver.

Jean's next question to her parish audience made clear that faith and sex were equally taboo: "What other books would you hesitate to read in public? *The Kinsey Report*? *The Police Gazette*? *Naked and the Dead*? Margaret Mead's new *Male and Female*?" The Bible ranked, she suggested, on the same level as girlie magazines, Norman Mailer's raw prose, and detailed descriptions of the sex lives of Pacific Islanders in terms of social offensiveness. The Christ Church Bible discussion group hoped to remove some of that stigma in order, according to the program's mission statement, to "reintroduce family and personal use of the Bible in the home."[37]

Jean and her Christ Church friends need not have worried. The taboo on public professions of Christian faith was on its way to being lifted, and, in fact, the rumblings of an evangelical backlash against the Golden Rule "statism" of Roosevelt's New Deal had been making slow but steady inroads for at least a decade. Roosevelt routinely used biblical allusions to translate his sweeping reforms into a language Americans could understand, declaring in his inaugural address, for instance, that his administration would sweep the moneychangers from their high seat in the temple of civilization.[38] In keeping with a Social Gospel model of Christianity, Roosevelt chose parables that emphasized the state as duty-bound to feed the hungry and clothe the needy.

American business interests, dismayed by the New Deal's creation of a "welfare state," sought to parry this biblical thrust with one of their own. Roosevelt's administration, they declared, had made a "false idol" of the state, perverting the emphasis of Christ's teachings from manly individual salvation toward a feminized collectivism. Reasserting a Robert Wade–like prosperity gospel reading of America's free-market Christian destiny was essential to reclaim the soul of the nation. Historian Kevin Kruse dates the decisive turn in the national Christian narrative to the fiery speech-cum-sermon delivered by H. W. Prentis, Jean's former boss at Armstrong Cork and president of the National Association of Manufacturers, before the US Chamber of Commerce in 1940. Faith, not "economic facts," Prentis thundered, was essential to "check the virus of collectivism" threatening to overrun the country and reestablish business as the standard bearer of America's founding Christian values.[39]

Harry Truman provided a crucial link in this turn toward a closer pact between Christianity and the state when he sought to energize the forces of anticommunism by appealing to a Manichean opposition between the "religion" of dialectal materialism and Christianity. His 1947 announcement of the Truman Doctrine—that the United States would henceforth provide aid to countries struggling with internal or external interference with democracy, in a bid to check Soviet expansion—was followed by a 1948 State of the Union address that emphasized America's strength lay not merely in its economy or its democratic tradition, but in its "spiritual" values. On Christmas Eve of 1950, Truman reminded a radio audience that "democracy's most powerful weapon is not a gun, a tank, or a bomb. It is faith— faith in the brotherhood and dignity of man under God."[40]

If Ike's crusade-studded rhetoric three Christmases later was thus not entirely new, it nonetheless marked a decisive shift in the push and pull between Social Gospel and prosperity gospel Christianity that had defined the national narrative over the first half of the twentieth century. It denoted a turn away from the use of scripture by way of analogy, as a rhetorical tool to legitimate secular institutions, and a turn toward a definition of the American experiment as distinctively faith-based and Christian. In much the same way as the communist threat was envisioned as a satanic force or "virus" lying in wait, so Christian faith was imagined as America's secret weapon: freedom-dealing kryptonite to the Soviet superman of collectivism. John Foster Dulles, Eisenhower's secretary of state and himself a virulent anticommunist, perhaps best summed up this new mode of imagining the red menace: only a spiritually vigorous and Christian America, Dulles opined, would be equipped to "resist the penetration of alien faiths" such as communism.[41]

Jean had a Dulles-style parable of American faith that she liked to pull out from time to time in her speeches. She had a friend whose daughter had married a diplomat assigned to the Bulgarian embassy; she was having a baby, and found herself behind the Iron Curtain when she went into labor and needed an emergency

Caesarian. The sanitary conditions in the drafty hospital operating room were appalling: "No anesthetics. No medicine," Jean recounted grimly. The Greek nurse on duty gave her courage to go on, however, by whispering in her ear: "Show them you're an American."[42] Faith in the American way, Jean hinted, would not only see the young woman through pain, but even through sepsis if she only believed fervently enough. Anticommunist faith was, in some sense, a form of magical thinking: wishing something hard enough just might make it come true.

Roosevelt and Truman had initiated a rhetorical rapprochement between church and state, but Eisenhower codified the pact, officially investing previously secular civic rites with Christian content. In the decade and a half following Prentis's rousing speech denouncing economic fact in favor of faith, corporate leaders would partner with preachers and politicians to establish America as "one nation under God." Jean preserved a letter dated October 31, 1952—the eve of the presidential election—from Walter Williams, chairman of the Citizens for Eisenhower-Nixon Committee, thanking her for all she had done for Ike's campaign. "Regardless of the outcome," Williams encouraged her, "each of us has the inner satisfaction of knowing that the cause we have been fighting for is indeed a great crusade."[43] Once elected, Eisenhower sealed the rhetorical crusade into law. In 1954, Congress voted to add the words "Under God" to the Pledge of Allegiance, and in 1956 it ratified "In God We Trust" as the country's official motto.[44]

Ike's was a strange brand of religion. A good gauge of its oddness might be found in "God's float," designed for his 1953 inaugural parade. Featuring a square white edifice shaped to suggest an indeterminate house of worship, it was topped with a gold dome and rod that, in the words of the parade's organizer, was ambiguous enough that spectators "will be unable to tell whether there's a cross or a beam of light at the tip of the rod."[45] A snarkier commentator noted that, in aiming to represent all religions, "it had the symbols of none," and "looked like nothing whatsoever in Heaven above, or in the earth beneath, except possibly an oversized model of a deformed molar left over from some dental exhibit."[46]

But God's float was indeterminate by design, not by accident. The vigorous reinvention of America's Christian past had to avoid too blatant a violation of that other pillar of American identity, religious pluralism. It was not faith in a particular creed that was of the essence; rather, it was faith in faith itself, belief in believing, that mattered. The genial vagueness of Eisenhower's indeterminate crusade was precisely its attraction: who could be against it? Americans' strength and secret Communist-slaying weapon lay in their being a people of faith; it would be counterproductive to be too precise about its content. The fact that this faith resisted dissection or critical reflection was precisely its point. Indeed, those who sought to question it or garner a clearer definition of what, exactly, Americans were being asked to believe in were accused of being fancy-pants elitists, "those who dwell with words and phrases," as Eisenhower once dismissed them. "Faith seems to be too simple a thing for some people to understand," he complained.[47]

Eisenhower was the first president specifically marketed as a television personality by public relations and admen; he was also the first to so consistently rely on the language of Christian faith revival in his campaign. These two aspects of his candidacy were not unrelated. On the contrary: appealing to a contentless faith, a vague, oceanic surge of fellow feeling mingled with patriotic pride, was uniquely effective in swelling support for a candidate running on the power of personality rather than a specific and clearly articulated set of policies. Eisenhower, according to William Lee Miller, presented himself as "the negation of all that is meant by politics"—its messiness, its complexity, its incivility.[48] "Faith" was a perfect information shortcut for potential voters, a piece of easily digestible personal information from which they could construct a narrative and infer policy. This turn in politics is what one might expect of a culture in which popularity, teamwork, and a species of private, inoffensive likability had become the lingua franca of public engagement.

Eisenhower tapped into the American spiritual awakening at mid-century; Jean did the same. In a speech at a 1956 Food Forum conference, Jean canvassed recent "depth psychologist" research on what motivated housewives to buy one food product over another. The first motivator was "newsiness," "still the hottest word you can put into a headline, Mr. Gallup says."[49] The second motivator was "fun." And the third, Jean announced, without missing a beat, was "a strong reaching out for religion." She continued: "Maybe it's reassurance. Maybe it's nostalgia. But whatever it is, women want to find some way to be a little bit of use in the world." So, in addition to offering housewives soups in new flavors or serving dishes or cupcakes with a funny icing smile on top, advertisers might satisfy the consumer's spiritual longing by suggesting "that they bake two cakes and give one to a neighbor. Something like that."[50]

Jean sought to put her depth research to the test by floating an advertising campaign that would tie Betty Crocker to the ambient national Christian revival. In an undated memo, she announced, "I believe Betty Crocker could spearhead a GREAT AMERICAN BAKING REVIVAL." "There's a nostalgia in the air," Jean mused, "emotion waiting to catch on to something." Betty Crocker could fill this wordless emotional emptiness with a worthy object: baking. "She wouldn't begin it," Jean was quick to point out. Any religious revival worth its salt depended on spontaneity—the spirit moves you, and you catch fire. Anything suspected of being orchestrated behind the scenes would smack of inauthenticity. Rather, Betty would "simply act as though it is an accepted fact that baking is back," Jean advised. "And I think if we do it right, we could make it a reality."[51]

10

The Power of Positive Thinking

The species of Christian faith popularized at midcentury was of a very peculiar sort. Psychiatrists, businessmen, and ministers converged to forge a cultural recipe that took the country's long-standing love affair with religious faith and repackaged it as a quasi-medicalized, technocratic project to secure American "peace of mind" and productivity. Jean signed on to the project. Her files include copious typewritten notes on a range of now-forgotten figures who worked in the overlapping realms of industrial psychology, marketing, and sociology, including Henry C. Link, W. W. Charters, and husband-and-wife team Harry Allen and Bonaro Overstreet. All were armchair entrepreneur-psychologists who peddled Christianity-infused formulae for industrial efficiency, well-adjusted "successful living," or both. All were prolific writers and public speakers whom Jean followed, read, and quoted in her advertising work.

To read through Jean's extensive forays into the evangelical-inspired literature of self-help and "motivation," both in the workplace and in the hundreds of speeches she delivered before women's clubs, is to track just how pervasive this cultural idiom was at midcentury. It is also to track how a theology of salvation through salesmanship—what Jean liked to call the cultivation of a "Personal Public Relations Program" for peak individual and national well-being—managed to become a new form of secular faith.

Carefully preserved in Jean's folder "Wedge Ideas, 1943–1955," is the transcript of a speech delivered on June 4, 1943, before a gathering of the Association of National Advertisers, entitled "Brands, A Major Contribution to Social Progress and World Harmony." The author of the speech, Henry C. Link, PhD, was a practicing psychologist and vice president of the Orwellian-sounding Psychological Corporation. Link's speech yokes tried-and-true Progressive shorthand ("Social Progress and World Harmony") with that most vigorous of free-market icons: the Brand.

Link trotted out the usual liberal equivalence between market choice and political choice, with brand loyalty living proof that in a democracy, consumers were free to "vote" with their pocketbook every bit as much as citizens were free to vote at the ballot box. "More people elect Campbell soup every month than elect the president every four years," he observes. But in an increasingly secular age, brand loyalty represented "not so much a materialistic as a spiritual . . . phenomenon," an act of faith on which "people are daily staking their comfort and their money." Indeed, Link suggested, "we might say, without disrespect, that if the people of America had as much faith in the doctrines of the church as they have faith in nationally advertised brands, this country would be a far more religious country." Take Coca-Cola, for instance. "[Coca-Cola's] use represents an act of faith in which all men, regardless of nationality, are friends," he suggested. Brands "transform mental confusion into mental harmony" and "convert social distrust into mutual understanding."[1] Globally, Link suggests, people have more faith in a can of Campbell's soup or a bottle of Coca-Cola than they have in "the system of international law that is supposed to govern nations."

Link's Psychological Corporation is a perfect illustration of how salesmanship, free-market faith, psychiatry, and Christianity blended at midcentury. The Psychological Corporation was granted a charter by the state of New York in 1921 with the object of advancing the field of applied psychology. Describing the corporation's mission, psychologist J. McKeen Cattell singled out the development of standardized psychological tests to measure employee fitness and scholastic aptitude as among the organization's top priorities. Cattell surmised that just as advances in the hard sciences led to a quadrupling of America's industrial output during the Industrial Revolution, so investment in the science of "personality testing" would repay itself many times over in the form of increased industrial efficiency and wealth production. "Hours of labor, fatigue, interest, good will, efficiency and the like," Cattell proposed, are all problems that psychological testing can measure and solve.[2]

And indeed, the field of industrial psychology garnered enthusiastic support from business executives haunted by the specter of labor agitation in the wake of the Bolshevik Revolution. Industry-funded psychological studies of the "maladjusted" worker advanced the view that labor agitation was less a political expression than regressive emotional "acting out" by individual laborers. By studying workers' moods and attitudes, altering work schedules, and providing counseling, management could mitigate such problems as boredom, fatigue, and frustration, a potent weapon in the fight against unions.[3] Alternatively, managers could screen out "agitators" before they even hit the factory floor. After the passage of the National Labor Relations Act in 1935 barring hiring discrimination based on union membership, managers skirted the law by using personality inventory tests not to predict worker performance, as purported, but to sniff out (and turn away) likely union sympathizers.[4]

Applied psychologists worked in partnership with industry and government to formulate personality and intelligence tests that would standardize military and industrial behavior. The discipline exercised, then, an essentially conservative cultural function, even as it touted itself as the "objective" scientific study of human behavior. Cattell's description of the Psychological Corporation, claiming that applied psychology was the royal road to social progress, corroborated this conflation of individual social adjustment and national well-being. "To get the best kind of people and to put them in the situations in which they will behave in the way best for themselves and for others," he asserted, is essential in the drive toward "the satisfaction of human needs and the promotion of human happiness."[5] Engineering good behavior and adjustment to the industrial mechanism was key to ushering in God's Kingdom.

Henry C. Link's first book, *Employment Psychology: The Application of Scientific Methods to the Selection, Training, and Rating of Employees* (1919), was swiftly followed by a tome on *The New Psychology of Selling and Advertising*, and then a memoir-style exhortation on the mental and even physical health benefits of Christian faith (his 1936 *The Return to Religion*). Together, they sketch an itinerary that makes sense within the context of the increasingly overlapping spheres of psychiatry, industrial relations, advertising, and Protestant "pastoral care." Link's own personal return to faith came as a result of his work as a psychotherapist: after fifteen years and 4,000 patients, he realized that his counsel to troubled souls invariably harked back to the biblical parables of his childhood.[6]

That the science of psychology should have led Link back to faith was no accident. Psychology, he asserted, teaches us that people are happy and well adjusted when they are liked; they are liked when they unselfishly extend themselves to, and seek to please, others. Psychologically speaking, Jesus was the very picture of well-adjusted mental health: an unselfish "extrovert" to a "degree that few can hope to achieve," "highly aggressive in making social contacts." The story of Jesus's life is "a story of winning friends," of "forever changing the water of existence into the wine of social intercourse."[7] (Immediately after this analogy, Link suggested bridge and ballroom dancing as excellent therapy for recovering introverts.)

This canonization of the sociable Jesus from the mid-1920s onward was something of a cottage industry in American business circles. Bruce Barton was perhaps the first to reclaim Jesus for Roaring '20s capitalism in his bestselling 1925 biography of the Nazarene, *The Man Nobody Knows*. Barton's rereading of scripture revealed Jesus as the ultimate personality man: gregarious, fun-loving, magnetic, muscular. In his chapter "The Sociable Man," Barton put to rest the stereotype of the long-faced Jesus, inviting the reader to imagine, instead, "how he loved it all—the pressure of the crowd, the clash of wits, the eating and the after-dinner talk."[8] Of all the miracles Jesus performed, Barton argued, the one most characteristic was the replenishment of the wine at the marriage feast at Cana. When the bride's mother whispered tearfully in Mary's ear that there was no more wine, Jesus "glanced across at [her] wistful face . . . [and] remembered that the event was the one social triumph of her self-sacrificing life." Instantly, his decision was made: he used his inner powers to "keep a happy party from breaking up too soon, to save a hostess from embarrassment" by filling the twelve empty jugs not just with wine, but with wine of the finest vintage. Jesus was no kill-joy; on the contrary, he was life of the party.[9]

Psychologist Harry Allen Overstreet hopped on Barton's Jesus bandwagon in his 1925 published series of lectures, *Influencing Human Behavior*—a book that Jean assiduously read and annotated, typing up three pages of notes on it. "Life is many things; it is food-getting, shelter-getting, playing, fighting, aspiring, hoping, sorrowing," Overstreet preached. "But at the center of it all it is this: it is the process of getting ourselves believed in and accepted."[10] Yet this did not mean, necessarily, that we were all base egoists. Lincoln, Socrates, and Jesus were all extraordinarily skilled, in different ways, in making their personalities "effective." In the immortal words of Dale Carnegie—a fervent fan and popularizer of Overstreet's pseudoacademic lectures—"looking at the other person's point of view and arousing in him an eager want for something is not to be construed as manipulating that person so he will do something that is only for your benefit and his detriment." Rather, each side "gain[s] from the negotiation," he concludes brightly.[11]

Among the nuggets of wisdom Jean retained from *Influencing Human Behavior*: when speaking to a crowd, "Never make the audience feel inferior"; "Study other people in terms of habit-systems" to understand their motivations; and "Use the good will technique—highbrow way of saying Golden Rule!"[12] The *Wedge* articles Jean wrote often sounded like a cross between a Sunday School sermon and a correspondence course for aspiring salesmen—which, of course, was exactly how she needed them to sound.

Link's "Brands, A Major Contribution to Social Progress" appealed loosely to the old Progressive mantra of democratized consumption as guarantor of universal Christian "sociability" and peace. Nonetheless, in *The Return to Religion*, Link was careful to clarify that while the well adjusted will strive to embody the Prince of Peace's "good will technique" in their personal lives, transferring it to social planning is a tell-tale sign of deviance. "One of the most common symptoms of an inferiority complex or of personal failure is the desire to change the social order," Link warned. This was a classic case of projection, he said, focusing blame on society's failings rather than turning the critical gaze inward. Indeed, many of Link's most emotionally disturbed patients betrayed a troublesome desire to "become social workers" (a tendency he was able, happily, to defuse in "hundreds" of cases). Even worse: with the advent of the New Deal, it appeared "as though the whole country were suffering a radical inferiority complex," turning the individual into a ward of the state and depriving him of "responsibility for himself and his own deeds."[13] Sociability, if it was not to destroy the very subjects it purported to help, was a precept best confined to the private realm of the dance parlor and the bridge table.

Along similar lines, a growing cadre of evangelical Christians and their corporate allies intuited that the old Progressive lingo of "harmony" and "mutual understanding" could be replaced with a more red-blooded defense of rugged individualism and privatized, faith-based self-realization. By the mid-1950s, such dated appeals to social harmony had begun to smack of sissified statism at best, communism at worst. The acme of this renewed Cold War twist on the American prosperity gospel was surely the ministry of Norman Vincent Peale, whose Marble Collegiate Church and adjacent Religio-Psychiatric Clinic blossomed from a small outfit ministering to Depression-wracked New Yorkers in the 1930s to a full-blown spiritual-industrial complex by the mid-1950s. Peale, the son of a Methodist pastor, was an early and outspoken critic of both the New Deal at home and communism abroad (two projects he claimed were suspiciously similar in scope and worldview). Americans must "choose between the Church and the Reds," Peale thundered repeatedly from his pulpit. The New Deal abetted the Communist advance, even if indirectly, by convincing citizens that salvation was to be found in the State rather than in God Almighty. "In the old days people flocked to church to pray to God that the evidences of His displeasure might pass. . . . Today they pray to the government to write another code," Peale fumed.[14]

Peale's 1952 publication of *The Power of Positive Thinking* detailed in ten easy steps how health and wealth, both personal and national, was best achieved through Christian faith-infused "positive thinking." The book was an almost instantaneous bestseller. Much of the book is warmed-over Oliver Swett Marden, the Gilded Age prosperity gospel guru whose dollops of wisdom were served up regularly in Robert Wade's Pennsylvania Business College promotional pamphlets. All of the familiar nineteenth-century New Thought touchstones reappear, from William James's pronouncement that human beings can "alter their lives by altering their attitudes of mind," to energy metaphors comparing the mind to a power-producing plant that need only be sufficiently plugged into God to hum profitably along.[15] But where Marden and his Depression-era successor Dale Carnegie retained a largely secular tone, the Reverend Peale resolutely affirmed that the All-Supply was to be found in Jesus Christ our Lord and Savior, and the successful man would accept no substitutes.

While earlier self-help gurus had favored electrical energy metaphors, Peale compared the power of prayer to the power of the atomic bomb. "Just as there exist scientific techniques for the release of atomic energy," he theorized, "so are there scientific procedures for the release of spiritual energy through the mechanism of prayer." In the context of the Eisenhower presidency and its weaponization of faith as the country's best defense against godless Communists, Peale's atomic metaphor takes on even deeper resonance. Properly deployed, prayer could "blast out all defeat and lift a person above all difficult situations."[16] Peale's ten-step plan for releasing one's inner powers involved visualization ("Stamp indelibly on your mind a mental picture of yourself as succeeding") and chant-like repetition of biblical verses ("Ten times each day practice the following affirmation, repeating out loud if possible. 'I can do all things through Christ which strengtheneth me' (Philippians 4:13)."[17] Increased wealth and business success were, of course, among the gifts that would naturally flow in as a result.

Commentators of all stripes acknowledged that postwar American culture, basking in material plenty yet living in the shadow of the A-bomb, was peculiarly marked by nervousness, anxiety, and "neuroticism." Peale found this an unmanly state of affairs, and one that the power of prayer could, not surprisingly, fix. In his chapter "Relax for Easy Power," Peale revealed that according to a drug manufacturer he knew, "every night in these United States more than six million sleeping tablets are required to put the American people to sleep." "What a pathetic situation," he scoffed. His own church had noticed this uptick in "tension" as the "prevailing malady of the American people," and responded with a double-barreled strategy of assigning psychiatrist-pastor teams to suffering parishioners at their wellness clinic. Under the supervision of the remarkably named Dr. Smiley Blanton, a psychiatrist would analyze and diagnose each patient's neurosis before passing him on to the pastor, who would then apply, "in scientific and systematic form, the therapies of prayer, faith, and love."[18]

This quasi-pastoral therapeutic vocabulary echoes advertising's endlessly recycled appeals to the same themes. Jean's own work on Teaberry gum aimed to promote the product as a therapeutic cure for the inevitable tensions of modern life—like prayer, or perhaps in combination with it, chewing a stick of Teaberry gum was plugged as a way to "un-tense" and regain power over anxiety-producing situations. "A central phrase for any of their advertising might well be 'Time for Teaberry's,'" Jean suggested in a memo summing up a recent brainstorming session for the client. "This could be developed on a 'Steady your nerves' theme with pictures of nervous moments and the phrase 'Time for Teaberry's' or the same pictures and the phrase 'Steady your Nerves with Teaberry's.'"[19] Suggested scenarios included a husband helpfully proffering a stick of Teaberry gum to his young wife before she takes her driver's test and a best man giving one to the nervous groom before he walks down the aisle. Another approach to the motif might feature photographs showing Teaberry gum mixed in among the effects of rich and famous people known for successful nerve mastery: Teaberry glimpsed in Vivien Leigh's makeup kit, in Olympian swimmer Eleanor Holm's locker, or on J. P. Morgan's lunch tray, casually strewn across the financial pages.

Alternatively, Jean closed out the memo, the gum manufacturer could go with a "Relax with Teaberry's" campaign. "Relax is a stopper word, a proven headline stopper on other accounts," she counseled. Why not his-and-her cartoons showing relatable "nightmare nerves" scenarios that could be easily remedied with Teaberry's? "Man at office desk, three phones ringing, heads popping in four different doors, messengers and secretaries crowding desk—'Time to Relax with Teaberry's." Or: "Woman at telephone, boy pounding on door, children fighting on floor, dog gnawing rug, kettle boiling over—"Time to relax with Teaberry's."

In both her personal and professional lives, Jean worshipped at the altar of Bruce Barton's sociable Jesus. A folder in her papers labeled "Personal: Inspiration 1948–1965" is filled with newspaper clippings, prayer cards, and retyped quotations that caught her interest; they frequently found their way into her client speeches and advertisements. A sampling includes a quotation from John Donne's "For Whom the Bell Tolls" ("No Man is an Island"); St. Francis of Assisi's "Prayer for Peace" ("Lord, Make Me an Instrument of Thy Peace"); and psychiatrist Karl Menninger's definition of mental health ("Maintain an even temper, an alert intelligence, socially considerate behavior and a happy disposition").[20] And, of course, Dr. Peale puts in an appearance: one of his weekly columns for the *Sunday Herald Tribune*, titled "Confident Living: How to Meet Difficult Situations." Look down on your life obstacles from a "high spiritual altitude," Peale coaches. "From there, it will look small in comparison to the power of faith—and it *is* small."[21] This clipping appears alongside one touting the "Mind as a Wonder Drug." Never forget, the columnist coaches, that every human being "is a reservoir of anxieties and troubles that may affect his health." Bacteria and metabolic disturbances are real enough—but maintaining a positive outlook is at least half the battle when it comes to health.

Such a relentlessly sentimental worldview, when joined with the free-market faith so prevalent at midcentury, helps explain how Jean could write an article in praise of family togetherness for a mainline Protestant Christian magazine that differed little in tone and theme from a talk she gave to a furniture company on how to market "relaxing" recliner chairs. Jean's essay "The New Togetherness," which appeared in the *Christian Herald* in 1955, rehearsed the familiar sentimental theme of the nuclear family as a microcosm of the larger Family of Man, such that private expressions of love and kindness between husband and wife become tokens of a loosely Christianized peace on earth. Jean opened by recounting a touching scene that she had witnessed recently while riding the bus to work. A young couple got on and the husband, after paying the driver, moved to the rear of the bus and called back to his wife in an "affectionate, cheery voice," "'Come on back, Honey. There's a better seat here—where we can be together.'" The togetherness that "starts with a man and a woman," she suggested, is so "rich and warm and glowing" that it can radiate across the whole neighborhood and then, "rightly used, can help to remake the world."[22]

In a roughly contemporaneous speech she gave to the Barcalo Corporation in 1956, Jean brainstormed a dozen or more ways in which the company might market its "BarcaLounger" recliners to middle-class Americans. "What else is new in today's picture of the good life?" she asked rhetorically, before leaping in to answer: "Togetherness." "People are doing things in pairs," she elaborated— working in pairs, cooking in pairs, relaxing in pairs. "And what an opportunity that is to sell two chairs instead of one," she proffered. "Sell togetherness," she urged, "His and Her chairs for His and Her moments of quiet, peaceful relaxation."

She went on to emphasize that in today's crazy-mixed-up world, "everybody's living too fast, feeling all wound up. Everybody feels that he needs to relax." Today's consumer is looking for "peace"— and the BarcaLounger is teed up to sell it. "If you can wrap up a piece of peace, tie it with a ribbon, sell it on a silver platter—you've got customers aplenty," she assured her audience. "Peace there is in the good life—peace that's hard to find at home." And here Jean reached back into her prosperity gospel past and pulled out a perfect biblical adage, one Bruce Barton himself would have been proud of: "Blessed are the peacemakers! Blessed in sales."[23]

The premium that Peale et al.'s theology of self-realization placed on profit and productivity—both material and spiritual—made it naturally attractive to American corporate culture. Some of BBDO's top brass, including Bruce Barton and Alex Osborn, implemented secular versions of Peale's motivational speeches in the workplace. Founding BBDO partner Osborn, in particular, published a steady stream of self-help "creativity" manuals throughout the 1940s and '50s. Debuting with a spunky wartime pamphlet, *How to Think Up*, Osborn churned out in quick succession *Your Creative Power* (1948), *How to Wake Up Your Mind* (1952), *Applied Imagination* (1953), and *The Goldmine between Your Ears* (1955).

"Each of us has an Aladdin's lamp which psychologists call creative imagination," Osborn postulated in *How to Think Up*. "I have learned by experience that imagination, like muscle, can be built up by exercise." "This truth is accepted by more and more psychologists," he asserted, and "business is learning that Tom, Dick and Nellie can be coached and coaxed to think up new ideas."[24] He continued on to provide a three-step program by which any workplace could host a "think-up conference" to boost productivity. BBDO, he confided, had evolved a "successful device for group thinking" called a "brainstorm supper." A mixture of managers and younger staff from among the company's 500 employees were invited to supper in the company dining room. "The executive in charge carves the beef and serves the salad," he described, while "our attractive dietician makes all feel at home" (the dietician's attractiveness acting as stimulus, apparently, to the free flow of ideas).[25] After pie and coffee, the problem to be tackled was aired and the ideas began to fly. The ground rules were simple: no criticism "until all ideas are in"; "wildness is wanted," or "the crazier the idea, the better"; and simple ideas could be joined into compounds to "make a 'wow.'"[26]

Osborn's book took off, and in 1945 he was asked by *Reader's Digest* to write an article on how "the average person" might employ the corporate brainstorming technique in his or her personal life. He asked Jean whether she could cull from her female staff some "actual illustrations or case histories" of personal brainstorming in action.[27] Jean responded with a list: a woman who brainstormed ideas for how she might make pin money; a woman who sought to reduce bickering in the house by instituting a "Family Improvement Society" where behavior problems were tossed out on the table, and all members encouraged to brainstorm ways of solving them.

Osborn's "think up" technique was so popular that by 1947, BBDO was conducting hour-long buffet lunch brainstorms, open to all employees, devoted to hammering out ideas for selected client issues: how to promote a company's centennial; how to get Chiquita Banana more brand visibility. Jean composed a speech laying down specific, step-by-step advice for how to lead a "mass brainstorm" session with up to one hundred participants. "The basic difference between a group brainstorm session and a New England town meeting," she explained, "is that the brainstorm seeks a practical, down-to-earth course of action, not an academic, balanced opinion." No place for "wise guys" bent on criticism or "holding forth"; "in short, for bores!" "NO CRITICISM," she reiterated. "The leader's job is to smile, to say 'swell!,' to grab ideas as they pop and translate them into rapid practical applications for the record."[28] The evocation of Peale's self-help theology was more than clear.

Osborn's technique drew on Freudian psychology and its deep dive into the mysteries of the unconscious mind. If Peale focused on God as the sole source of unrealized spiritual and financial potential, Freudian-inspired pop psychology prized the unconscious for its unconventionality, its alliance with spontaneous action rather than ponderous, rational thought processes. Osborn (and Jean's) own rhetoric castigating uptight "bores" who would proffer an "In other words, . . ." or a "But that's not feasible . . ." appears at first glance to fly in the face of corporate group-think. To let the mind roam, to create a democratic space where board room executive and steno pool typist break bread and freely exchange ideas, might have seemed a radical innovation in office culture at the time. But ultimately, creativity is given a pass always, and only, in the service of the bottom line. To "make a 'wow,'" in Osborn's gimmicky formulation, actually just meant to make a profit.

Predictably, Jean closed out her report on the lunch brainstorms by noting their positive effect on worker morale. Participants reportedly returned to their desks "rested, refreshed, alert"—ready to work more efficiently.[29] Building on Osborn's technique, Jean went on to craft a series of "pep talks" to young women copywriters in her department. One of these was a presentation urging them never to forget to "look around and learn something" from their colleagues. "Pop in through open doors, pop out with wider horizons," was Jean's cheerful advice. Sure, every job has its ups and downs, moments where you feel stalled and stymied. But "as long as you are still growing," Jean urged, her "little sprouts" should stay put—because there is "good GROWING weather in BBDO!"[30]

In her speeches to outside women's groups, Jean tweaked the masculine self-help model of a Peale or an Osborn to suit her audience's more domestic concerns. In a 1959 article for the trade magazine *Forecast for Home Economists*, "How are your Personal Public Relations?" Jean encouraged women to pay attention to "the small amenities that oil the wheels of human relations."[31] Jean walked her audience through a four-point checklist to help them keep track of their inner growth: 1. Look yourself up! 2. Warm yourself up! 3. Think yourself up! 4. Grow yourself up! After first making sure you appear fresh, clean, crisp, and "nice to be near," give a moment of thought to how you make others feel. "Watch a friendly, outgoing person," Jean counseled. "What's the secret of her charm?" You know yourself—it is that she exudes a "warm, genuine, receptive interest" in others.

In another, similarly themed speech to a dietician's club, after coaching her audience on ways to grow into better workers ("Ask yourself . . . Am I laying bricks? or helping to build a cathedral?"),[32] Jean pondered, "Can you use these same business techniques to enrich your private life?" "Think yourself up," she urged, "think for yourself what can I do this week, this hour, this day, this minute to make my home brighter, my family happier, my friends stronger?" Becoming a "gayer, brighter, easier to live with person" would bear fruit in professional settings as well: "Any good habits you acquire in the process of making your life more fun come in handy in the process of making your life more productive."[33]

She continued the growth theme in another speech, "Keep Reaching! That's the Way to Grow." Quoting Robert Browning's line—"Ah, but a man's reach should exceed his grasp, or what is heaven for?"— Jean then tweaked it for women: "A woman's reach should exceed her grasp—to bring heaven-on-earth a little nearer."[34] Whether it was reaching beyond one's humdrum musical tastes to try out a Bach concerto or throwing some "chopped green pepper or pimento" into Sunday morning's scrambled eggs, any housewife-mother could engage in little "daily stretching[s] of the mind" that would "make your mothering more rewarding." Perhaps sensing, however, that throwing "a bit of sliced almond in the instant pudding" wasn't precisely the kind of soul growth most housewives craved, Jean shifted focus and closed the speech by urging her audience to "reach for the big things, as well as the small." "Are you too tired to pray, too skeptical to believe, too scornful to trust?" she asked. Instead, reach out to find the "inner strength and peace" in the "source books" that guided our ancestors: for instance, this verse from Matthew 7:7: "'Ask and you shall find; knock and it shall be opened unto you.'" There's never a time in a woman's life where it is too late to "reach out and grow."[35]

Like Peale, Jean had little use for worriers. And so Jean, too, got in on the advice market for how to "break the worry habit," the title of a chapter from *The Power of Positive Thinking*. She developed an eight-point program for "how to worry successfully," which writer Marguerite Clark included in her 1962 self-help book *Why So Tired? The Ways of Fatigue and the Ways of Energy*. In a feature story titled "Learn How to Worry Right," a columnist interviewed Jean to glean tips on how to organize "brooding, fussing, fuming and stewing into a constructive plan."[36] Everyone should draw up a "worry list," Jean coached, breaking down big worries into smaller components; then,

FIGURE 14. Undated photograph of Jean Rindlaub giving a speech.

"nibble at the little ones" until they feel more manageable. Her signature invention, however, was what she called a Worry Wheel:
write down all your worries on 3" × 5" notecards, tack them to a
wheel, and "give it a whirl." Devote the week to single-mindedly
chipping away at the first worry your finger lands on. When you spin
the wheel again one week later, Jean promises, "it will be amazing
how often you'll find most of the worries have resolved themselves."

11

Chiquita Banana and the Politics of Kitsch

In November 1956, the United Fruit Company, the multinational banana conglomerate, hosted its sixth annual Food Forum conference at the Hotel Pierre in New York. A wide range of panelists, from nutritionists and social scientists to food writers and home economists, gathered to take stock of what Americans were eating, why they were eating it, and how they might be persuaded to eat otherwise. As United Fruit was one of BBDO's most high-profile accounts, Jean was among the invited speakers. Her speech focused on how to use creative marketing to capitalize on the basic fact that "the American stomach is elastic," and "the American housewife's mind is flexible."[1] These two propositions, taken together, meant that creating a new niche for an old food product—like bananas—was bounded only by the creativity and culinary audacity of its marketing team.

Also among the speakers there was Edward Bernays, a personal and professional acquaintance of Jean's as well as United Fruit's principal public relations counsel since 1940. His speech, "The Study of Man and His Food Habits," rifled through a grab bag of psychology and "motivation research" pointing out that eating was often emotional rather than rational. Among his findings: food carried with it unconscious "sexual possibilities," with men drawn to such red-blooded foods as roast beef and steak, and women gravitating toward symbolically lighter fare: "salads, whip cream, and soufflé."[2] If those insights sound as though pulled out of a hackneyed Freudian guide to dream symbolism, it wasn't by accident: Bernays was

Sigmund Freud's nephew (a fact that, despite his lack of any formal psychological training, lent him an aura of prestige in the marketing world). Jean good-naturedly objected to Bernays and other "depth research" marketing specialists focusing on individual psychological drives rather than the broader social meaning of food. "Mr. Bernays' Uncle Freud may have all kinds of reasons why one woman settles for oodles of noodles and another spells out her emotions in bland chicken rice," she joked. But when it came to baking a cake or a loaf of bread, "no woman bakes for herself alone." Rather, she bakes out of the "depth" of her love for a husband or child.[3]

Jean was far from dismissing Bernays and his brand of depth research wholesale. Indeed, in her own Food Forum talk, Jean cited recent depth findings that the American housewife was drawn toward foods that promised either to (a) distract her from boredom or (b) salve her vaguely felt need for religion—two psychological insights (apparently interchangeable) a food marketer could use to advantage.[4] Whatever differences Jean and Bernays might have had, they *did* agree that the social and emotional contexts of food could be manipulated—in United Fruit's case, to encourage more banana consumption.

But Bernays's role at the corporation went well beyond helping advertising colleagues like Jean figure out how to monetize the elasticity of the American stomach; it even went beyond promoting the company's "civilizing" mission abroad and the benefits of banana eating at home—the usual wheelhouse of the PR man. The United Fruit Company's banana business depended on the fact that they were semifeudal landowners in Central America and the Caribbean, where they harvested their tropical fruits. In Guatemala, United Fruit (dubbed by locals "El Pulpo," "The Octopus") was more than simply a foreign investor; it formed, for all intents and purposes, a shadow government and had depended since its founding on cozy relations with the country's military dictators. When Jacobo Arbenz came to power in 1951, only the second of Guatemala's democratically elected presidents, he passed a sweeping Agrarian Reform Law with United Fruit's vast landholdings as its target. Overnight, the company's half-century-old colonial ecosystem was threatened.

Having long persuaded the American public of United Fruit's status as a model global citizen and civilizing force, Bernays now got to work persuading them—along with key appointees in the State Department and CIA—of the necessity of a US political and military intervention in Guatemala to remove Arbenz from power. And while Bernays operated behind the scenes in this for United Fruit, Jean acted as the conglomerate's media-friendly front person. She helped craft the face of the company through the figure of Chiquita Banana: that paragon of silly, sexy Latin insouciance who reminded Americans, with a flirtatious toss of her turbaned head, to eat their fruits and vegetables. But the two campaigns—one covert and politico-military, the other broadcast on page and screen as entertainment—were in fact halves of a single strategy to enforce American political and economic interests abroad.

The origins of the United Fruit Company can be traced to the day in 1870 when Lorenzo Dow Baker, a schooner captain who ran cargo between the Caribbean and Boston, docked in Jamaica on one of his regular runs. A street market vendor offered him 160 bunches of still-green bananas for twenty-five cents apiece; as he had extra room in his hold, Baker took a chance on the exotic fruit. Landing in New York, he was able to unload his stock for three dollars a bunch—a tidy profit that kept him coming back for more. Encouraged by the growing popularity of the fruit, Baker went all-in for bananas, partnering with a Boston shipping agent, Andrew Preston, to form the Boston Fruit Company in 1885. Soon, its operations spread to Cuba and Santo Domingo, but it still couldn't keep up with demand. Worse, piecemeal production by local farmers was inefficient and untrustworthy.

The solution was vertical integration. Like many corporations during this period, the Boston Fruit Company saw the advantages of taking control of all phases of production, from raw materials to distribution.[5] This meant the company needed to acquire its own plantations and its own transportation network to ferry the cargo from the inland jungle to the coast for export. In 1899, Baker and Preston partnered with Minor Keith, who had spent his career building and maintaining railroads in Costa Rica, Guatemala, and neighboring countries, to create the United Fruit Company.[6]

By the 1930s, United Fruit was not only the largest employer in Guatemala, but the largest landholder and, as sole owner of the Atlantic port city of Puerto Barrio as well as the railroads leading to it, effectively controlled the nation's international commerce. And it was wildly profitable. By brokering deals with Guatemala's strongmen dictators, the company operated virtually tax-free in the country, ensuring ample dividends to its American shareholders. Critically, it knew it could rely on the State Department in case of local interference. In 1904, Teddy Roosevelt proclaimed a corollary to the Monroe Doctrine, stating America's right to intervene in the commercial and economic affairs of its Latin American neighbors. "Any country whose people conduct themselves well can count upon our hearty friendship," he opened. On the other hand, "chronic wrongdoing, or an impotence which results in a general loosening of the ties of civilized society may . . . require intervention by some civilized nation"—in other words, the United States.

United Fruit, too, touted itself as a "civilizing" force, bringing a backward jungle country into the twentieth century through capital investment in infrastructure: the roads, rail, and port cities. Workers on its plantations, the company liked to boast, enjoyed conditions better than those of most farm laborers in Guatemala, with decent housing, schools, and medical clinics provided by the company. In 1914, Frederick Upham Adams, kicking off a book series titled "The Romance of Business," composed a paean to the corporation as embodying "that instinctive spirit which ever has urged the American to face and conquer the frontier."[7]

America's aggressive interventionist policy earned it a dim reputation in Latin America. Franklin D. Roosevelt, anxious to shore up open markets in the midst of the Depression and secure the Americas against fascism, softened his predecessor's Big Stick into what came to be called the Good Neighbor policy. In 1933, he committed the United States to a policy of increased commercial and economic ties and vowed to respect the political sovereignty of South American nation states. Roosevelt became a cult hero in Central America, his "four freedoms" speech a guiding light in countries racked by political instability and autocratic regimes.

Its own civilizing protestations to the contrary, by the 1930s the United Fruit Company was widely seen as a cutthroat corporate megalith, even in America, and its zealous president —the swashbuckling Sam "The Banana Man" Zemurray—as a "seamy operator," in the words of one commentator.[8] So, in 1940, Zemurray hired Edward Bernays to help humanize the company. It was time to align the company's public image more closely with the new neighborly rhetoric of hemispheric solidarity—to a degree.

Bernays had launched his career as a theater press agent, drumming up American audiences for such foreign imports as the Ballets Russes and Italian tenor sensation Enrico Caruso, before moving on to plug causes as varied as Lucky Strike cigarettes, Ivory Soap, and Calvin Coolidge.[9] Much like Bruce Barton, Bernays grasped early on the key role that mass media would play in politics. "The conscious and intelligent manipulation of the organized habits and opinions of the masses is an important element in democratic society," Bernays wrote in his 1928 pamphlet *Propaganda*. "Those who manipulate this unseen mechanism of society constitute an invisible government which is the true ruling power of our country." In all his dealings, he sought to educate, simplify, and amplify a message with his desired audience. Propaganda, in his view, was simply a targeted form of information; it did not imply deceit or manipulation.[10]

For United Fruit, Bernays coined a condensed way of referring to a hazily defined region—"Middle America"—and founded a Middle American Information Bureau to churn out articles devoted to it. He then pipelined that information to Latin American and American journalists and businessmen in the form of a weekly "Latin American Report," among other vehicles.[11] These efforts dovetailed with an intensive cultural outreach program by the US State Department. In 1940 Franklin D. Roosevelt created the Office of the Coordinator of Inter-American Affairs (OCIAA), headed by Nelson Rockefeller, and charged with promoting "cultural diplomacy" between the hemispheres so as to strengthen a neighborly spirit of Pan-American solidarity. The OCIAA's Motion Picture division partnered with Hollywood studios to feature Latin American stars and content, introducing Latin culture to a larger American public.

Carmen Miranda, aka "The Brazilian Bombshell," was inarguably Hollywood's most successful south-of-the-border import. Miranda was a well-known radio and film star in her native Brazil in the 1930s, popularizing the *samba*. While she was white and of Portuguese descent, Miranda's signature look—flowing, brightly colored skirts and a turban—was intended to imitate a poor African market girl from Bahia, a figure often associated with carnival. It was in this guise—all shaking hips, gaudy costume bangles, and a turban piled high with fruit and flowers—that she made her American debut. Her first vehicle, Twentieth Century Fox's *Down Argentine Way* in 1940, was a box office hit, and was followed quickly by *That Night in Rio* and *Week-End in Havana* in 1941. In these films (and in the 1943 apotheosis of the wartime camp musical genre, *The Gang's All Here*), Miranda was regularly cast as a nightclub singer whose sexually suggestive stage act was tempered by her "backstage" persona as a feisty but ultimately lovable girl: prone to fits of jealousy and temper, but genial, loyal, and gentle as a child once appeased.[12]

Her role in *That Night in Rio* is emblematic of her status as a Good Neighbor ambassador. The opening scene features her, dazzling in a silver skirt and headdress, in a Rio nightclub belting out "Chica Chica Boom Chic" in Portuguese. From stage right a convertible rolls up; a tall, mustached man in a white naval uniform (Don Ameche as Larry Martin, her boyfriend) salutes the crowd and dispenses a formal Yankee greeting: "My friends, I send felicitations/ To our South American relations/May we never leave behind us/ All the common ties that bind us." He then launches into an English translation of Miranda's song, whose exotic, primitive "chica boom" charm is not lost even on the civilized northerner: "Come on and sing the Chica Chica Boom Chic/That crazy thing, the Chica Chica Boom Chic/It came down the Amazon from the jungles/Where the natives greet everyone they meet/Beating on a tom-tom/. . . It don't make sense, the Chica Chica Boom Chic/But it's immense, the Chica Chica Boom Chic."

Backstage, Carmen accuses Larry of having flirted with another woman; she chatters wildly at him in mile-a-minute Portuguese before lobbing a gold-spangled shoe at his head. Larry tries to calm her down. "Now listen, I've been trying to teach you English for six months. You can't learn it unless you speak it, and you can't speak it when you get excited." At just that moment a package arrives for Larry; Miranda, convinced it is a gift from another woman, rips it out of his hands and scratches him in the process. "Now look what you've done, you little jaguar, you've ripped me to shreds!" "Quick, get me some iodine before the fever sets in," he yells to his man servant. The package turns out to be a shiny new bauble for Carmen herself. She is overcome with happiness and begs Larry's forgiveness. "Oh Larry, why you don't tell me?" she asks him, batting her eyelashes contritely. "Oh, my terrible temper. I should not have lose him!" To which he quips, good-naturedly, "Oh, you haven't lost him, baby, he's still there. All he wants is a little break!"

Carmen Miranda gave North Americans permission to indulge in a cleaned-up, whitened fantasy of sultry African "jungle" rhythms. Her performances were brimming with "color" and sexuality, but her otherness was ultimately rendered harmless by the comedic force of her childlike, lisping persona. She was less the equal of her Yankee partner than his endearing, uncivilized ward—not unlike the relationship between the United States and Central America itself, as United Fruit saw it.

Throughout the '20s and '30s, United Fruit had had great success marketing the banana as "the healthy fruit," touting its nutritional value, naturally germ-free packaging (its peel), and ease of digestion, making it the perfect food for babies and the elderly.[13] But by 1944, as the Allies looked toward victory, the company started casting about for a catchy way to ramp up banana consumption after war's end. It took its problem to BBDO. And from there hatched the idea of Chiquita Banana, a samba-dancing carnival figure who hawked bananas.

The jingle and the voice came first. In a 1950 interview, United Fruit advertising head R. G. "Pat" Partridge recalled the day in 1944 when "two slightly groggy young men emerged from the [BBDO] music room with Chiquita Banana." "Garth Montgomery, lyricist, handed the script to a vocal office girl, swept a handful of paper clips into a Dixie cup to simulate a maraca, and composer Len MacKenzie whammed out the catchy score."[14] The song was an immediate hit, far beyond its use in advertisements, playing on more than 300 radio stations nationwide, recorded by nine different studios, and published in sheet music form in the *American Weekly*.

Given the "valuable property" that the Chiquita character proved to be, Partridge explained, branching out into film and television had to be done carefully: "What if the transition from vocal to vocal-visual was a let-down to viewers who might have their own mental picture of Chiquita? We decided an actual person wouldn't do; it would have to be a drawing."[15] Though all of the 155 cartoon mock-ups presented for consideration were "gay and ingratiating," Partridge admitted, "somehow they all looked like a Latin lovely you'd seen somewhere before." A banana-human hybrid was hit on as the best way to visually embody Chiquita's south-of-the-border charm.

For all of Partridge's claims that the cartoon character had to break free of generic "Latin lovely" stereotypes, the eventual Chiquita Banana was quite simply Carmen Miranda in fruit form: from the cornucopia straw hat, to the belly-baring red skirt, to the droopy bedroom eyes fringed with black lashes. In the series of eighty-second spots set to debut in film houses and then on television, Chiquita sashayed suggestively across the screen, hands on hips or twirling her wrists in stylized samba style, and ended each segment with Miranda's trademark wink at the camera.

In the original Chiquita segment, the opening image shows a white steamship—a nod to United Fruit's notorious Great White Fleet—with the smoke from its stack spelling out "Chiquita Banana" against a blue sky. The next shot cuts to Chiquita disembarking, met by smiling tuxedo-and-sash-clad ambassadors and flashbulb-popping paparazzi. The message of Pan-American goodwill and

FIGURE 15. Jean's work for United Fruit involved designing Chiquita Banana "service" advertisements teaching American homemakers how to use bananas for creative cookery.

cultural exchange mimics the Good Neighbor solidarity showcased in Miranda's films. In collaboration with apple producers, BBDO manufactured a riff on the original jingle announcing Mr. Apple as Chiquita's paramour: "I'm Chiquita Banana, and I've got a beau/A chap from North America you ought to know/Now his name is

Mr. Apple and he has such taste/He's a favorite on whatever table that he's placed." The cross-cultural romance between a firecracker Latina and a staid Yankee admirer would have been immediately familiar to audiences as a classic Carmen Miranda plot.

So iconic was the figure that in 1952, Butterick published a sewing pattern for a Chiquita Banana Halloween costume in girls and misses' sizes. The costume was toned down, of course, to suit the more puritanical northern soul—no bared midriff, but a long skirt and sash, scoop-necked blouse with short puffed sleeves, and a wide-brimmed hat, stamped with a United Fruit Chiquita Banana seal. The catalog urged women to create a costume that "will have you dancing the mambo."[16]

Jean worked closely with United Fruit's Pat Partridge, acting in some cases as a mediator between him and BBDO. "Mr. Partridge is on a strange warpath," Jean warned colleague Charlie Brower in a March 4, 1954, memo. "He seems to think that because of things like Chiquita Banana and his new 'Doctor' ads and his all round loyalty to BBDO he has helped to build us into a very good company—and no one has ever thanked him." Jean suggested that to smooth his ruffled feathers, Brower and President Ben Duffy "come down someday and have a banana lunch and hear the gospel."[17]

Partridge also gave Jean her marching orders for what she should talk about at the annual Food Forum conferences. Jean opened her 1953 speech by poking gentle fun at Partridge's corporate–Ivy League stiffness, playing plebe to his patrician. Pat had given her a title for her talk, she recounted drolly, a "most impressive Hotchkiss cum Harvard cum Fruit Boat title," one that "almost breaks down into rhythmic blank verse": "What meals/or courses thereof/out of the 21/meals of the week/in any particular family/is it open/to the food manufacturer/or food writer/to influence?" Jean then looked up brightly and rephrased the question: "'Oh, yes, Pat, I see exactly what you mean,'" "You mean what do they eat WHEN—and when do they eat WHAT?"[18]

The banana-driven concoctions that came out of BBDO's kitchen under Jean's leadership pushed the boundaries of the palatable even by the standards of the 1950s. In an attempt to nudge bananas out of the dessert ghetto, one recipe suggested bananas dipped in egg, rolled in cornflake crumbs, and deep fried as a side for roast meat; another, bananas smeared in mustard, rolled in ham slices and baked, then topped with a cheese sauce. "Chiquita Banana Says: You Can Do a Lot with Baked Bananas!" runs one magazine ad. While the sultry Chiquita dominates the top of the page, the margins feature a toned-down Chiquita *sans* fruit turban and in an apron, offering helpful serving tips to homemakers. "Serve as a vegetable: Baked Bananas"; "Pack a Punch in your Lunch: Banana Peanut-Butter Sandwiches"; "For 4 o'clock Fatigue: Bananas Flecked with Brown."

What the Carmen Miranda/Chiquita Banana archetype didn't show, however, was the brutal realpolitik that lay beneath the surface of the Good Neighbor rhetoric. In 1944, the same year that BBDO and United Fruit emerged victorious with the Chiquita jingle, another kind of victory was being won in Guatemala: a political revolution that would test America's Good Neighbor commitment, on paper, to encouraging democracy and the sovereignty of the nations in its "backyard."

The Guatemalan revolution in 1944 ironically was inspired partially by Roosevelt's Good Neighbor policy and America's attempts to clean up its negative image as a colonial presence in Central America. In particular, Guatemala's rising middle class of shopkeepers and school teachers chafed against the nation's feudal strictures. They had been heartened by the "Four Freedoms" speech and, in the spring of 1944, took to the streets, demanding an end to military dictator General Jorge Ubico's fourteen-year reign and supporting free and fair elections. The protests ultimately toppled the general and brought an exiled schoolteacher, José Arévalo, to power in 1945, with 85 percent of the popular vote—the nation's first democratically elected president since independence in 1822.[19]

President Arévalo piqued the ire of United Fruit, and its friends and lobbyists in Congress, almost from the get-go. His 1947 Labor Code guaranteed the right of workers to unionize, bargain collectively, and strike; it also established minimum wages and regulated child labor. In 1949 and 1950, senators of both parties in Congress assailed the Guatemalan government for its failure to protect the interests of United Fruit and its American investors, alleging "Communist" infiltration of the Arévalo administration.[20] Worse was yet to come: in March 1951, Jacopo Arbenz succeeded Arévalo, swept into office on a platform promising agricultural reform in a country where 70 percent of the land belonged to a mere 2 percent of the population.[21] Ninety percent of the country's workers were rural farming peasants, and a program of land redistribution, turning subsistence tenant-farmers into landowners, was widely seen as the only long-term solution to Guatemala's economic and social stagnation. United Fruit, the country's largest single landholder, was an obvious target of the policy.

United Fruit had reason to be worried. Under the favorable monopolistic conditions conceded by General Ubico, between 1942 and 1952 the company had increased its assets by 133.8 percent and paid stockholders nearly sixty-two cents for every dollar invested. "It was," recalled Edward Bernays, "a highly profitable venture," largely because "the company was conducted like a private government."[22] Bernays had been among the first in the United Fruit fold to sound the alarm when Arbenz ran for the presidency in 1950. He predicted that Communist-inspired movements were going to spread across the region and that the company had better inform the American public of the looming threat to compel the US government to "take steps to improve the situation."[23] As in all his public relations work, he approached the business of propagandizing scientifically. "The whole matter of counter-Communist propaganda is not a matter of improvising," he wrote to United Fruit's publicity chief. What was needed was "the same type of scientific approach that is applied, let us say, to a problem of fighting a certain plant disease."[24]

The first volley in Bernays's propaganda war came in 1950 when he arranged with the *New York Herald Tribune* and with his close friend, Arthur Hays Sulzberger of the *New York Times*, to dispatch journalists to Guatemala, where they met with United Fruit officials to discuss the political situation. "Communism in the Caribbean" was the title of the five-part series eventually splashed across the front pages of the *Tribune*. Sulzberger didn't have to rely solely on Bernays for his Guatemalan scoop; the newspaper kingpin's college roommate, Richard Patterson, was US ambassador there, and Patterson gave him an earful of anticommunist conspiracy theory when Sulzberger visited him in 1950. When Patterson resigned his post later that year, he dispatched a private letter to United Fruit head Sam Zemurray advising him to "launch an all out barrage [*sic*] in the U.S. Senate on the bad treatment of American capital in Guatemala."[25]

In 1951, at Bernays's request, Sulzberger commissioned another round of *Times* articles on the progress of the "Reds" in Arbenz's government; they piqued the interest of other major news outlets, including *Time, Newsweek, U.S. News & World Report*, and *Atlantic Monthly*, which also dutifully dispatched reporters to the region. Bernays was more than happy to show them around. Between 1952 and 1954, Bernays organized five press junkets—two-week "fact finding" trips, as he called them—on which reporters were, according to one account, "shepherded on elaborately choreographed tours of Fruit Company facilities, and talked to local politicians who were sympathetic to the company's plight."[26]

The ax finally fell in March 1953, when the Arbenz government reclaimed 200,000 acres of United Fruit's uncultivated land, offering $627,572 in bonds in return—the price per acre the company had declared that year for tax purposes. The company was outraged. On April 20, 1954, the US State Department—Secretary of State John Foster Dulles himself had close ties with the company—lodged a formal complaint with the Arbenz government on behalf of United Fruit, demanding almost twenty-five times the offered price. Guatemalan officials entered into talks with the United States.[27] But by then, the company and its allies in the State Department were already taking matters into their own hands.

"I have the feeling that Guatemala might respond to pitiless publicity in this country," Bernays had conjectured in 1950 as he drew up his campaign.[28] In the end, Guatemala didn't respond to "pitiless publicity"—Arbenz went boldly ahead with his land expropriations anyway. But Bernays had achieved his goal just the same. By 1954, both the mainstream mass media and the back channels of government had been saturated with articles and hack-job secret "reports" drawn up by United Fruit's hired public relations firms, all warning of a Communist plot afoot in Guatemala. When the CIA finally made its move to remove Arbenz, public opinion was already on its side.

Official approval for a covert CIA-backed coup in Guatemala— code name Operation Success—was granted by Eisenhower in August 1953.[29] A plan to assassinate Arbenz was abandoned for fear of making him a martyr. Instead, beginning in January 1954, director of field operations Colonel Albert Haney decided to pursue the very Bernaysian course of launching a campaign of psychological warfare against Arbenz. It had the advantage of being cheaper and less diplomatically unpleasant than outright military intervention. Haney would first wage a radio and leaflet propaganda campaign designed to terrorize and confuse the Guatemalan populace. The destabilizing information blitz would crescendo in a mock "invasion" by Guatemalan patriots come to liberate the country from its Communist fetters (in reality, 300-some disgruntled hired Guatemalan exiles and mercenaries amassed on the Honduran border and awaited the CIA's orders). A handful of unmarked planes would strafe public buildings in the capitol to add a dash of unpredictable firepower to the mix. The CIA would jam Guatemala's radio stations and transmit its own signal, "The Voice of Liberation," announcing the imminent invasion and the fall of Arbenz. Using the combined forces of radio, airpower, and a patched-together "insurrectional army," US operatives would mount a convincing fiction: a coup manufactured to look like an inside job.[30]

But before the coup could be launched, the CIA needed one last element: the character of "Liberator" himself, a Guatemalan who could lead the charge to take back the country from the Reds. In a private meeting with CIA director Allen Dulles, a representative from United Fruit was assured that whoever replaced Arbenz would be prohibited from going ahead with land seizures; Dulles even encouraged the company to take part in the search for a Liberator. They finally landed on Colonel Carlos Enrique Castillo Armas, an anti-Arbenz military man living in exile after his own actual attempted coup in 1950. He was a man with no strong ideological bent beyond nationalism and anticommunism, a perfect cipher for US interests.

As an added bonus, as Operation Success propaganda chief Howard Hunt later commented, he "had that good Indian look about him.
He looked like an Indian, which was great for the people."[31]

The sham coup was, against all odds, successful. The combined
assaults sowed panic and disorder across the country. Arbenz held
out for ten days; on June 27, 1954, he went on the radio for one last
time to concede defeat. The victory of Castillo Armas was touted in
the US press as a major win for democracy and freedom. Eisenhower,
in welcoming Castillo Armas's new ambassador to the United States,
waxed eloquent: "The people of Guatemala, in a magnificent effort,
have liberated themselves from the shackles of international Communist direction, and reclaimed their right of self-determination,"
he beamed.[32]

"Bananas go brightly for breakfast," Jean observed in her 1956 United
Fruit Food Forum talk, but they are even better in lunchtime muf-
fins and salads. So why not try bananas butter-browned as a side
vegetable or blended in a curry for supper? Widening the scope of
acceptable banana-eating practices—pushing the fruit into heretofore uncharted times and places and condiment schemes—boosted
United Fruit's bottom line *and* gave American housewives something that, according to Jean's market research, they desperately
needed: fun, diversion, a way to conquer domestic tedium through
creative cookery. From her perspective, it was a win-win.

The win was not as clear from the Guatemalan side. Once in power,
Colonel Castillo Armas showed himself less malleable to US direction
than promised. Instead of steering a center-right course, he resur-
rected some of Ubico's worst specters, tapping the deposed general's
hated secret police chief to head his security forces. He disenfran-
chised the illiterate (two-thirds of the population); canceled agrarian reform; and outlawed political parties, labor unions, and peasant
organizations. Castillo Armas's assassination in 1957 led to a decade
of political turmoil and escalating violence in Guatemala that, by the
decade's close, had resulted in more than 10,000 civilian deaths.[33]

A folder in Jean's papers labeled "Article Ideas" includes a series of
undated mimeographed sheets with typewritten notes for projected

articles. They all circle loosely around the idea of "the American abroad" in the context of the Cold War, and how private citizens can make friends for their country and the American Way of Life through personal gestures of goodwill and peace. "Would it be possible," muses one note, "to develop a 'National Books for Asia Committee' like 'Shoes for Korea,' gifts from the American people? Write to Bernays about this."[34]

"Shoes for Korea" was a humanitarian program developed under the Eisenhower administration during the Korean War, a way of signaling goodwill toward the innocent civilians caught in the cross-hairs of international politics. And, indeed, Jean's instincts were right: Bernays was precisely the person to contact about such a project. He suggested similar overtures in the messy aftermath of the Guatemalan coup, proposing United Fruit establish a tourist information bureau for the region, encourage a pen pal exchange between US and Guatemalan students, or sponsor postgraduate programs for Guatemalan medical students in the United States. Such outreach efforts, Bernays offered, would help establish "goodwill with the people of Guatemala at this time with due reference to the United Fruit Company getting a share of the credit."[35]

Jean's default setting, when face-to-face with the messy workings of politics and economics, was always to universalize the personal. Humans are all the same on the inside, she reasoned—susceptible to the timeless human heart-tug of joy and pain. Any reckoning with real-world unpleasantness was always kept at bay by brandishing this fetish of the private individual who, on his own, generally wished his neighbor well. "The image of America projected around the world cannot be projected by the government," another snippet in Jean's "Article Ideas" series warns. "It must be projected by you. Stimulate private activity of individuals." In another note she observes, as though rehearsing an argument for the benign nature of national propaganda, that "no information program can ever be better than the actions of the people that information program represents."[36] "Good folk" could not help but do good.

Sentimentality, as Hannah Arendt knew, is not the opposite of political violence; on the contrary, it is its most reliable and amiable facilitator. That is because sentiment (and its cognates: folksiness, niceness, "personality," "goodwill") is the natural enemy of thought. It sides with force against criticism; feeling against facts. It is willing to run roughshod over evidence and, indeed, evolved in the nineteenth century as a popular mode of public discourse specifically for this purpose. Jean's sentimental cult of domesticity, by which feminine "outreach" provided weak resistance to the rough masculine violence of political and economic reality, was not only effective in quieting conflict at home. It worked wonders in the sphere of geopolitics as well.

Americans thought Chiquita Banana was funny; more, they thought she was sexy. She was Mr. Apple's exotic girlfriend who spoke adorable pidgin English. She taught housewives how to serve up tasty vitamins to their growing children and how to keep bored husbands entertained with increasingly baroque banana casseroles. Surely the men running the company behind Chiquita must be good sorts, too.

12

A Second Look at the Second Sex

The year Jean retired from BBDO, 1963, also saw the publication of Betty Friedan's *The Feminine Mystique*, a book popularly credited with sparking "second-wave" feminism and the women's liberation movement. "The problem lay buried, unspoken, for many years," Friedan opens her manifesto. "Each suburban wife struggled with it alone. As she made the beds, shopped for groceries, matched slip-cover material, ate peanut butter sandwiches with her children, . . . she was afraid to ask even of herself the silent question—'Is this all?'" For those who like tidy narratives, the symbolism aligns. Jean earned her bread by selling American women domestic bliss and, failing that, salving the housewife's misery through the compensatory pleasures of consumption. Friedan articulated the "problem that has no name," giving women permission to voice the unhappiness they had for so long been told to keep quiet.[1] That Jean should disappear into the proverbial sunset just as a new feminist day was dawning appears poetic justice.

Yet history isn't always so neat. At the very same time as East Coast women's lib was so spectacularly catching fire, a conservative counterfeminist movement in California and the Sunbelt was quietly gathering steam as well. When cowboy boot-wearing, red-baiting, libertarian Arizona senator Barry Goldwater stole the 1964 Republican presidential nomination away from the usual cast of moderate party insiders, it was women who had done the grass-roots work to make it possible. Goldwater's nomination marked a watershed moment for the Republican Party, presaging a shift away from its traditional anchor in genteel East Coast wealth and laissez-faire economics and toward its more populist, small-government, Bible-beating fringe.[2]

Jean's free enterprise boosterism and appeals to sentimental domestic rhetoric would appear, at first glance, to make her a natural ally of the conservative Sunbelt housewives and their "folksy, nationalist, maternal style," as Michelle Nickerson has characterized this emerging group of activists.[3] Yet this was not the case. By the mid-1960s, Phyllis Schlafly had emerged as de facto head of the socially conservative wing of Republican Party women; in 1972, she called out the newly passed Equal Rights Amendment as an elitist plot to "destroy morality and the family."[4] During the same period, Jean accepted a position as vice president of the National Council of Women (NCW), a progressive national organization promoting women's rights; by 1976, she was writing pro-ERA copy against Schlafly's efforts to derail the amendment's final ratification. "Who Says We Live in the Land of the Free? Not until You Vote for the ERA!" ran one slogan Jean generated for a poster or TV spot. "If you care about your family," urges another tagline, "strengthen it with the ERA."[5] Where Schlafly led a revolt against the inclusion of a party plank opposing racial discrimination in voting and housing at the 1960 Republican National Convention, Jean wrote a 1965 article for the NCW's monthly bulletin educating her readers on the realities of racial discrimination in housing, and how they could mobilize to prevent it in their communities.

How are we to understand Jean's apparent renunciation of her earlier conservative, privatized, free-market politics and sentimental focus on the nuclear family? The answer lies in what Nancy Cott has called the "Janus-faced" legacy of American women's political activism since the nineteenth century. On the one hand, nineteenth-century woman-centered reform movements pioneered a pro-statist political style that allowed women to enter the public sphere as defenders of maternal "family values." Woman's status as caretaker of all God's children gave her permission to expand her maternal reach beyond the four walls of her home and into her larger community, in partnership with the state.[6] At the same time, a parallel track of staunchly antistatist women activists decried a meddling federal government as the greatest threat to the sacred family circle, where such traditionally American "family values" as independence, local governance, and religious instruction were nurtured.[7]

Both groups of women activists claimed to be fulfilling their gendered role as guardians of virtue, upholding their maternal duty to protect and care for the American family. But the precise nature of these maternalist values—and how to achieve them politically— would remain a source of heated debate throughout the twentieth century. Indeed, with 52 percent of white women voting for Donald Trump in 2016—a candidate enthusiastically endorsed by a ninety-two-year-old Schlafly, who hailed him as America's "last hope"— this bitter political divide continues to define contemporary American politics today.

Women activists were among the first in the country to call attention to the ills of urban industrialized society as structural rather than individual in nature, a product of bad institutions rather than bad souls. Recounting her experiences at Hull House in 1890s Chicago, Jane Addams lamented the "piteous dependence of the poor upon the good will" of wealthy private citizens in the days before municipal and state governments stepped up to alleviate poverty in the cities. She recalled the case of one immigrant cleaning woman whose daughters, having succumbed to the "vices" of Chicago, became unwed mothers struggling to secure financial support from absentee fathers. "She did not need charity, for she had an immense capacity for hard work," Addams clarified. What she needed, instead, was "the aid of the State attorney's office, enforcing the laws designed for the protection of such girls as her daughters."[8] Faith in private charity and the invisible hand of the market, Addams and other early social reformers intimated, was not a viable solution to modernity's problems. Women would prove a major mobilizing force behind Progressive Era efforts to expand state-mandated protections for American families, inaugurating the modern "welfare state."[9]

This model of a maternalist state was resisted, almost from the get-go, not only by men who feared a feminization of politics but by women who believed their political duty was to keep decision-making private, local, and family-based. If "classical" liberals and laissez-faire conservatives in the early decades of the twentieth century lobbied for small government, they did so largely from an economic standpoint: the federal government should refrain from interfering with personal property and the free-market mechanism. It was women who expanded the conservative platform to include vigorous opposition to a federal welfare state, which they regarded as an elitist, "globalist" plot to usurp private parental control over the nuclear family. The Bolshevik revolution and Red Scare panic it touched off on the home front worked to strengthen what Michelle M. Nickerson has termed American "housewife populism," with its signature paranoid-style blend of "patriotic" antiradicalism and antistatism.[10] One of this group's first political victories came in 1924, when massive grassroots organizing by women helped defeat passage of a child labor amendment to the Constitution. The amendment, which would have granted Congress power to "limit, regulate, and prohibit the labor of persons under eighteen years of age," was condemned by conservative women's groups as a ploy to "substitute national control . . . for local and parental control, [and] to bring about the nationalization of children."[11]

Women proved their political usefulness to the Republican Party once again during the 1950s, when white suburban housewives and mothers mobilized to get Eisenhower elected in 1952. Postwar Republican women cheerfully took up their gendered position as secretaries and "housekeepers" for male Republican Party leaders by organizing grassroots fundraisers and letter-writing campaigns; running voter drives; manning polling stations; and, in one popular program with the cutesy title "Operation Coffee Cup," hosting meet-and-greets in the comfort of their own homes where Republican candidates could chat with local voters. Moreover, under the leadership of Elizabeth Farrington as head of the National Federation of Republican Women between 1948 and 1952, it was women who began nudging the party as a whole to the right on social issues, urging their more moderate Republican brothers to adopt the traditionally feminine (and evangelical) political style of the "moral crusader" to attract new membership.[12]

So when, in his 1960 manifesto *The Conscience of a Conservative*, Barry Goldwater decried the Welfare State as a dangerous "instrument of collectivization" poised to rule with an iron fist as tight as any "oriental despot," conservative women had already been primed to heed the call.[13] Against the backdrop of a nascent feminist movement, Republican men and women alike sought a way to attract women to their ranks. "The conservative feels that the family is the natural source and core of any good society," pronounced political scientist Russell Kirk in his 1957 book *The Intelligent Woman's Guide to Conservatism,* and knows that "when the family decays, a dreary collectivism is sure to supplant it." It is by virtue of their instinctive family-centeredness, Kirk asserts, that women can be called the truly "conservative sex."[14] And indeed, it was troops of cowboy-hatted and white-gloved "Goldwater Gals" that helped propel the outsider candidate to victory at the 1964 Republican National Convention.

It was into this charged political atmosphere that Jean stepped when she took her leave of Madison Avenue in 1963. Upon retiring she immediately took on an enormous slate of volunteer work, producing public relations copy and other literature for organizations as diverse as the Girl Scouts, the National Safety Council, the Fresh Air Fund, and her local Teaneck Community Chest. Some of Jean's contributions to charity and other "uplift" organizations remained therapeutic and local in scope, still animated by a faith in the power of individuals to improve their characters and thus their material and spiritual fortunes. But other volunteer engagements, in particular her work for the NCW and Church Women United, committed her to a brand of large-scale domestic "community housekeeping" in the style of Jane Addams and the early women's reform movements.

The NCW was founded in 1888 by suffragists Susan B. Anthony and Frances Willard to mark the fortieth anniversary of the Seneca Falls Women's Rights Convention, with the goal of establishing an umbrella organization to bring together the country's multitude of women's clubs. The NCW's founding statement declared, "We the women of the United States, sincerely believing that . . . an organized movement of women will best conserve the highest good of the family and the State, do hereby band ourselves together in a confederation of workers committed to the overthrow of all forms of ignorance and injustice, and to the application of the Golden Rule to society, custom, and law."[15] When the Fourteenth Amendment failed to bring equality under the law to women as well as freed slaves, the post–Civil War women's movement had doubled down on its effort to make their voices felt in the public sphere through the back channels of voluntary associations. It was at the heart of this same National Council of Women that, eighty years after its founding, Jean first began to question her faith in the power of private market behavior to bring about social change.

American women in the postwar era married younger and had more children more quickly than the preceding generation, a domesticating trend that was paradoxically matched by an upsurge in the number of women combining child rearing with employment: by 1960, more than 40 percent of women with children between the ages of six and eighteen worked for pay. Jean had spent the midpart of her career documenting (and helping her clients to target) this increasingly common "two-job woman." As part of an attempt to understand the momentous demographic shifts that had been taking place over the previous two decades, in 1961 President John F. Kennedy created the Presidential Commission on the Status of Women to study—with the goal of improving—the legal, civic, economic, and social status of American women.

From start to finish, the language framing the commission and its mandate revealed uncertainty about how to classify America's modern woman. Chairwoman Eleanor Roosevelt's inaugural address lauded the commission's mission statement, its commitment to seeing "many of the remaining outmoded barriers to women's aspirations . . . disappear," and closed with the ambiguous hope that in the near future, "all Americans will have a better chance to develop their individual capacities to earn a good livelihood and to strengthen family life." The commission's final report, released on October 11, 1963, reaffirmed the demographic trend by which more and more wives and mothers were entering the workforce and, accordingly, put forth policy recommendations designed to help women better balance their dual roles as homemakers and workers. These included recommendations for equal pay for equal work, publicly funded day care, and paid maternity leave.

Still, the language of the report was marked by ideological tensions: it wavered between calls to recognize women as equal participants in the economic and professional life of the nation, and reassuring the audience that this would not entail the neglect of their traditional homemaking duties. The first section of the report, "Education and Counseling," called for an expansion of job opportunities and job counseling for women. Yet a brief heading at the end of the section labeled "Preparation for Family Life" rushed to reassure readers that, "widening the choices for women beyond their doorstep does not imply neglect of the education for responsibilities in the house." Rather, "at various stages" during their lives, girls of all economic backgrounds should receive instruction in respect to "physical and mental health, child care and development, human relations within the family."[16]

Jean was intrigued by the commission's findings (she would go on to be named editor for New York State's own "Status of Women" report), and borrowed part of its name for a talk she gave to women at Teaneck Presbyterian Church in the spring of 1964: "The Status of Women—and YOU." Jean said that America had "come to a stocktaking time," "pulling out a lot of things we used to take for granted and taking a fresh, hard look at them." She encouraged her listeners to read the commission's report—it was published as a mass market paperback—and other proto-feminist rumblings as well. On her list: Mary Beard's 1946 *Woman as a Force in History* and, surprisingly, "that recent and bothersome and sometimes too true book *The Feminine Mystique* by Betty Friedan."[17]

Overall, Jean's 1964 speech, just a year after her retirement, is an odd document. In it she continues to rely on the facile, universalizing, "consensus-building" jargon that had worked so well for her in her advertising endeavors. She encouraged her audience to recognize that, despite all that had changed for women since their mothers' generation, women of all types and times remained unwaveringly family-centered. After asking her audience to jot down "the thing [they] are most worried about," Jean joked that she didn't need a crystal ball to intuit that, "your biggest single worry, I am very sure, is very, very personal"—"your health, your family's health, your children." Thus had it ever been and would continue to be, Jean assured them. She even milked her audience for something akin to nostalgia for an older social order, evoking the collapse of the extended family network and the working woman's increased burden as a result. "The life of the average woman today is full of problems . . . her mother never knew," Jean lectured. "We have lost that close-knit family under one roof," a time when "one could always borrow an aunt or a grandmother to keep an eye on the baby." The result, Jean lamented, is that as recently as 1958, more than 400,000 children under the age of twelve "were completely unsupervised while their mothers worked full time." (Jean herself, of course, had not had this problem.)

And yet the speech just as quickly pivoted from such universalizing sentiment to a call for political engagement. "You and I can be shocked" by the statistic concerning unsupervised children, Jean temporized, and "I think we should be." But she insisted such shock was pointless unless it prompted public action, to "help the three million women who are sole breadwinners for children under six." Alongside her habitual sentimentalizing rhetoric ("That we keep surprising ourselves, that we keep reaching," Jean the positive thinker concluded, "is the Status of Women I *really* care about"), Jean issued a call to her audience of (largely) conservative churchwomen to "get involved" in militating for such crucial women's issues as greater access to public office, state-funded childcare, and equal pay for equal work.[18]

Three months after Jean delivered this speech, the cause of women's civil rights was given a sudden and wholly unexpected boost with the passage of the Civil Rights Act of 1964. Included in the bill was a last-minute provision, inserted by Republican senator Robert Byrd, adding "sex" to the categories protected against discrimination. Commentators have wrangled ever since over whether the amendment was intended as a joke (either at the expense of African Americans or women) or serious. Either way, women were quick to jump at the opportunity to see it enforced. And, surprisingly, among these women was Jean Wade Rindlaub.

As we have seen, throughout the 1940s and '50s Jean consistently emphasized that professional women should "shut up"; assume disparities in pay or promotions were due to poor performance, not gender bias; and laugh off—or get real about—sexual advances ("Are you *sure* he tried to make a pass at you?"). This stance reached its apogee in her 1955 speech at Westover School, the all-girl boarding school in Connecticut where her daughter, Anne, was a high school student. Entitled "Is There Any Room for *Women* in the Executive Suite?" the talk largely answered in the affirmative—but was threaded with Jean's usual wariness of women who sounded the call for inclusion too shrilly or who sought a career for narrow, selfish reasons. She began by acknowledging that a "visiting anthropologist . . . from Mars" come to assess the ratio of women to men in executive positions on Earth would, indeed, find an imbalance. But the responsibility for this disparity, Jean insisted, fell pretty squarely on women's shoulders. An entire class of women "who *want* to stay in a low-pressure job"—who see a job as no more than a stepping-stone until a marriage proposal or a baby comes along—skew all the statistics, she explained. Were our hypothetical anthropologist to bracket this mass of what she dubbed "mark-time women," he "might find women doing better."[19]

But one decade later, Jean's thinking on women's rights in the workplace had undergone a complete reversal. Her archive contains drafts of an article dated November 1965 lauding the inclusion of women in the new civil rights bill. A slightly amended version of this draft, "You Can Help Change the Climate for Women," was published in the February 1966 issue of Radcliffe College's alumnae bulletin. "The sudden and surprising inclusion of sex in Title 7 of the Civil Rights Act gives organized (and even disorganized) women an opportunity and an obligation to break down walls that have kept women second-class citizens," Jean opened her editorial. The obligation was real and pressing: "men have already appeared before the House Labor Committee suggesting the repeal" of the sex provision, making it imperative that women "act now if they are to preserve the long-overdue legal rights and privileges that are now within their grasp."[20]

"What can one woman do?" Jean queried—before listing ways women could make their voices heard. First up: "Write a letter of protest to every newspaper in your home town and your business town," objecting "strenuously but politely to the illegal method of classification by sex." Newspaper job listings had found a "tidy way to evade the law," continuing to advertise positions by gender with the disclaimer that such presorting offered greater "convenience" to job seekers. "Qualified female job-seekers should apply for positions listed "Help Wanted: Men" anyway, Jean counseled; "if you find any evidence that you are not being considered for the job because of your sex," report it to the Equal Employment Opportunity Commission. Ditto for women who were already employed: they must make an honest assessment of all the ways their professions treat women differently from men—from separate seniority rules, to men-only executive dining rooms, to exclusion of women from management training tracks—and protest. All of these things counted as discrimination, Jean schooled her readers, "cause for complaint and, if necessary, for legal procedure."[21]

By 1965, Jean had pivoted from warning women that workplace troubles were mostly of their own making to educating them on how to recognize discrimination and to call it out—with a lawsuit, if necessary. What had changed? The *Radcliffe Quarterly* article and its drafts give us a clue. After graduating from Westover in 1956, Jean's daughter Anne had matriculated at Radcliffe College. She married midway through college, in 1958, and began a family. Not content to be a stay-at-home mother, however, by 1966 Anne was enrolled as a PhD candidate in Harvard's Department of Linguistics. Jean's archive includes a report Anne compiled in response to a sociological study that attempted to tabulate "what needs doing in a household," as well as "who is presently doing these tasks and in how much time and at what cost to the homemaker." The authors of the study contended that, in a culture where women were increasingly asked to "perform two roles," "society must find ways to reduce the cost to the homemaker and to society." Anne heartily endorsed the report's mission: "As a full-time graduate student with two young children," she opened her remarks, "I couldn't agree more."[22] In contrast to Jean, who had been able to rely on her aunt to take over the major tasks of childcare while she worked, Anne had no such help in managing her double duty.

Jean closed her *Radcliffe Quarterly* article by recounting a recent conversation with "a Radcliffe mother." "'I realized that I had been living with the fact of second-class citizenship all my life,'" the mother admitted. "'I had been rather proud that I was not one of those women who get up on a soapbox and fight for the whole female sex. I had been rather pleased that I could hold my own in man's world.'" And then, all of a sudden, she realized this wasn't good enough for her daughter and that she was "ready to fight for more . . . for her."[23] Earlier drafts of the article, however, record slight variations. In one, the mother remarked of her daughter, "She has a good brain, a sound education, a real contribution to make to her life and her times"— why then, the mother concluded with obvious frustration, should she have to live out her life battling the "insidious, invisible" curse of "faint praise" for all she does? In another, Jean crossed out "I want something more than that for my daughter" and scribbled in "something more than second class performance from my daughter." In these handwritten edits, it becomes clear that the "Radcliffe mother" is none other than Jean herself—and the conversation took place not with a friend, but with her own conscience.

At the same time as her ideas about women's workplace rights were shifting, Jean was also revising her approach to questions of poverty and wealth distribution. In his 1964 State of the Union address, President Lyndon B. Johnson declared "an unconditional war on poverty in America," pledging to raise up "that one-fifth of all American families with incomes too small to even meet their basic needs." Johnson's Food Stamp Act of 1964 was quickly followed by the Social Security Act of 1965, which created Medicare and Medicaid for the benefit of the elderly and the poor. In addition, the Economic Opportunity Act of 1964 created job-training programs and established the Office of Economic Opportunity, to implement the antipoverty programs. When Johnson addressed the First Annual Conference on Women in the War on Poverty in May 1967, he recognized the crucial role women activists had always played in the nation's great reform movements. "Long before there was an official, Federal 'war on poverty,' . . . women's groups were fighting poverty in the neighborhoods and legislative halls," he opened. And continuing on: "Many of the early victories in the struggle against poverty were won because the women cared enough to work, to plan, and to make their influence felt," citing the battle for compulsory education and the battle against child labor as two wars that "women carried on and that women won." Now, he urged them, it was time again for "women's work": "to teach, to heal, to awaken the conscience of this great Nation" by again taking up the pro-statist, maternalist legacy of her reform-minded forebearers.[24]

Jean's work with the National Council of Women brought her directly into contact with Johnson's War on Poverty. At first glance, Jean's prosperity gospel upbringing and free-market faith make her an unlikely candidate to endorse Johnson's program. Yet looking closely at her early religious training, the possibility of such a shift was always present. From earliest childhood Jean had been taught to understand, with Matthew, that the poor we have always with us (Matthew 26:11)—and that this imposed certain duties upon her. From her account books, we know that Jean was committed to tithing, contributing a hefty portion of her monthly salary to her church and an ever-evolving slate of charitable causes. In a speech she once delivered to the women of her local Christ Church congregation, Jean reminisced how as a child each week in Sunday School she had been given a "Golden Text" to learn by heart. "They have stuck with me" she avowed, allowing she was struck by "how many of the Golden Texts have to do with this subject of poverty and responsibility." And she went on to quote them: "Be ye kind to one another, tenderhearted, forgiving one another," ran one; "Feed my lambs," another. And the most sacred of all: "Do unto others as you would that they should do unto you." "With only slight differences of wording," Jean informed her church ladies, "the Golden Rule appears in every single one of the world's great religions."[25] This was one of

Jean's favorite New Testament passages, and one whose universality she was committed to demonstrating. In her "Personal: Inspiration" folder is filed a typewritten sheet labeled "The Golden Rule in Ten of the World's Great Religions," recording variations on the theme as it reappeared across cultures, from Buddhism to Islam to Sikhism.[26]

What changed in retirement, then, were not Jean's core values but her understanding of what it took to put them into practice. Private charity, no matter how well-meaning or extensive, was not enough to change systemic inequalities. A turning point in Jean's evolution on thinking about poverty, "minorities," and economics came at the Second Annual Conference of Women in the War on Poverty in Washington, D.C., in May 1968. This conference coincided with Martin Luther King's Poor People's March. The overlap may have been unintentional, but it did not go unnoticed by the organizers of either event. The recent assassination of King shed an even starker light on the inextricability of systemic racism and poverty in the United States. Thousands of poor people converged on the Southwest Mall and built a makeshift tent encampment, christened Resurrection City, just a block and a half from the Washington-Hilton where the well-heeled Women in the War on Poverty delegates congregated. The contrast was sobering.

At the conference, Reverend Maurice Dawkins hailed the Poor People's March as yet another step in the quest for justice that had begun with the civil rights marches earlier in the decade, when "the visible walls of segregation, like the walls of Jericho, came tumbling down." But "instead of crossing over into the Promised Land," Dawkins cautioned, "we found that we were still in the wilderness. Poverty was revealed as the enemy we had not overcome." Like other speakers, Dawkins drew on the twin history of reform as "women's work" and as God's work to inspire the congregants in the face of modern poverty.[27]

Upon returning home, Jean wrote up minutes from the conference for the NCW bulletin as well as a shorter version as a column addressing "What One Woman Can Do about POVERTY." The missive opened with a reading list: Michael Harrington's classic 1962 study of American poverty, *The Other America*; the recently released

Kerner Report, a government-commissioned study of urban race riots from 1963 to 1967. After listing ways women could get involved in fighting poverty, Jean appended this dictum: "You can resolve not to criticize welfare mothers . . . or the Poor People's March until you have gone to Washington or visited one of the churches on the line of march, and understand something of the simplicity, of the sincerity, of the need that prompts individual marchers."[28]

A speech that Jean delivered to a chapter of Church Women United in Teaneck during this crucial period gives the measure of her new commitment to educating the public on the "problem" of poverty. The challenge in this age of affluence, she suggested to her solidly middle-class audience, was how to share their prosperity with those whom prosperity had bypassed. What causes poverty, she queried? There are a number of "easy answers," she suggested.[29] "It's all Communist," is one: "If there are riots against intolerable, insoluble, complicated problems, it's all communist," she ventriloquized. Or, "people could get work if they wanted it." "That's another easy answer—easier than thinking," she lectured.

She then rolled out statistics that, if anyone took the time to look at them, would dispel such lazy shortcuts. "Easier to look at the rolls of 7 million people on welfare as 7 million people wasting the good taxpayer's money than to break down the list . . . to show how many of those people are small children, how many are mothers who must stay with their children, how many are men and women 65 and older," Jean enlightened them. Of the 7 million, only 58,000 were even eligible to work. "Think about the percentage of 58,000 to 7 million—and you will understand a little better what the welfare rolls are composed of." And here Jean slipped into her jeremiad voice, the one she had used, just a decade earlier, to whip up advertisers' sense of their sacred duty to spur consumption: "Stop to think—judge not that ye be not judged—before you use that easy answer."[30]

In this period Jean wrote a number of texts explaining to a lay audience how welfare works and exposing the falsity of the most common welfare myths. To the well-publicized images of welfare mothers in "Cadillacs and mink coats," Jean responded evenly that such cases of fraud accounted for "one half of one percent of all welfare recipients." To the specter of African American women as welfare-incentivized "brood mares," drummed into the national consciousness in 1965 by Louisiana Senator Russell Long, Jean cited statistics proving that multiple pregnancies were tightly correlated with poverty—not a feint for government handouts. And finally, Jean enlightened her audience on the semantics of "relief" and "subsidies": "Some of the wealthiest industries receive subsidies in the form of tax abatement," she countered. "The oil industry, for example, receives a tax abatement of 27% that runs into the hundreds of millions of dollars a year." And yet the public recoils at the notion of "relief" for the poor.[31]

One cannot get much farther away, ideologically, from Robert Wade's Prosperity Gospel than a little tome Jean recommended at the end of her Church Women United address: Henry Clark's "troubling, exciting, stimulating book," *The Christian Case against Poverty*.[32] Clark outlines the history of thinking about poverty within the Christian tradition and explains how one prevalent contemporary American attitude—that poverty is an individual and private ill, to be dealt with by individuals rather than the public collectively—has its origins in a historical and economic reality that is far in the past. Robert Wade's kind of philosophical disquisition on the Christian case for private prosperity, Clark argues, no longer apply. "This is not the kind of temporary poverty that a little more prosperity in the national economy or a little more diligence on the part of the poor will erase: it is structural and permanent, more likely to increase than decrease in the years ahead." These poor are not temporarily but permanently out, and "only extraordinary measures can reclaim them from the desolate shores of the other America."[33]

In working for economic justice, Jean also came face-to-face with the brutality of American racial apartheid. The NCW worked in partnership with the National Council of Negro Women (NCNW), and Jean composed a column for the NCW newsletter—part of a series she titled "What One Woman Can Do!"—that explicitly addressed how whites could join the fight for civil rights, making their opinion heard in the marketplace, in the workplace, and in their local communities. Write to the heads of companies in which you hold stock for a commitment to increasing the hires of African Americans, Jean urged. Speak to the head of your department at work to "express the hope that your company will open its doors wide to Negro employees." Volunteer to do work for your city's Fair Housing Committee. Stock your local library with a "list of reading material on Civil Rights."[34]

In the same newsletter, Jean also addressed the question of racial minority representation in the mass media—or, rather, its conspicuous lack. This was an issue Jean had tried and failed to tackle once before. In 1960, BBDO piloted a new project encouraging its clients to include "extra dimension" service messages in their advertising— associating their products with anything from "get out the vote" blurbs to plugs for nature conservation. Asked her thoughts on the idea, Jean recounted how she and her team on the Campbell's Soup account had once designed an ad campaign showcasing racial integration. The proposed posters pictured "children of all races, each eating soup," with the caption "All America's Children Love Soup for Lunch." The result? "Killed by the boys downstairs," Jean noted dryly. "I doubt if it ever got to management."[35] Given the firm's renewed interest in "service advertising," however, Jean suggested ways they might try again: "Could we be the first agency to get a client to drop a man or a woman of another race quietly into every group picture?" she queried. "It is one thing to run ads in *Ebony*—it is another and more courageous thing to run ads of beautiful Negro girls and handsome men as a matter of course in *Life* and the *Post*." She goes on to note that BBDO might not be in any position to preach to their clients about the value of diversity, however. "Wouldn't we have to begin this one at home?" she countered. "I for one think one real proof of dedication to awareness would be to make an earnest attempt to get half a dozen bright Howard girls into our secretarial ranks, . . . make an earnest effort to broaden our own racial patterns."[36]

When, eight years later, Jean turned her mind again to the problem of racism in her NCW newsletter, she was sure to include media as among those American institutions that had to be taken to task.

"A child is bound to grow up with a distorted, one-dimensional view of American life if he sees an all-white world depicted in movies, television, magazines, newspapers," Jean warned. "Make yourself felt" by writing to television stations and their sponsors with approval when they include African American characters on their shows.

In a 1968 letter Jean addressed to her senator, Harrison Williams, she thanked him for his recent missive to constituents on the subject of "the Negro and higher Education." Jean agreed with Williams that education was key to black social mobility. But she couldn't help thinking that the call for education was putting the cart before the horse. She recalled attending a national nutrition conference during the Depression where all the experts clamored that the poor had to be educated on the nutritional value of milk, meat, fruits, and vegetables. And yet it wasn't until World War II boosted the economy that those people actually went out and bought, in any significant quantities, the nutrition-rich foods they had been taught to prize. "They didn't need education, it turned out—they needed money," Jean observed. A negative income tax, she went on to suggest, "designed to put money in the pockets of the poor," was the only realistic way to expect increased rates of black attendance in higher education.[37]

Jean had been appalled by the assassination of Martin Luther King Jr., referring to it as "the recent deep sorrow" in a June 17, 1968, letter to a fellow woman activist. In the letter, Jean floated the idea of creating a "simple white booklet" honoring fallen "Civil Rights Martyrs." "Inside," she elaborated, "on the left-hand page would be a picture of one man—name, date of birth, date and place of death; on the right-hand page would be a brief biography." The heart of the book, Jean explained, would be found in a bolded paragraph at the bottom of each page "telling exactly what has been done about his death (Name of killer; tried by an all-white jury; date. No conviction)." "I think this is a deeply needed book," Jean mused. "We know the names. We can say them over like a litany. But then we forget.... It seems to me that the course of history might be altered if we could get wide circulation for a simple booklet making it very clear that the cause of justice, in most cases, has not been served."[38]

In a letter one month later to the same friend, Jean recounted how disturbed she had been at the Women in the War on Poverty meeting upon seeing a delegate from Kentucky muttering, "'I would not have come if I had thought they were going to talk about that Martin Luther King.'" In what appears a prescient glimpse into the "Southern strategy" that Richard Nixon would exploit to such success in the presidential election that fall, Jean mused: "The thing that really worries me . . . is the new 'skillful silence,'" she remarked. "I felt it first in Washington . . . —important people, intelligent people, people at the heads of major groups, arch-conservatives many of them, who have learned not to talk, but to sit quietly and listen, and still go away unconvinced. It is this group—the new underground of the right—that I have a feeling will show up at the polls."[39]

Jean's innocuous profile as a white, middle-class defender of homemakers and domesticity gave her credibility among those "Main Street" housewives who might have been on the fence politically, caught between the two competing political styles available to women during this turbulent period. In much the same way as her intuitive grasp on gender norms during the 1950s allowed her to pivot between male and female points of view in her ad copy, so now Jean's ideological fluidity on questions of social justice and feminism afforded her buy-in with a demographic that more overtly liberal organizers might not have been able to reach. In a 1964 letter addressed to Corienne Robinson Morrow, an early civil rights activist and a key voice in pushing forward legislation for equal housing, Jean proposed that the NAACP or CORE (Congress of Racial Equality) sponsor an informal "Walk a Mile for Freedom" campaign as a less high-stakes way, short of joining a sit-in or Freedom Ride, for concerned citizens to show their support for civil rights. The event could be organized over several weeks in the summer in cities across the country, Jean brainstormed, with a traveling "Freedom Scroll" to be signed by each participant once he or she had completed the mile. "It seems to me that a lot of people who would be distressed by the idea of jamming traffic or chaining themselves to posts would feel impelled to pick up a sign and walk a mile," Jean reasoned. "And that they would feel uncomfortable about the quiet, relentless march of good people going on day after day through the summer."[40] Jean knew from long experience that the civil rights protesters' direct, albeit nonviolent, defiance of the law would scare off women trained to perform a rigorously "quiet," private, and unobtrusive femininity. In this letter, she proposed a recruiting tactic that might work on more middle-of-the-road civil rights converts. "Dream? Naïve? Or possible?" She left it up to her civil rights colleagues to decide.

Similarly, her deep understanding of the conservative mindset led her to caution fellow activists to tread lightly in making political appeals. Her proposed column entitled "What One Woman Can Do!" for the NCW's newsletter would mount a stealth attack on "the new underground of the right," as Jean termed it. By first offering chatty, hands-on ways for the reader to get involved in the fight for fair housing, for instance, or opposition to South African apartheid, the column could then expand to "gradually include more and more material about the far right without ever starting out with a 'rightist' label that immediately alarms some of our conservative friends," Jean suggested. This was just one of many "steps we might take against the danger on the right," she concluded.[41]

Jean ended her missive by referencing a book recently published by the Anti-Defamation League, *The Danger on the Right*, that she insisted was required reading for all concerned Americans. The book cataloged the growing power of what its authors called "the Radical American Right," spearheaded by the John Birch Society, as well as the "Extreme Conservatives" who provided useful cover for their more fringe fellow travelers. The cheerful economic liberalism and free-market faith that Jean had championed during her career appeared now to have mutated into something darker. The authors of *The Danger on the Right* closed their study by chiding "true conservatives" such as William F. Buckley, who continued to "blink at the Radical's game out of either softness or blindness."[42] Nothing less than the future of the republic depended on cutting right-wing extremists off at the root.

Jean agreed. In brainstorming how the new "underground of the right" might be brought around, she sensed that more education was needed at the grassroots level. But, at times, she found it difficult to remain optimistic. "It is hard to know where to begin," she confessed to a friend. "It is such a peaceful-*looking* country, in the country."[43] Jean's genial faith in an America of "good folk" and the Golden Rule had been shaken. Not all, she discovered, was as it seemed in the dark fields of the republic.

The Service Ideal, Revisited

In her postretirement speeches to industry insiders, Jean continued to try to "believe in advertising," that most deep-seated of faiths that had guided her career. But after her years working with the National Council of Women at the forefront of their antipoverty, pro–civil rights platform, one senses her heart was no longer in it. Typical of this waning faith is a speech she gave in the summer of 1967 to a group of young advertisers, entitled "How Advertising Looks to Me Now That I Don't Write It Anymore." Even as she is, ostensibly, talking about belief in advertising, it is as though she cannot help but lapse back into belief in what she calls "realer" things.

In an obvious allusion to the standard love-and-kisses advertising strategy she used throughout the 1950s, Jean confides: "I usually stand up on a soapbox and explain that people have little, intimate, personal worries—my job, my raise, my children, my house."[1] Yet increasingly, she notes, it is impossible for people to ignore the world outside their doors. "For quite a while now, Vietnam has no longer been that big, impersonal, far away thing" it once was. "It has rather suddenly become the boy next door, . . . [and it] comes into the living room every night at eleven." "I know you can't control the climate of your ads," she concedes, and she is "thankful you haven't had to start to produce some of the sentimental drivel we did in older wars." But she is troubled by the fact that were a "man from Mars" to drop in and take a look at American advertisements, he would find "few bits of evidence that we are a nation at war." Somehow, admen and adwomen must find a way to register the gravity of current events, not to sidestep them or, worse, trivialize them with a jingle. These are surprising words indeed coming from the author of Oneida's "Back Home for Keeps" advertisements, quintessential heart-tug copy that sought to convert wartime emotions into silverware sales.

What Jean misses when she looks at today's advertising, she says (admitting that it sounds, even to herself, "terribly square"), is "service—helpfulness," something beyond mere slickness. At first, her concept of service seems not to have moved much beyond her earlier notions of helping the beleaguered housewife cope, to "give a woman a little help in fitting [the product] quietly into the pattern of her life, into her needs, into her wants, into her problems."[2] And yet no sooner has she argued that the best companies will show that they have listened—and tried to respond to—the consumer's hopes and dreams than she veers off into entirely different territory. "Let's listen to somebody else," she suggests, and quotes the Reverend Otis Moss Jr. talking to Mayor Walton Bachrach in the midst of riot-torn Cincinnati: "'Oh, how wonderful it would have been if you had listened to our dreams and understood our aspirations.'" The implicit comparison between the civil rights leader's dream for racial justice and the housewife's dream for a richer, easier life shocks by its incongruity. And yet the odd shift in tone feels less like Jean's habitual sentimental overreach and more like an attempt to throw up a bridge between the two halves of her life, to forge a common language between youthful ad writing and postretirement social activism. To find some way that advertising's cherished catch phrases—"service," "help," "listening," "responsibility"—might be given new meaning.

In her advertising days, Jean had been a leading proponent of market research as the best way to sell. One of her biggest pet peeves was what she called "high hat" types, locked up in their ivory Madison Avenue towers, trying to puzzle out on their own what American housewives wanted without bothering to go directly to the source. "Ask her," Jean tirelessly advocated. "Let her tell you what she wants. Let her help you plan."[3] Listen when she talks, and believe what she tells you.

In her 1967 speech, however, Jean landed on a very different example of market research and the importance of knowing one's audience: Reverend George Webber, a Protestant minister who opened a mission-oriented outreach in East Harlem in 1948. "He went with a lot of normal natural notions about the poor," Jean explains: that with hard work and a little positive thinking, they could turn their lives around. "And then he lived in East Harlem and it wasn't like that," she remarks flatly. In a book recounting his East Harlem experience, *God's Colony in Man's World*, Webber explained how he and his fellow missionaries had to learn to speak a new language to meet their constituents' needs. "The normal pattern of community organization on the crowded tenement blocks was the store, laundry, or social club," Webber noted on first moving into the neighborhood. This led to the use of storefront churches, a notion foreign to the white suburban places of worship from which many volunteers came.[4] In Webber's ability to listen to need, even when it was expressed in an unfamiliar language, Jean finds an analogy for admen: "Is there a chance that you, like George Weber [*sic*], are carrying around a lot of misconceptions about your market?" she queries. "And would it be a good idea to go out and find out?" For the second time in her speech, Jean begins by speaking about advertising and market demographics and ends up talking about our duty to the poor, the widow, and the orphan (Isaiah 10:2)—a very different kind of service.

Jean's most surprising admission is yet to come, however. After exhorting her audience to work for something they believe in, she muses: "We were simple-hearted, in my youth. We believed that we were doing a good thing just helping people smell better. . . . Or get better meals faster. Or make housework easier. We believed that American business created jobs and that jobs were good things, they put money into pockets, and money in pockets was a fine thing." Here, Jean summarizes the free-market faith for which she had been missionizing all her life. "Well, that was a long time ago," she confesses. "Even I know now that all of this was simplistic thinking." She urges these fledgling ad makers to "get in there and fight" for something they believe in. "I wish you the deep joy of believing in what you are doing," she concludes, "because I know how bitter life can be when you have lost that belief." It sounds very much like a recantation.

In her life as an advertiser, Jean believed she was doing her nation the service of more efficiently matching up consumers and producers, thereby facilitating economic growth: creating jobs, putting "money in pockets" where it hadn't been before. What Jean struggles with in this speech is, in effect, the collapse of her faith in economic liberalism's incrementalist dream, whereby a self-regulating market would fuel an ever-expanding economy and, eventually, guarantee a place in the sun to all of God's children. This was a dream that, toward the end of her life, Jean could no longer believe in.

"Sentimentality . . . is the mark of dishonesty," James Baldwin once wrote. It betokens an "aversion to experience," a refusal to look reality squarely in the face. Jean's career-long attachment to the treacly rhetoric of home and hearth, "love and kisses," had been deeply felt; it had also, she recognized in retrospect, functioned as a strategy of political evasion. At the end of Jean's 1968 letter describing her idea for a civil rights martyrs' book, she allowed herself to hope that the rising generation would be better equipped to fight the good fight. "At least, I keep being thankful we are raising an adventuresome breed of children," she proffered. She recounted that she had recently read her five-year-old granddaughter "Goldilocks and the Three Bears." The little girl had listened patiently, only to respond: "You know, Granny, I never understand why the little girl ran away. She could have played with the little bear. And they could have given her tea, or something!" "Maybe," Jean concluded hopefully, "the next generation won't run away."[5]

Acknowledgments

This study has its origins in my last book, *Oneida: From Free Love Utopia to the Well-Set Table*, during research for which I discovered that Jean Wade Rindlaub of BBDO created Oneida Limited's wartime "Back Home for Keeps" advertisements. Combing through her archive at the Schlesinger Library, I was fascinated by the odd blend of business enthusiasm and Christian belief that animated her work, themes I recognized from my own family story. I decided to dig into the connection more deeply, and I ended up writing this book.

I thank the University of Southern California's Dana and David Dornsife College of Letters, Arts and Sciences for supporting my research. My deepest thanks to the National Endowment for the Humanities, which granted me a 2017–2018 Public Scholar Fellowship, and to Peter Mancall, who, in his capacity as dean, helped arrange my leave of absence. I also thank my home department at the University of Southern California, the Writing Program, for their enthusiastic and unstinting support of my book-writing endeavors, particularly John Holland and Norah Ashe McNally, former and current directors of the program. I could not have applied for the NEH grant without the generous recommendations of Karen Haltunnen and Ann Fabian, scholars extraordinaires on nineteenth-century America, whose smarts and flair for good storytelling have deeply influenced my own way of writing history.

To my agent, Rob McQuilkin, thank you for believing in my project and for helping it find a perfect home. At the University of Chicago Press, undying thanks to my editor, Tim Mennel, who, among other things, de-purpled my prose and made it much more read-able, even to me. Thank you to Susannah Engstrom for her patience with my frequent pleas for deadline extensions. Thank you to the Arthur and Elizabeth Schlesinger Library on the History of Women in America for many fruitful visits in the archive. I especially appreci-ate the help I received from Schlesinger librarian Diana Carey, who helped me navigate the image selection and reproduction process. Thank you to other staff at the University of Chicago Press: Tamara Ghattas, Lauren Salas, and Carrie Olivia Adams. Your professional, punctual, and always cheerful advice along the way made this last phase of the book a pleasure.

Thank you to my comrades-in-writing, Erika Nanes and Kate Levin; our delightful writing group sessions kept me on track and always reminded me why I write, even though it is hard. An equal thank you to Katie Mather, whose feminist and eco-driven fiction has been a delight to share. She is a truth teller in my life and keeps me honest (and reminds me to laugh at myself). Julie Park was tire-lessly generous in providing support, pep talks, and suggestions for better writing practice during the whole course of the book.

My father, Giles Wayland-Smith, guided me through my last book but didn't live to see this one to completion. This is a great sorrow for me, but at the same time, this book continues the tangled story of Christianity, community, and capitalism that he devoted much of his life to thinking about. To me, his voice is everywhere in its pages. To my mother, Kate Wayland-Smith, who taught me early on that Mother's Day was a racket, and how to the tell the difference between real love and sentimentality. To my sister, Sarah Wayland-Smith, who held and still holds the family together and who, during summers, did the (often thankless) labor of watching my children so I could write.

Finally, thank you to Jake, Sophia, and Lydia. You were patient with the most absent-minded and cranky manifestations of my book-writing self, and for that I am endlessly grateful.

Notes

Introduction

1 Tierney's book jacket bills the memoir as a woman's riposte to the male tell-all confessions that preceded it, notably David Ogilvy's *Confessions of an Advertising Man* (New York: Atheneum, 1963), and Jerry della Femina's *From Those Wonderful Folks Who Gave You Pearl Harbor: Front Line Dispatches from the Advertising War* (New York: Simon and Schuster, 1970).

2 Patricia Tierney, *Ladies of the Avenue: The Advertising Agency Jungle . . . Defoliated by an Insider, a Successful Woman Copywriter* (New York: Bartholomew House, 1971), 43.

3 See Mary Wells Lawrence, *A Big Life in Advertising* (New York: Knopf, 2002), and Jane Maas, *Madwomen: The Other Side of Life on Madison Avenue in the '60s and Beyond* (New York: Thomas Dunne Books, 2012).

4 Judann Pollack, "Jane Maas, Copywriter Considered 'The Real Peggy Olson,' Dies at 86," *AdAge*, November 20, 2018, https://adage.com/article/agency-news/jane -maas-real-peggy-olson-dies-86/315695/.

5 Maas, *Madwomen*, 159.

6 Tierney, *Ladies of the Avenue*, 44.

7 "Don't Wait—Marry the Man!," box 12, folder 2, Papers of Jean Wade Rindlaub [hereafter cited as JWR].

8 Speech to Advertising Club, January 1948, box 17, folder 2, JWR.

9 Quoted in James Weinstein, *The Corporate Ideal in the Liberal State: 1900-1918* (Boston: Beacon Press, 1968), x.

10 James Baldwin, "Everybody's Protest Novel," in *Uncle Tom's Cabin*, by Harriet Beecher Stowe, ed. Elizabeth Ammons (New York: W. W. Norton, 1994), 496.

11 "Never Trust a Woman's Viewpoint," Dupont Clinic, August 1945, box 16, folder 12, JWR.

12 Speech to the Pharmaceutical Association, February 7, 1952, Biltmore Hotel, box 17, folder 7, JWR.

13 "Never Trust a Woman's Viewpoint."

14 Marilyn Morgan, "Recipe for Success: Jean Wade Rindlaub's Influence on American Women's Ideals," in *We Are What We Sell: How Advertising Shapes American Life . . . and Always Has*, vol. 2, *Advertising at the Center of Popular Culture: 1930s–1975*, ed. Danielle Sarver Coombs and Bob Batchelor (Santa Barbara: Praeger, 2014), 1–20.

Chapter One

1   Letter of recommendation from G. W. Williams, July 9 1895, box 42, folder 2, JWR.
2   R. M. Wade, Speech to Committee on the Brotherhood of the Presbytery, n.d., box 42, folder 6, JWR.
3   Letter of recommendation from G. W. Williams.
4   Letter signed J. M. Wade, October 3, 1895, box 41, folder 18, JWR.
5   "Wade's Pennsylvania Business and Shorthand College" brochure, 1903, box 42, folder 3, JWR.
6   "Wade's Pennsylvania Business and Shorthand College."
7   Pennsylvania Business College Circular, April 16, 1912, box 42, folder 4, JWR.
8   "United Fruit Cookbook Conference, November 5, 1954," box 18, folder 3, JWR.
9   Max Weber, *The Protestant Ethic and the Spirit of Capitalism* (London: Allen and Unwin, 1930), 163, 177.
10 See Daniel L. Dreisbach, "The 'Vine and Fig Tree' in George Washington's Letters: Reflections on a Biblical Motif in the Literature of America's Founding Era." *Anglican and Episcopal History* 76, no. 3 (September 2007): 299–326. Eric Foner gives the definitive account of the rise of republican ideology in antebellum America and its role in legitimizing the long-stigmatized status of wage labor as "free labor," thus stymying early critiques of capitalism. See *Free Soil, Free Labor, Free Men: The Ideology of the Republican Party Before the Civil War* (Oxford: Oxford University Press, 1995). On post–Civil War optimism that the factory system and material abundance for all would strengthen republican values and civic virtue, see John Kasson, *Civilizing the Machine: Technology and Republican Values in America 1776–1900* (New York: Grossman, 1976).
11 O. A. Brownson, *The Laboring Classes: An Article from the Boston Quarterly Review*, 3rd ed. (Boston: Benjamin Greene, 1840), 10.
12 Brownson, *Laboring Classes*, 12, 21.
13 Foner, *Free Soil*, xxi. For two works canvassing early critiques of capitalism and market society in Jacksonian America, see Carl J. Guarneri, *The Utopian Alternative: Fourierism in Nineteenth-Century America* (Ithaca, NY: Cornell University Press, 1991), and Charles Sellers, *The Market Revolution: Jacksonian America, 1815–1846* (New York: Oxford University Press, 1991). Both Guarneri and Sellers seek to reconstruct the complexity of social and economic thought in America during this period before the consolidation of free-market orthodoxy.
14 Foner, *Free Soil*, 23.
15 R. M. Wade, Speech to Committee on Brotherhood of the Presbytery, box 42, folder 6, JWR.
16 R. M. Wade, Speech titled "Our Duty to the Poor," box 42, folder 6, JWR.
17 R. M. Wade, Speech to Sunday School teachers, box 42, folder 6, JWR.
18 Wade, Speech to Sunday School teachers.
19 For an account of the "progressive" current in American politics from the rise of the trusts through the New Deal, see Richard Hofstadter, *The Age of Reform* (New York: Random House, 1955).
20 Daniel Rogers discusses the tension between these two visions of the "New World"—as wilderness requiring the hard toil of "clearing" versus Golden Age paradise—in *The Work Ethic in Industrial America, 1850–1920* (Chicago: University of Chicago Press, 1979), 1–5.

21 Cited in David Potter, *People of Plenty: Economic Abundance and the American Character* (Chicago: University of Chicago Press, 1954), 105.

22 On the importance of the "abundance narrative" in America, see Potter's *People of Plenty*. Other treatments that focus specifically on abundance and rise of consumer culture are Jackson Lears, *Fables of Abundance: A Cultural History of Advertising in America* (New York: Basic Books, 1994), and William Leach, *Land of Desire: Merchants, Power, and the Rise of a New American Culture* (New York: Vintage Books, 1993). John F. Kasson charts the intersection of republican ideology and technological innovation as key to American utopian and more generally "progressive" thought in *Civilizing the Machine*.

23 Simon N. Patten, *The New Basis of Civilization* (New York: Macmillan, 1907), 9. For a discussion of Patten in intellectual and historical context, see Daniel M. Fox, *The Discovery of Abundance: Simon N. Patten and the Transformation of Social Theory* (Ithaca, NY: Cornell University Press, 1967). See also Leach's excellent discussion of Patten's influence on consumer culture in *Land of Desire*, 231–44.

24 Patten quoted in Leach, *Land of Desire*, 236. Martin J. Sklar gives a fascinating account of how the shift from what he calls proprietary-competitive capitalism to corporate capitalism was imagined as an evolutionary passage to a higher form of development, leaving behind the "wastes" of the earlier competitive model to attain the maturity of "cooperation." *The Corporate Reconstruction of American Capitalism: The Market, the Law, and Politics* (Cambridge: Cambridge University Press, 1988). Couched in these evolutionary terms, corporate capitalism could be seen as more inclusive and "socialized" than its earlier forms: "In its very centralizing and standardizing characteristics, corporate capitalism was inclusive of social diversity in a way that proprietary capitalism was not and could not be. Its partisans, accordingly, called corporate capitalism progressive" (22). Gabriel Kolko similarly argues that "Progressivism was initially a movement for the political rationalization of business and industrial conditions, a movement that operated on the assumption that the general welfare of the community could be best served by satisfying the concrete needs of business." *The Triumph of Conservatism: A Reinterpretation of American History, 1900–1912* (New York: Free Press, 1963), 3.

25 Walter Rauschenbusch, *Christianizing the Social Order* (New York: Macmillan, 1912), 45. Samuel Zane Batten takes a similar tack, calling on readers to recognize that the kingdom of God "is a kingdom and a society; it is not an anarchy of good individuals, but a fellowship of brothers." *The Social Task of Christianity: A Summons to the New Crusade* (New York: Fleming H. Revell, 1911), 84.

26 Susan Curtis has written the definitive work on how Social Gospel thinkers and institutions helped consolidate as well as validate a consumption ethic in early twentieth-century America; see *A Consuming Faith: The Social Gospel and Modern American Culture* (Baltimore: Johns Hopkins University Press, 2001).

27 Quoted in Leach, *Land of Desire*, 243. This conflation of moral and material progress is evident even earlier in antebellum republican ideology, where economic development, social mobility, and the spread of democratic institutions appeared linked in the more general march of "civilization" and "progress." See Foner, *Free Soil*, 38–39.

28 Samuel Haber devotes a chapter of his study on scientific management and the Progressive movement to prominent advocates of economic and political liberalism; see *Efficiency and Uplift: Scientific Management in the Progressive Era*

1890–1920 (Chicago: University of Chicago Press, 1964; Midway repr., 1973), chap. 5, "Three Reformers of Reform." On the Progressive movement's contribution to the emergence of a new model of the state based on the "engineering of consent" and faith in managerial experts, see William Graebner, *The Engineering of Consent: Democracy and Authority in Twentieth-Century America* (Madison: University of Wisconsin Press, 1987).

29 See Roland Marchand, *Creating the Corporate Soul: The Rise of Public Relations and Corporate Imagery in American Big Business* (Berkeley: University of California Press, 1998), esp. chap. 5.

30 Earnest Elmo Calkins, *Business the Civilizer* (Boston: Little, Brown, 1928), 51.

31 Haber, *Efficiency and Uplift*, ix–xii.

32 See Curtis, *Consuming Faith*, 23.

33 For an interpretation of the Progressive period that argues its signature achievement was the essentially conservative one of establishing "business control over politics," rather than "political regulation of the economy," see Kolko, *Triumph of Conservatism*. James Weinstein advances a similar thesis in *The Corporate Ideal in the Liberal State: 1900–1918* (Boston: Beacon Press, 1968). According to Weinstein, "liberalism in the Progressive Era—and since—was the product . . . of the leaders of the giant corporations and financial institutions that emerged astride American society in the last years of the nineteenth century" (xv). Even Hofstadter, who takes a much more generous stance toward the Progressive movement and its reformist impulse, ultimately concludes that the federal measures adopted to check the power of the trusts had no real teeth, nor were they designed to. "It is impossible not to conclude that, despite the widespread public agitation over the matter, the men who took a conservative view of the needs of the hour never lost control" (*Age of Reform*, 252).

34 See Carole Srole, *Transcribing Class and Gender: Masculinity and Femininity in Nineteenth-Century Courts and Offices* (Ann Arbor: University of Michigan Press, 2010), 108.

35 Pennsylvania Business College, n.d., brochure, box 42, folder 3, JWR.

36 Pennsylvania Business College brochure.

37 Pennsylvania Business College pamphlet, "A Challenge," October 1909, box 42, folder 5, JWR.

38 "Challenge," 10.

39 "Challenge," 2, 8.

40 T. DeWitt Talmadge, *From Manger to Throne: Embracing a New Life of Jesus the Christ and a History of Palestine and its People* (Philadelphia: Historical, 1890), 1. For an excellent overview and bibliography of this push to remake the effeminate Victorian Jesus into a magnetic "organization man," see Curtis, *Consuming Faith*, 80–88.

41 Orison Swett Marden, *The Masterful Personality* (New York: Thomas Y. Crowell, 1921), 98, 23.

42 Marden, *Masterful Personality*, 28, 276.

43 Pennsylvania Business College Circular, April 16, 1912, box 42, folder 4, JWR.

44 Pennsylvania Business College brochure. In his comprehensive account of the "managerial revolution" in American business, Alfred D. Chandler Jr. documents how modern corporate enterprises replaced earlier market mechanisms regulating supply and demand, thereby becoming "the most powerful institutions in the American economy," as well as "the most influential group of [economic] decision

makers." See *The Visible Hand: The Managerial Revolution in American Business* (Cambridge, MA: Harvard University Press, 1977).

45 Alan Trachtenberg argues convincingly that during the Gilded Age, "corporate life . . . was still too new for Americans to recognize except in the familiar but already outmoded language of individualism." *The Incorporation of America: Culture and Society in the Gilded Age* (New York: Hill and Wang, 1982; rev. ed. 2007), 5.

46 Finance ledgers, Box 3, folder 5, JWR.

Chapter Two

1 "Policy Committee Has Strenuous Day," *Armstrong Jobber*, March 1, 1927, box 1, folder 4, JWR.

2 Advertising Department memo, January 23, 1929, box 13, folder 9, JWR.

3 "McCoy Uses Linoleum Floors Throughout his New Home," *Armstrong Jobber*, box 1, folder 4, JWR.

4 Catharine E. Beecher and Harriet Beecher Stowe, *The American Woman's Home*, ed. and intro. Nicole Tonkovich (New Brunswick, NJ: Rutgers University Press, 2002), 25. See also Kathryn Kish Sklar, *Catharine Beecher: A Study in American Domesticity* (New Haven, CT: Yale University Press, 1973).

5 Nancy Cott's *The Bonds of Womanhood: "Woman's Sphere" in New England, 1780–1835* (New Haven, CT: Yale University Press, 1977), helped shape a generation of historical scholarship on the influence of the nineteenth-century "cult of domesticity" on evolving American gender roles. Equally important to my study of how the Victorian domestic canon was tweaked to keep up with the evolution of capitalism in the twentieth century is Ann Douglas's 1977 study, *The Feminization of American Culture* (New York: Noonday Press, 1998). Douglas argues that midcentury disestablished ministers and disempowered middle-class women joined forces to exert a major cultural influence through the back-door channel of popular sentimental literature. Touting the civilizing virtues of the "matriarchal values of nurture, generosity, and tolerance" in defiance of market values, these women ended up, ironically, reinforcing the very system of power relationships they set out to protest. "The sentimentalization of theological and secular culture was an inevitable part of the self-evasion of a society both committed to laissez-faire industrial expansion and disturbed by its consequences" (12).

6 Beechers, *American Woman's Home*, 167.

7 On the emergence of a proto-feminist consciousness in nineteenth-century women's literary organizations, and their appeal to feminine virtue "to justify their departure from the home to exert special influence on the male sphere," see Karen J. Blair, *The Clubwoman as Feminist: True Womanhood Redefined, 1868–1914* (New York: Holmes and Meier, 1980), 4.

8 See Rosalind Rosenberg, *Divided Lives: American Women in the Twentieth Century* (New York: Hill and Wang, 1992; rev. ed. 2008), chap. 2, "Domesticating the State: 1901–1912"; Robyn Muncy, *Creating a Female Dominion in American Reform, 1890–1935* (New York: Oxford University Press, 1991).

9 For a historical overview of American women and their access to public power, see Glenna Matthews, *The Rise of the Public Woman: Woman's Power and Woman's Place in the United States, 1630–1970* (New York: Oxford University Press, 1992).

10 Christine Frederick, *The New Housekeeping: Efficiency Studies in Home Manage-ment* (New York: Doubleday, Page, 1914), viii, ix. For a comprehensive biography placing Frederick in historical context, see Janice Williams Rutherford, *Selling Mrs. Consumer: Christine Frederick and the Rise of Household Efficiency* (Athens: University of Georgia Press, 2003). For an analysis of "housework technology" and its complex relationship to gender from the Industrial Revolution through the postwar period, see Ruth Schwartz Cowan, *More Work for Mother: The Ironies of Household Technology from the Open Hearth to the Microwave* (New York: Basic Books, 1983). See also Susan Strasser, *Never Done: A History of American House-work* (New York: Pantheon, 1982).

11 *For Top Executives Only: A Symposium*, ed. J. George Frederick (New York: Busi-ness Bourse, 1936), 55.

12 Frederick, *New Housekeeping*, 204.

13 Frederick, *New Housekeeping*, 215, 217, 224, 215.

14 Frederick, *New Housekeeping*, 227–28.

15 See Lizabeth Cohen, *A Consumer's Republic: The Politics of Mass Consumption in Postwar America* (New York: Random House, 2003), chap. 1, "Depression: Rise of the Citizen Consumer."

16 Cohen, *Consumer's Republic*, 22.

17 On the "centrality of gender in Red Scare patriotism," see Kim E. Nielsen, *Un-American Womanhood: Antiradicalism, Antifeminism, and the First Red Scare* (Columbus: Ohio State University Press, 2001), 13.

18 See Nielsen, *Un-American Womanhood*, esp. chap. 2, "Bolshevik in the Shape of a Woman."

19 Nielsen, *Un-American Womanhood*, 89. See also Muncy, *Creating a Female Domin-ion*, chap. 5, "Contraction and Dissolution of the Female Dominion."

20 Sharon Hartman Strom, *Beyond the Typewriter: Gender, Class, and the Origins of Modern American Office Work, 1900–1930* (Urbana: University of Illinois Press, 1992), 188.

21 See Margery W. Davies, *Woman's Place Is at the Typewriter: Office Work and Office Workers, 1870–1930* (Philadelphia: Temple University Press, 1982), 80.

22 On the cultural debate surrounding the suitability of women clerical workers in the nineteenth century, see Davies, *Woman's Place*, chap. 5 "The Ideological Debate." For a particularly trenchant analysis of the double bind of seeking "respectability" in the workplace, see Carole Srole, *Transcribing Class and Gender: Masculinity and Femininity in Nineteenth-Century Courts and Offices* (Ann Arbor: University of Michigan Press, 2010), chap. 5, "Typewriter Girls and Lady Stenographers: The Challenges of Respectability," 129–59.

23 Srole argues that female office workers strove to blend the "ambition, independence, and self-control of the businesswoman with the modesty and caring of the lady" (*Transcribing Class and Gender*, 12). On working-class women and stereotypes, see Amal Amireh, *The Factory Girl and the Seamstress: Imagining Gender and Class in Nineteenth Century American Fiction* (New York: Garland, 2000).

24 Letter from Rindlaub to Miss Hildegarde Fillmore, November 27, 1946, box 12, folder 4, JWR.

25 "Weekly Feature: To Girls on the Way Up," n.d., box 12, folder 1, JWR.

26 "My Hobby Is Imagination," n.d., box 12, folder 4, JWR.

27 "My Hobby Is Imagination."

28 Talk to Girls Club of Advertising Department at DuPont, June 3, 1947, box 17, folder 1, JWR.

29 See Simone Weil Davis, *Living Up to the Ads: Gender Fictions of the 1920s* (Durham, NC: Duke University Press, 2000), 82.

30 Davis, *Living Up to the Ads*, 88.

31 Quoted in Roland Marchand, *Advertising the American Dream: Making Way for Modernity, 1920–1940* (Berkeley: University of California Press, 1985), 34–35.

32 See Marchand's treatment of advertising's early self-fashioning in *Advertising the American Dream*, esp. 1–16.

33 Roland Marchand, *Creating the Corporate Soul: The Rise of Public Relations and Corporate Imagery in American Big Business* (Berkeley: University of California Press, 1998).

34 Davis, *Living Up to the Ads*.

35 Talk to Girls Club of Advertising Department at DuPont.

36 Intra-office memo from Jean Rindlaub to Mr. Feland, November 23, 1948, box 1, folder 14, JWR.

37 On the way, corporations, including advertising agencies, incorporated themes from the Social Gospel and Progressive movements to humanize and sell their mission, see Curtis, *Consuming Faith*, and Davis, *Living Up to the Ads*. Davis's chapter 1, "Uplift and the Bottom Line," is a particularly trenchant analysis of how advertising blended the rhetoric of masculine profit motive with the rhetoric of feminine "social uplift" to sell itself to the public.

38 Finance Ledgers, box 3, folder 5, JWR.

39 "Don't Wait—Marry the Man," box 12, folder 2, JWR.

40 Typewritten speech honoring Rindlaub, dated October 23, 1958, box 1, folder 1, JWR.

41 Marilyn Mercer, "Drive and Dedication Distinguish Ad Agency V.P.," *New York Herald Tribune*, March 1, 1960, box 1, folder 5, JWR.

Chapter Three

1 "Advertising, Or the Story of Susy," n.d., box 14, folder 9, JWR.

2 See Kathy Peiss, *Hope in a Jar: The Making of America's Beauty Culture* (New York: Henry Holt, 1998), 144.

3 Stephen Fox, Roland Marchand, and Jackson Lears are indispensable sources on the history of American advertising. See Fox, *The Mirror Makers: A History of American Advertising and its Creators* (Urbana: University of Illinois Press, 1984); Marchand, *Advertising the American Dream: Making Way for Modernity, 1920–1940* (Berkeley: University of California Press, 1985); and Lears, *Fables of Abundance: A Cultural History of Advertising in America* (New York: Basic Books, 1994).

4 Frank Presbery, *The History and Development of Advertising* (Garden City, NY: Doubleday, Doran, 1929), 617.

5 Quoted in James Harvey Young, *The Toadstool Millionaires: A Social History of Patent Medicines in America Before Federal Regulation* (Princeton, NJ: Princeton University Press, 1961), 4.

6   Peter Benes, *For a Short Time Only: Itinerants and the Resurgence of Popular Culture in Early America* (Amherst: University of Massachusetts Press, 2016), 23–24.

7   Brooks McNamara, *Step Right Up*, rev. ed. (Jackson: University Press of Mississippi, 1995), 66–67.

8   Young, *Toadstool Millionaires*, 39.

9   Young, *Toadstool Millionaires*, 82.

10   Robert Jay, *The Trade Card in Nineteenth-Century America* (Columbia: University of Missouri Press, 1987), 3. See also Ellen Gruber Garvey, *The Adman in the Parlor: Magazines and the Gendering of Consumer Culture, 1880s to 1910s* (New York: Oxford University Press, 1996).

11   John Fanning Watson, *Methodist Error; or, Friendly Christian Advice to Those Methodists, Who Indulge in Extravagant Emotions and Bodily Exercises* (Trenton, NJ: Fenton, 1819), 17, 31. For an excellent account of the convergence of entertainment and faith in nineteenth-century America, see R. Laurence Moore, *Selling God: American Religion in the Marketplace of Culture* (New York: Oxford, 1994). Moore examines how the disestablishment of religion, combined with the vigorous spirit of democracy and economic *laissez-faire* of the opening decades of the nineteenth century, "threw religion into a free-for-all competition for people's attention" (43). On the carnivalesque strand in early Christianity, see Lears, *Fables of Abundance*.

12   Dr. Benjamin Dolbeare, *Dow's Family Medicine: Invalid's Manual* (1836), https://archive.org/details/101182862.nlm.nih.gov/page/n1.

13   For a detailed examination of how early modern European traditions of magic and alchemy were blended with Christianity in colonial America, see Jon Butler, "Magic, Astrology, and the Early American Religious Heritage, 1600–1760," *American Historical Review* 84, no. 2 (April 1979): 318.

14   On the syncretism of pagan "folk" magic and Christian beliefs in early modern Europe, see Keith Thomas, *Religion and the Decline of Magic: Studies in Popular Beliefs in Sixteenth- and Seventeenth-Century England* (New York: Penguin, 1971).

15   See Alan Taylor, "The Early Republic's Supernatural Economy: Treasure Seeking in the American Northeast, 1780–1830," *American Quarterly* 38, No. 1 (Spring, 1986): 8. See also Chris Lehmann, *The Money Cult: Capitalism, Christianity, and the Unmaking of the American Dream* (Brooklyn: Melville House, 2016). Lehmann contends that the dominant motif in American religious life has always been "the strange symbiosis of the calculating Puritan conscience and the vernacular worship of the many totems of our unique New World prosperity" (xxi).

16   Quoted in Peiss, *Hope in a Jar*, 16. Madame Bayard, *The Art of Beauty: or Ladies' Companion to the Boudoir* (London: Weldon, 1876), 35.

17   Bayard, *Art of Beauty*, 51.

18   Alexander Walker, *Beauty: Illustrated Chiefly by an Analysis and Classification of Beauty in Women* (London: H. G. Bohn, 1846), 4, 13.

19   Quoted in Marilyn Thornton Williams, *Washing "The Great Unwashed": Public Baths in Urban America, 1840–1920* (Columbus: Ohio State University Press, 1991), 13.

20   William Horsell, *Hydropathy for the People: With Plain Observations on Drugs, Diet, Water, Air and Exercise* (New York: Fowlers and Wells, 1850). Horsell refers to what appears to be the definitive treatise on "water cure," published in 1843: Edward Johnson's *Hydropathy: The Theory, Principles, and Practice and the Water Cure* (London: Simpkin, Marshall, 1843). Madame Bayard quotes directly (without attribution) from this manual in her treatment of skin care.

21 Horsell, *Hydropathy*, 158–59.

22 Bayard, *Art of Beauty*, 33.

23 While the water-cure movement may have been of dubious medical credibility, it dovetailed with a decidedly more rational national undertaking: the building of large-scale municipal water and sewage systems to bring indoor plumbing into America's middle-class homes. By the 1890s, growing acceptance of the germ theory of disease by the medical establishment and an increasingly clean-obsessed public made the matter of access to baths a public health priority and fueled a push by middle-class reformers to build public baths in poor, congested urban centers. See Williams, *Washing "The Great Unwashed."*

24 Advertisement for "Jap Rose," *Ladies' Home Journal*, January 1910.

25 For an interesting analysis of the exploding market for soap among middle-class American consumers in the 1890s, in particular soap's relationship to the larger "cleanliness" reform movement, see James D. Norris, *Advertising and the Transformation of American Society, 1865–1920* (New York: Greenwood Press, 1990), chap. 3, "Any Fool Can Make Soap."

26 Advertisement for Packer's Tar Soap, *Ladies' Home Journal*, March 1912.

27 Advertisement for Packer's Tar Soap, *Ladies' Home Journal*, March 1915.

28 Ad for Woodbury Soap, *Ladies' Home Journal*, April 1918; ad for Pears Soap, *Ladies' Home Journal*, August 1915.

29 Advertisement for Sunkist, "Rinse with Lemon," *Ladies' Home Journal*, November 1919.

30 Advertisement for Woodbury's Soap, *Ladies' Home Journal*, November 1919.

31 Advertisement for Woodbury's Soap, *Ladies' Home Journal*, November 1915.

32 Advertisement for Woodbury's Soap, *Ladies' Home Journal*, December 1918.

33 Advertisement for Resinol Soap, "The Joy of a Perfect Skin," *Ladies' Home Journal*, February 1919.

34 Intra-office memo from Jean Wade Rindlaub to Mr. Page, Mr. Palmer, Mr. Durstine, February 14, 1936, box 9, folder 5, JWR.

35 Advertisement for Lux Soap, *Ladies' Home Journal*, September 1936.

36 Laura Clark, "How Halitosis Became a Medical Condition with a 'Cure,'" Smithsonian.com, January 29, 2015, https://www.smithsonianmag.com/smart-news/marketing-campaign-invented-halitosis-180954082/.

37 See Marchand, *Advertising the American Dream*, 17–20.

38 Intra-Office memo from JR to George Bushfield, cc: Dave Danforth, Squibb Account, 4/2/40, box 9, folder 5, JWR.

39 "Wildroot Speech," Biloxi, December 29, 1949, box 16, folder 2, JWR.

40 "Wildroot Shampoo" sketches, box 7, folder 4, JWR.

41 "Wildroot Shampoo" sketches.

42 "Boy Sights Gal! Kisses Same!" John W. Hartman Center for Sales, Marketing and Advertising History, Duke University Library, Digital Depository.

43 "Face Dandruff," March 3, 1939, box 9, folder 4, JWR.

44 "Face Dandruff."

45 "You've Got to Watch Out for Advertising," *Wedge*, vol. 54, no. 2, box 15, folder 1, JWR.

46 Article for New York Woman, "So You Want to Be Thin!", box 12, folder 1, JWR.

47 See, for instance, her reference to herself as a "fat Dutchman" in a speech at a 1956 United Fruit Cookbook conference, box 18, folder 6, JWR.

48 Anne Rindlaub, "Through the Looking Glass," ca. 1954, box 43 Oversize, JWR.
49 "You've Got to Watch Out."

Chapter Four

1   For a history of the rise of mass market cosmetics, see Kathy Peiss's foundational study, *Hope in a Jar*, esp. chap. 4, "The Rise of the Mass Market."
2   For Factor's biography, see Fred Basten, *Max Factor: The Man Who Changed the Faces of the World* (New York: Arcade, 2008).
3   See Carolyn Kitch, *The Girl on the Magazine Cover: The Origins of Visual Stereotypes in American Mass Media* (Chapel Hill: University of North Carolina Press, 2001), chap. 6, "The Flapper." Peiss also documents the gradual conquest by cosmetic manufacturers of the pages of mainstream women's magazines. *Ladies' Home Journal*, for instance, devoted less than one percent of each issue to beauty in the 1920s; by the mid-1930s, beauty editorials in women's magazines were *de rigueur*, with syndicated "beauty experts" openly endorsing cosmetics by name (125).
4   See Peiss, *Hope in a Jar*, chap. 5, "Promoting the Made-Up Woman," 146–47.
5   See Basten, *Max Factor*, 28.
6   Memo to R. B. Barton and S. A. Harned, "Hudnut," February 14, 1939, box 1, folder 8, JWR.
7   For a history of the Hollywood fan magazine, see Anthony Slide, *Inside the Hollywood Fan Magazine: A History of Star Makers, Fabricators, and Gossip Mongers* (Jackson: University Press of Mississippi, 2010).
8   Al Hughes, "'Li'l Gawgia' Gets Glamour!" *Photoplay*, March 1932, 66–67.
9   Warren Reeve, "She's One in a Million!" *Photoplay*, February 1932, 110.
10 Reeve, "She's One in a Million!" 110.
11 Jan Fisher, "If You Want to Be a Glamorous Beauty," *Photoplay*, November 1937, 5.
12 Adela Rogers St. Johns, "Joan Crawford, Starring in the Dramatic Rise of a Self-Made Star," *Photoplay*, October 1937, 26.
13 Hughes, "'Li'l Gawgia,'" 67.
14 Carl Vonnell, "A World-Famous Psycho-Analyst Tells Just What Makes Them Click," *Photoplay*, April 1932, 30.
15 "Any Woman Can Be Beautiful," By Sylvia, *Photoplay*, February 1932, 30.
16 Oliver Swett Marden, *The Masterful Personality* (New York: Thomas Y. Crowell, 1921), 28.
17 Marden, 108.
18 Marden, 25.
19 Marden, 3.
20 Marden, 172.
21 Marden, 98, 26.
22 Dale Carnegie, *How to Win Friends and Influence People*, rev. ed. (New York: Gallery Books, 1981), xx.
23 Hughes, "'Li'l Gawgia,'" 67.
24 On the advertising strategy of blurring editorial content with merchandising in women's magazines, see Peiss, *Hope in a Jar*, 124–26.
25 For an excellent analysis of the Hollywood "star machine" during the golden age of film, see Jeanine Basinger, *The Star Machine* (New York: Random House, 2009),

75. Basinger explores the key role that "type" played in streamlining the Hollywood factory products (including a fascinating look at "malfunctions").

26 Rex Morton, "New Latin Lover Stirs Hollywood," *Motion Picture Magazine*, September 1935, 56.

27 "The New Art of Society Make-Up, by Max Factor," Cosmetics Booklet, 1929, http://www.cosmeticsandskin.com/booklets/max-new-art-1929.php.

28 Armand "Find Yourself" Cosmetics Booklet, 1929, http://www.cosmeticsandskin.com/booklets/find-yourself-1929.php.

29 Tangee Make-Up, "How to Avoid that 'Made-Up' Look!" *Photoplay*, December 1936, 105.

30 Advertisement for Max Factor, "This Hollywood Make-Up," *Motion Picture Magazine*, September 1936, 39.

31 Letter from JWR to Sherman K. Ellis and Co., August 21 1939, box 1, folder 8, JWR.

32 "New Loveliness for You: Marvelous, the Eye-Matched Makeup," 1936, box 7, folder 1, JWR.

33 Memo to R. B. Barton and S. A. Harned, "Hudnut," February 14, 1939, box 1, folder 8, JWR.

34 Memo, "Hudnut."

35 Delores del Rio advertisement for Marvelous Makeup, *Photoplay*, December 1937.

36 "Hollywood's Four Most Beautiful Women," *Photoplay*, October 1937, 34.

37 James Reid, "Which Stars Are Doomed by Color?" *Motion Picture Magazine*, August, 1936, 35.

38 Virginia T. Lane, "Steffi Duna Is a Perfect Type for Color," *Motion Picture Magazine*, August 1936.

39 Quoted in Basten, *Max Factor*, 110.

40 On the racialized history of cosmetics in cinema, see Sarah Berry, *Screen Style: Fashion and Femininity in 1930s Hollywood* (Minneapolis: University of Minnesota Press, 2000), chap. 3, "Hollywood Exoticism"; Kirsty Sinclair Dootson, "'The Hollywood Powder Puff War': Technicolor Cosmetics in the 1930s," *Film History* 28, no. 1 (2016): 107–31. On Delores del Rio as ambiguously raced in the context of Hollywood films of the 1920s and '30s, see Joanne Hershfield, *The Invention of Delores del Rio* (Minneapolis: University of Minnesota Press, 2000).

41 Quoted in an article, "'Beauty Micrometer' Analyzes Facial Flaws for Makeup," that appeared in the January 1935 issue of *Modern Mechanix*. The Beauty Calibrator was proudly on display at the grand opening of the Max Factor Studio in Hollywood on November 26, 1935; see Basten, *Max Factor*, 89.

42 See Nell Irvin Painter, *The History of White People* (New York: W. W. Norton, 2010), esp. chap. 7, "The White Beauty Ideal as Science," 59–71. In the context of a segregated America, the classical white body of the Apollo Belvedere was converted into an icon for Anglo-American white supremacy after the Civil War; see Kirk Savage, *Standing Soldiers, Kneeling Slaves: Race, War, and Monument in Nineteenth-Century America* (Princeton, NJ: Princeton University Press, 2017).

43 Peiss devotes a chapter of *Hope in a Jar* to the obvious imbrication of mass market, "standardized" cosmetics and white supremacy (chap. 7, "Shades of Difference"). "For African Americans, commercialized beauty was not only an aesthetic . . . matter, but, from the outset, explicitly a problem of politics" (203).

44 See Sarah Berry's excellent analysis of race, exoticism, and the construction of eth-nicity in 1930s Hollywood in *Screen Style*, 94–141; see also Hershfield, esp. chap-ters 1 and 2.

45 Basten, *Max Factor*, 40–42.

46 Dootson, "'Hollywood Powder Puff War,'" 107. Dootson excavates the little-known history of the "Powder Puff War" between Max Factor and Elizabeth Arden, demonstrating how Factor won out not only because Arden's makeup was more costly and labor-intensive to apply but because it failed "to maintain a light skin tone for Caucasian consumers" as well as Factor's Pan-Cake Make-Up (120).

47 On the cosmetic industry's use of "natural" as a euphemism for "white," see Susannah Walker, *Style and Status: Selling Beauty to African American Women, 1920–1975* (Lexington: University of Kentucky Press, 2007), 82.

48 "New Loveliness for You: Marvelous, the Eye-Matched Makeup," 1936, box 7, folder 1, JWR.

49 Madison Grant, *The Passing of the Great Race; or, The Racial Basis of European History*, 4th rev. ed. (New York: Charles Scribner's Sons, 1922), 24, 31.

50 "New Loveliness for You."

Chapter Five

1 "Main Street . . . and How to Find Your Way Back," *Reporter of Direct Mail Advertising*, September 1959, box 12, folder 7, JWR.

2 "Main Street . . ."

3 Nell Irvin Painter, *The History of White People* (New York: W. W. Norton, 2010), 134.

4 William Graebner analyzes the shift in the United States between roughly 1870 and World War I toward "democratic social engineering," a new model of instituting social control based on group-process "consensus building" and technical exper-tise to replace the nineteenth-century focus on more coercive state and religious authority. *The Engineering of Consent: Democracy and Authority in Twentieth-Century America* (Madison: University of Wisconsin Press, 1987).

5 Sarah Igo's *The Averaged American: Surveys, Citizens, and the Making of a Mass Public* (Cambridge, MA: Harvard University Press, 2007), is indispensable reading on opinion polling, the rise of "social scientific ways of knowing" (13), and "averageness" as a key cultural, political, and economic concept in midcentury America. I rely heavily on her analysis in this chapter. Equally trenchant is Wendy L. Wall's analysis of America's midcentury "consensus culture" (5), whose origins she traces to post-Depression turmoil among both conservatives and progressive liberals amid the rise of the "alien" European political specters of fascism and com-munism, the influx of new immigrant groups, and the economic devastation of the Depression. See *Inventing the "American Way": The Politics of Consensus from the New Deal to the Civil Rights Movement* (Oxford: Oxford University Press, 2008).

6 See, for example, Warren I. Sussman, "The Culture of the Thirties," in *Culture as History: The Transformation of American Society in the Twentieth Century* (Washington, DC: Smithsonian Institution Press, 2003). Sussman describes the 1930s as an era in which America went in search of itself, producing "the most overwhelming effort ever attempted to document in art, reportage, social science, and history the life and values of the American people" (158).

7   For the racial politics of twentieth-century immigration within the context of a segregated America, see David R. Roediger, *Working Toward Whiteness: How America's Immigrants Became White* (New York: Basic Books, 2005).

8   See Wall, *Inventing the "American Way,"* 27–31.

9   Quoted in Igo, *Averaged American*, 105. I choose Gallup here as representative of the much wider polling field that emerged in the 1940s and that included such other important innovators as Archibald Crossley and Elmo Roper.

10 Igo, *Averaged American*, 118–19.

11 George Gallup and Saul Forbes Rae, *The Pulse of Democracy: The Public-Opinion Poll and How It Works* (New York: Greenwood Press, 1968), 13.

12 Gallup and Rae, *Pulse of Democracy*, 6.

13 Igo, *Averaged American*, 121–23.

14 Quoted in Graebner, *Engineering of Consent*, 42.

15 Sociologist Robert N. Bellah coined the term "civil religion" to describe the fact that, historically, "the separation of church and state has not denied the political realm a religious dimension" in the United States. See "Civil Religion in America," *Daedalus: Journal of the American Academy of Arts and Sciences*, special issue "Religion in America," 96, no. 1 (Winter 1967): 1–21. Will Herberg's landmark 1955 essay, *Protestant-Catholic-Jew*, suggests that religion in postwar America devolved into a contentless "faith in faith": "It is . . . this religion that makes religion its own object that is the outstanding characteristic of contemporary American religiosity." *Protestant-Catholic-Jew: An Essay in American Religious Sociology*, rev. ed. (Garden City, NY: Anchor Books, 1960). John Murray Cuddihy pushed Herberg's analysis further, suggesting that America's "civil religion" was indistinguishable from a "religion of civility," marked by "aggressive universalism" and a scrupulous attention to never "give offense." *No Offense: Civil Religion and Protestant Taste* (New York: Seabury Press, 1978), 6. See also Kevin M. Schultz, *Tri-Faith America: How Catholics and Jews Held Postwar America to its Protestant Promise* (Oxford: Oxford University Press, 2001).

16 "Talk to Community," August 28, 1946, box 16, folder 13, JWR.

17 Talk to Community executives on spring bridal fashions, n.d., box 16, folder 13, JWR.

18 Talk to Community executives on spring bridal fashions.

19 Talk to Community executives on "Community Is Correct," n.d., box 16, folder 13, JWR.

20 Talk to Community executives on "Community Is Correct."

21 "Background Facts About Homogenized," n.d., box 14, folder 1, JWR.

22 Quoted in William Leach, *Land of Desire: Merchants, Power, and the Rise of a New American Culture* (New York: Vintage Books, 1993), 239. Leach's book includes an excellent analysis of the gospel of standardization among Progressives; see also Jackson Lears, *Fables of Abundance: A Cultural History of Advertising in America* (New York: Basic Books, 1994), 160.

23 "Homogenization" was, obviously, a raced concept, and admission to the club was contingent on whiteness. The more than thirteen million immigrants from southern, eastern, and central Europe who flooded in between 1886 and 1925 were all ambiguously raced within the context of American apartheid: not black, but at the same time not quite white. See Roediger, *Working Toward Whiteness*, and Matthew Frye Jacobsen, *Whiteness of a Different Color: European Immigrants and the*

Alchemy of Race (Cambridge, MA: Harvard University Press, 1998), esp. chap. 3, "Becoming Caucasian, 1924–1965."

24 Quoted in Igo, *Averaged American*, 56.

25 See Igo, *Averaged American*, 126–39.

26 Igo notes that pollsters actually measured the population in carefully carved up demographic segments—"men, women, workers, immigrants, Southerners, migrants, housewives"—for the private use of corporate clients. "Yet when it came to the public consumption of their statistics, surveyors all but dissolved that same bundle of conflicting preferences and desires into a collective 'we'" (*Averaged American* 147).

27 "No Man Knows the Origin of the Marketplace," n.d., box 15, folder 6, JWR.

28 Quoted in Igo, *Averaged American*, 142, 143.

29 Quoted in Igo, *Averaged American*, 147.

30 Leila A. Sussmann, "Labor in the Radio News: An Analysis of Content," *Journalism Quarterly* 22, no. 3 (September 1945): 210.

31 Paul Lazarsfeld, "Remarks on Administrative and Critical Communications Research," *Studies in Philosophy and Social Science* 9 (1941): 2–16. See also William Albig, "Two Decades of Opinion Study: 1936–1956," *Public Opinion Quarterly* 21, no. 1, Anniversary Issue Devoted to Twenty Years of Public Opinion Research (Spring 1957): 14–22.

32 United Fruit Cookbook Conference, November 5, 1954, box 18, folder 3, JWR.

33 David Riesman, with Nathan Glazer and Reuel Denney, *The Lonely Crowd: A Study of the Changing American Character*, abridged and rev. ed. with a foreword by Todd Gitlin (New Haven, CT: Yale University Press, 2001), 48.

34 Riesman, *Lonely Crowd*, 83.

35 Arthur Kallet and F. J. Schlink, *100,000,000 Guinea Pigs: Dangers in Everyday Foods, Drugs, and Cosmetics* (New York: The Vanguard Press, 1932), 4.

36 "My Name is Jean Rindlaub and I Live a Double Life," *Daily News*, February 28, 1953, box 1, folder 4, JWR.

37 "Community," November 5, 1948, box 13, folder 15, JWR.

38 "I Shall Attend to My Little Errands of Love"; "Busy! Busy! Busy!" n.d., box 2, folder 11, JWR.

Chapter Six

1 Maureen Honey, *Creating Rosie the Riveter: Class, Gender, and Propaganda during World War II* (Amherst: University of Massachusetts Press, 1984), 32.

2 Wall, *Inventing the American Way*, 39, 38.

3 Three key studies treating this topic are Inger L. Stole, *Advertising at War: Business, Consumers, and Government in the 1940s* (Urbana: University of Illinois Press, 2012); Frank W. Fox, *Madison Avenue Goes to War: The Strange Military Career of American Advertising 1941–45* (Provo, Utah: Brigham Young University Press, 1975); and Robert Griffith, "The Selling of America: The Advertising Council and American Politics, 1942–1960," *Business History Review* 57, no. 3 (Autumn 1983): 388–412. Stole painstakingly documents how advertisers turned the unfavorable context of wartime into "a priceless opportunity to cement their place in postwar society" by launching a successful campaign on behalf of "favorable laws and regulations [that]

eliminated any realistic threat to the institution's role in the economic system" (2). This, Stole contends, was accomplished with "the enthusiastic support of the commercial media, especially the news media." For a comprehensive overview of the government's own "propaganda" efforts and its collaboration with national advertising and mass media during the war, see Alan Winkler, *The Politics of Propaganda: The Office of War Information, 1942–1945* (New Haven, CT: Yale University Press, 1978).

4 See Wall's excellent discussion of corporate-sponsored anti–New Deal public relations campaigns in the 1930s; *Inventing the American Way*, 48–62. On the active role that business elites played in countering Roosevelt's New Deal policies and establishing the conservative movement in the postwar period more generally, see Kim Phillips-Fein, *Invisible Hands: The Businessmen's Crusade Against the New Deal* (New York: W. W. Norton, 2009).

5 Quoted in Stole, *Advertising at War*, 20.

6 Stole, 11–12.

7 Stole, 28.

8 Stole, 43.

9 Stole, 44. See also Lizabeth Cohen on the advertising industry's use of red-baiting to attack the consumer movement and government campaigns to regulate advertising in the aftermath of the TNEC in *A Consumers' Republic: The Politics of Mass Consumption in Postwar America* (New York: Vintage Books, 2004), 54–61.

10 Quoted in Wall, *Inventing the American Way*, 59.

11 Stole, *Advertising at War*, 48.

12 Advertisement for Continental Can Company, box 32, folder 6, JWR.

13 Advertisement for Eat-Mor Cranberries, box 32, folder 10, JWR.

14 Honey, *Creating Rosie the Riveter*, 36.

15 Honey, *Creating Rosie the Riveter*, 21.

16 There exists an extensive literature on the role of American women in World War II and, in particular, the gendering of wartime work. Some feminist historians, like Maureen Honey and Elaine Tyler May, have documented the way women recruited into the workplace during the war were summarily sent back home at war's end, effectively stifling what could have been a turning point for women's equality in the workplace. See May's *Homeward Bound: American Families in the Cold War*, 20th ann. ed. (New York: Basic Books, 2008). Others, like Lizabeth Cohen, acknowledge the importance of women's role as "producers" in the wartime workforce, while also calling attention to the ways their traditional role as consumers was newly politicized by war, mobilizing them as "activist" consumers (what Cohen calls "consumer citizens") who could leverage their buying behavior to effect larger political goals. "Although Rosie the Riveter . . . may have dominated the official record of women's contribution to the Second World War, many more millions of women achieved new civic authority through their power as consumers" (*Consumers' Republic*, 63).

17 Honey, *Creating Rosie the Riveter*, 38, 48.

18 Quoted in Honey, 49.

19 Honey, 92.

20 Louise Page Benjamin, "Orders for the Girls at Home," *Ladies' Home Journal*, November 1943, 118.

21 Honey, 23.

22 Honey, 19.

23 "War vs. Non-War: A Study in Consumer Attitudes," n.d., box 9, folder 2, JWR.

24 "War vs. Non-War."

25 "War vs. Non-War." Robert B. Westbrook has argued that state propaganda during World War II relied largely on appeals to Americans' private interests and moral obligations, rather than to political obligations, to rally support for the war. Appeals to preserve the American "family" elicited particularly strong support. "Fighting for the American Family: Private Interests and Political Obligation in World War II," in *The Power of Culture: Critical Essays in American History*, ed. Richard Wightman Fox and T. J. Jackson Lears (Chicago: University of Chicago Press, 1993), 195–221.

26 "Excerpts from Letters to Hamilton Watch Company," May 5, 1943, box 1, folder 8, JWR.

27 George Frazier, "Jon Whitcomb and the Whitcomb Girls," *Good Housekeeping* 139, no. 3 (September 1954): 52–53, 177–81.

28 Jon Whitcomb, *All About Girls* (Englewood Cliffs, NJ: Prentice-Hall, 1962), viii.

29 Jon Whitcomb, "How I Paint a Picture," in *Famous Artists Course Lessons 1–24*, by Albert Donne et al. (Famous Artists Schools, n.d.), 6–24.

30 Letter to Community from T. Sgt. William E. Miller, December 3, 1944, box 16, folder 11, JWR.

31 Talk to Community, December 15, 1944, box 16, folder 11, JWR.

32 "Days of Decision," n.d., box 14, folder 9, JWR.

33 Cohen, *Consumers' Republic*, 56.

34 Cohen, *Consumers' Republic*, 127. Wall also discusses these so-called "purchasing power progressives" who emerged after WWI and who saw mass consumption as a liberating force; see p. 192–194.

35 Wall, *Inventing the American Way*, 173. According to Wall, the Advertising Council was instrumental in promoting a postwar "consensus" culture, one that reinvigorated faith in the free market as America's best social and economic equalizer.

36 Wall, 174.

37 Wall, 190.

38 Wall, 195.

39 Wall, 198.

40 See Cohen's discussion in *Consumers' Republic* of the way federal reconversion policies shaped postwar gender norms, in particular pp. 137–51: "The government buttressed a male-directed family economy by disproportionately giving men access to career training, property ownership, capital, and credit, as well as control over family finances" (137). See also May, *Homeward Bound*, esp. chap. 7, "The Commodity Gap: Consumerism and the Modern Home."

41 Talk to Community, August 28, 1946, box 16, folder 13, JWR.

42 Talk to Community.

43 "Never Trust a Woman's Viewpoint," speech to DuPont Clinic, September 1945, box 16, folder 12, JWR.

44 Letter to JWR from Ray Martin, June 11 1951, box 1, folder 9; letter to JWR from Harry W. Bennet, n.d., box 1, folder 11, JWR.

45 "Mother Named Advertising Woman of Year," n.d., box 1, folder 4, JWR.

46 "Ad Woman of the Year Successfully Manages Career and Family," *Printer's Ink*, n.d., box 1, folder 4, JWR.

47 "My Name is Jean Rindlaub," *Daily News*, February 28, 1953, box 1, folder 4, JWR.

48 Ruth MacKay, "White Collar Girl," *Chicago Daily Tribune*, March 8, 1946, box 1, folder 4, JWR.

49 James J. Nagle, "News of the Advertising and Marketing Fields," *New York Times*, March 7, 1954, box 1, folder 4, JWR.

50 Marilyn Mercer, "Advertising Woman Far from Average," *Houston Post*, March 22, 1960, box 1, folder 4, JWR.

51 "Ad Woman of the Year."

52 "Ad Woman of the Year."

53 "St. Louis Speech," June 10, 1951, box 15, folder 5, JWR.

Chapter Seven

1 "All the Rest of Your Natural Life," box 14, folder 9, JWR.

2 Letter from Bruce Barton to Mr. R. E. Zimmerman, October 21, 1952, box 1, folder 14, JWR.

3 See Roland Marchand, *Creating the Corporate Soul: The Rise of Public Relations and Corporate Imagery in American Big Business* (Berkeley: University of California Press, 1998), esp. chap. 3, "Corporate Morale in War and Peace: Advocacy, Industrial Statesmanship, and Humanization."

4 Marchand, 134. Marchand devotes an entire chapter of his book to Barton; see chap. 4, "A 'Corporation Consciousness': General Motors, General Electric, and the Bruce Barton Formula."

5 Marchand, 138–39.

6 Marchand, 152.

7 Newspaper clipping, Bruce Barton, "Advertising: Its Contribution to the American Way of Life," 1955, box 15, folder 3, JWR.

8 Marchand, *Creating the Corporate Soul*, 134.

9 On Barton and the "service ideal," see Marchand, *Creating the Corporate Soul*, 164–201. On the importance of the "servant leader" ideal to the development of the Walmart corporation, in particular, and to a gendered Christian ideology of postindustrial work in general, see Bethany Moreton, *To Serve God and Walmart: The Making of Christian Free Enterprise* (Cambridge, MA: Harvard University Press, 2009), esp. 100–124.

10 Material in n.d., box 7, folder 10 "Market Research: Betty Crocker 'Emotional Copy,'" JWR.

11 Material in n.d., box 7, folder 10 "Market Research: Betty Crocker 'Emotional Copy,'" JWR.

12 Inter-office memo from Jean Rindlaub to Mr. Feland, November 23, 1948, box 1, folder 16, JWR.

13 Speech to Advertising Club, January 1948, box 17, folder 2, JWR.

14 For a history of the Betty Crocker character, including detailed descriptions of her debut in radio and later transition to television, see Susan Marks, *Finding Betty Crocker: The Secret Life of American's First Lady of Food* (Minneapolis: University of Minnesota Press, 2007).

15 Papers of Adelaide Fish Hawley Cumming, 1922–1967 [hereafter cited as AFHC], folder 49, "Eastern Conference of Women's Advertising Clubs, 1956"; Speech

delivered February 5, 1956, "Betty Crocker: Pioneer Advertising Woman." Jeanette Kelly's role in the Betty Crocker persona is discussed in an article in *McCall's Food Service Bulletin*, April–May 1956, "Shop Talk: Betty Crocker's Voice of Experience," folder 59, "Promotional Material 1950–59," AFHC.

16 "Eastern Conference of Women's Advertising Clubs, 1956," AFHC.

17 Quoted in Marks, *Finding Betty Crocker*, 218.

18 "Copy Department, December 8, 1953, General Mills Talk," box 16, folder 4, JWR.

19 Memo to Ed Cachin from Jean Rindlaub, August 13, 1953, box 1, folder 14, JWR.

20 As recounted by Charles Bell, General Mills president, in a 1958 confidential memo to A. Z. Kouri, box 2, folder 1, JWR.

21 "Betty Crocker Presentation, March 30, 1953," box 16, folder 4, JWR.

22 "Copy Department, December 8, 1953, General Mills Talk," box 16, folder 4, JWR.

23 Memo to Ed Cachin from Jean Rindlaub, August 13, 1953, box 1, folder 14, JWR.

24 Letter from Walter R. Barry to Mr. B. C. Duffy, August 26, 1953, box 1, folder 14, JWR.

25 Memo from Jim Johnson to Charles Brower, October 22, 1953.

26 Speech to General Mills, February 10, 1956, box 16, folder 7, JWR.

27 Speech to General Mills, February 10, 1956.

28 "Betty Crocker Emotional Copy 1950–1963," box 7, folder 10, JWR.

29 Marks, *Finding Betty Crocker*, 221.

30 Magazine clipping, "Betty Crocker on Net Radio: Ultimate in Integrated Sell," *Sponsor*, December 27, 1954, folder 57, AFHC.

31 Speech to General Mills, February 10, 1956.

32 Marks, *Finding Betty Crocker*, 221.

33 Speech to General Mills, February 10, 1956.

34 Speech to General Mills, February 10, 1956.

35 Intra-office memo from Pat Tierney to Jean Rindlaub, January 28, 1955, box 14, folder 5, JWR.

36 Anita Colby, "Leave it to the Girls to Blast the Bomb!" box 1, folder 4, JWR.

37 "Betty Crocker Emotional Copy, 1950–1963."

38 "We Love LOVE!" April 16, 1954, box 14, folder 5, JWR.

39 Copy titled "From Betty Crocker," n.d., box 7, folder 11, JWR.

40 Article from *Science News Letter*, July 30, 1949, box 14, folder 6, JWR.

41 Article clipping, "Psychiatrist Says Man Needs Love in His Diet," n.d., box 8, folder 13, JWR.

42 For a thought-provoking discussion of "emotional capitalism," see Eva Illouz, *Cold Intimacies: The Making of Emotional Capitalism* (Cambridge, MA: Polity Press, 2007). Illouz argues that "the making of capitalism went hand in hand with the making of an intensely specialized emotional culture," by which "affect is made an essential aspect of economic behavior." Far from exiling emotion from the public sphere, capitalism ensures that "never has the private self been so publicly performed and harnessed to the discourses and values of the economic and political spheres" (4–5). Laurie Essig proposes that an American "ideology of romance" has been crucial to consolidating capitalism's unquestioned reign in the twentieth and twenty-first centuries in *Love Inc: Dating Apps, the Big White Wedding, and Chasing the Happily Neverafter* (Oakland: University of California Press, 2019). Like trickle-down economics, the lure of romance promises us that "things will get better" even in the face continued of evidence to the contrary.

Chapter Eight

1   Jon Whitcomb, *"How I Paint a Picture,"* in *Famous Artists Course Lessons 1–24,* by Albert Donne et al. (Famous Artists Schools, n.d.), 6–24.

2   On the centrality of sexuality to postwar constructions of American national identity, see Miriam G. Reumann, *American Sexual Character: Sex, Gender, and National Identity in the Kinsey Reports* (Berkeley: University of California Press, 2005). For Reumann, "Americans brought sexuality into the public arena in the decade and a half after the end of World War II, making it a political and social topic as well as a personal one" (5).

3   Margaret Mead, "Male and Female," *Ladies' Home Journal,* September 1949.

4   Mead, "Male and Female," 129.

5   Mead, "Male and Female," 143.

6   Reumann, *American Sexual Character,* 21.

7   "The mannish woman . . . may be treated as a man in disguise, and so forgiven her successes. But for the success of a feminine woman there are no alibis." Mead, "Male and Female," 151.

8   "Weekly Feature, To Girls on the Way Up," n.d., box 12, folder 1, JWR.

9   "To Girls on the Way Up."

10   "Electrical Women's Round Table," March 9, 1954, box 18, folder 3, JWR.

11   Memo from C. H. Brower to A. F. Osborn, May 10 1944.

12   "Never Trust a Woman's Viewpoint," speech to Dupont Clinic, September 1945, box 16, folder 12, JWR.

13   "United Fruit Cookbook Conference, November 5, 1954," box 18, folder 6, JWR.

14   "United Fruit Cookbook Conference, November 5, 1954."

15   "A Woman Takes a Look at the Woman's Viewpoint," May 9, 1944, box 16, folder 11, JWR.

16   "Woman Takes a Look at the Woman's Viewpoint."

17   "I Know Things About Your Husband," n.d., box 13, folder 9, JWR.

18   "How to Keep a Husband Happy," n.d., box 13, folder 9, JWR.

19   "I Know Things About Your Husband."

20   "Stay at Home Wives Need a Spanking!" n.d., box 12, folder 1, JWR.

21   "Wife—or Parasite?" n.d., box 12, folder 1, JWR.

22   "Wife—or Parasite?"

23   "Between the Lines: Ad Woman of the Year Successfully Manages Career and Family," *Printer's Ink,* n.d., box 1, folder 4, JWR,

24   "Woman—The Decision Maker," talk to the Association of American Soap and Glycerin Producers, 1953, box 12, folder 6, JWR.

25   "Wildroot Speech, Biloxi, 1949," box 16, folder 2, JWR.

26   Ann Douglas, *Feminization of Culture,* 12.

27   "Community, August 28, 1946," box 16, folder 1, JWR.

28   "The Gardner Agency Summary of Mrs. Middle Majority, *Tide,* September 23, 1949," box 11, folder 5, JWR.

29   Dr. Richard E. Gordon and Kathryn K. Gordon, and Max Gunther, "The Split-Level Trap," *Good Housekeeping* 152, no. 1 (January 1961): 35–50.

30   Gordon, Gordon, and Gunther, "Split-Level Trap," 37.

31   Gordon, Gordon, and Gunther, "Split-Level Trap," 46.

32   "Changing Women" brainstorm, n.d., box 8, folder 12, JWR.

33 "My Brother Has an Account in his Pocket," n.d., box 14, folder 9, JWR.
34 "My Brother."
35 "My Brother."
36 On the overlap between "containment"-driven national security and sexuality during the Cold War, see Elaine Tyler May, *Homeward Bound: American Families in the Cold War Era*, 20th ann. ed. (New York: Basic Books, 2008); Wini Breines, *Young, White, and Miserable: Growing Up Female in the Fifties* (Chicago: University of Chicago Press, 1992); *Not June Cleaver: Women and Gender in Postwar America, 1945–1960*, ed. Joanne Meyerowitz (Philadelphia: Temple University Press, 1994), esp. Donna Penn, "The Lesbian, the Prostitute, and the Containment of Female Sexuality in Postwar America," 358–81, and Wini Breines, "Beats and Bad Girls," 382–408.
37 Quoted in Robert D. Dean, *Imperial Brotherhood: Gender and the Making of Cold War Foreign Policy* (Amherst: University of Massachusetts Press, 2001), 68. K. A. Cuordileone analyzes the centrality of gender to political discourse in the Cold War and the evolution of a bipartisan "cult of masculine toughness" at home and abroad that briefly united conservative and liberal politics. *Manhood and American Political Culture in the Cold War* (New York: Routledge, 2005).
38 For an analysis of *The Vital Center* as a manifesto devoted to "toughening up" the feminized values of an earlier liberalism, see Cuordileone, *Manhood*, chap. 1, "Postwar Liberalism and the Crisis of Liberal Masculinity," 1–36.
39 For a fascinating look at the pressure gay men felt to "pass" in the 1950s, and the strong current within homophile culture to stigmatize feminine-coding gay men, see Craig M. Loftin, "Unacceptable Mannerisms: Gender Anxieties, Homosexual Activism, and Swish in the United States, 1945–1965," *Journal of Social History* 40, no. 3 (Spring 2007): 577–96.
40 Jean Wade Rindlaub, "The New Togetherness," in *Christian Herald*, 1955, box 12, folder 7, JWR.
41 Rindlaub, "New Togetherness."
42 On the way popular culture texts, including film and television, served as vehicles to explore contested gender roles in the 1950s, see James Gilbert, *Men in the Middle: Searching for Masculinity in the 1950s* (Chicago: University of Chicago Press, 2005). In his chapter devoted to the radio and television show *The Adventures of Ozzy and Harriet*, Gilbert gives a nuanced analysis of how the stock character of the "comic patriarch" helped viewers come to terms with masculinity in the newly "feminized" context of the suburban family home and mass consumption.
43 "Homemaker's Day Speech," Teaneck, New Jersey, 1957, box 19, folder 1, JWR.
44 "Speech to Toronto Ad Club," April 18, 1955, box 18, folder 4, JWR.

Chapter Nine

1 Talk to Betty Crocker/General Mills, February 10, 1956, box 16, folder 7, JWR.
2 Talk to Betty Crocker/General Mills, February 10, 1956.
3 Quoted in Craig Allen, *Eisenhower and the Mass Media: Peace, Prosperity, and Prime-Time TV* (Chapel Hill: University of North Carolina Press, 1993), 17.
4 John E. Hollitz, "Eisenhower and the Admen: The Television 'Spot' Campaign of 1952," *Wisconsin Magazine of History* 66, no. 1 (Autumn 1982): 27. On Barton's

political career, see Richard M. Fried, *The Man Everybody Knew: Bruce Barton and the Making of Modern America* (Chicago: Ivan R. Dee, 2005), esp. chap. 7, "Mr. Barton Goes to Washington," 159–92. On Barton's crafting of Coolidge's presidential image for the 1920 election, see Kerry W. Buckley, "A President for the 'Great Silent Majority': Bruce Barton's Construction of Calvin Coolidge," *New England Quarterly* 76, no. 4 (December 2003): 593–626. Buckley argues that "Barton's task, as he conceived it, was to introduce Coolidge as a political commodity, not by discussing the issues of the day but by presenting a personality with whom Americans could identify" (600).

5   Hollitz, "Eisenhower and the Admen," 27.

6   Hollitz, "Eisenhower and the Admen," 27. Bruce Barton was, in fact, correct in reading the increasingly nonpartisan nature of party politics beginning in the twentieth century. On the commodification of electoral politics in the twentieth century, and in particular the "packaging and sale of candidates to voter-consumers," see Robert B. Westbrook, "Politics as Consumption: Managing the Modern American Election," in *The Culture of Consumption: Critical Essays in American History, 1880–1980*, ed. Richard Wightman Fox and T. J. Jackson Lears, 145–73 (New York: Pantheon Books, 1983). Westbrook argues that a variety of forces, including antiparty progressive reform aimed at dismantling "machine" politics; the increasing popularity of bureaucratic interest groups such as unions or trade associations as means of pursuing economic or social interests; and displacement of the party press by mass journalism, gave rise to the increasingly "commodified" modern election cycle.

7   Hollitz, "Eisenhower and the Admen," 27.

8   William Lee Miller, *Piety Along the Potomac: Notes on Politics and Morals in the Fifties* (Boston: Houghton Mifflin, 1964), 9. Miller's extraordinary book is a collection of news articles he wrote chronicling the Eisenhower years. In "The Liking of Ike," Miller identifies the appeal of Ike as precisely his avoidance of politics: "The popularity of Mr. Eisenhower expressed the desire to avoid policies and ideas, to depend on a man, to get away from complexity that prevents the development of American political philosophies, including Mr. Eisenhower's own" (8).

9   Stephen C. Wood, "Television's First Political Spot Ad Campaign: Eisenhower Answers America," *Presidential Studies Quarterly* 20, no. 2, Eisenhower Centennial Issue (Spring 1990): 265–83.

10 Quoted in Hollitz, "Eisenhower and the Admen," 28.

11 Hollitz, 30.

12 Hollitz, 34.

13 Wood, "Television's First Political Spot Ad Campaign," 267, 268.

14 Hollitz, 31.

15 Wood, 269.

16 Wood, 271.

17 Wood, 271.

18 Hollitz, 37.

19 Hollitz, 37.

20 Quoted in Wood, 278.

21 Miller, *Piety Along the Potomac*, 60.

22 Miller, 62.

23 Quoted in Hollitz, 39.

24 The rise of a mass print culture and image production fundamentally changed the nature of democratic politics and the very idea of the public sphere. Frankfurt school theorists Theodore Adorno and Max Horkheimer introduced the idea of a "culture industry," the manufacture of standardized ideas and representations through mass media on the model of other industrial production, in their 1944 *Dialectic of Enlightenment*. In the American context, Daniel Boorstin's *The Image, or, What Happened to the American Dream* (New York: Athenaeum Books, 1962), analyzes the modern phenomenon of the "pseudo-event," in which the representation/circulation of an event in the mass media is granted more reality than the event itself. On the specific topic of politics, mass media, and "the image," see Kurt Lang and Gladys Engel Lang, *Television and Politics*, rev. ed. (New Brunswick, NJ: Transaction, 2002); Kathleen Hall Jamieson, *Packaging the Presidency: A History and Criticism of Presidential Campaign Advertising*, 2nd ed. (New York: Oxford University Press, 1992); Kathryn Cramer Brownell, *Showbiz Politics: Hollywood in American Political Life* (Chapel Hill: University of North Carolina Press, 2014); and Edwin Diamond and Stephen Bates, *The Spot: The Rise of Political Advertising on Television*, rev. ed. (Cambridge, MA: MIT Press, 1988).

25 "Eisenhower Broadcast to Mothers, October 31, 1952," box 12, folder 6, JWR.

26 "Eisenhower Broadcast to Mothers, October 31, 1952."

27 Allen, *Eisenhower and the Mass Media*, 21.

28 Allen, 23.

29 Allen, 25–26.

30 This anecdote is recounted in Allen, 33.

31 Dwight D. Eisenhower, "Remarks Upon Lighting the National Community Christmas Tree," Gerhard Peters and John T. Woolley, American Presidency Project, https://www.presidency.ucsb.edu/node/231512.

32 Christopher Lane, *Surge of Piety: Norman Vincent Peale and the Remaking of American Religious Life* (New Haven, CT: Yale University Press, 2016).

33 Miller skewers Eisenhower on this point. After campaigning on the idea of a "crusade" without an identifiable Holy City or Infidel, once he took office the rhetoric continued even after it was assumed that the object had been won. "This amorphous quality may be a product of the debilitating effect that the black arts of public relations and advertising have on words, particularly popular and/or honorable words like 'faith,' 'sincerity,' 'righteousness,' and 'morality'" (22).

34 "Panel Discussion, Christ Church," February 28, 1950, box 17, folder 4, JWR.

35 "Panel Discussion, Christ Church," February 28, 1950.

36 Cuddihy, *No Offense*, 7, 4.

37 "Panel Discussion, Christ Church," February 28, 1950.

38 Jonathan P. Herzog, *The Spiritual-Industrial Complex: America's Religious Battle against Communism in the Early Cold War* (Oxford: Oxford University Press, 2011), 32.

39 Prentis quoted in Kevin M. Kruse, *One Nation Under God: How Corporate America Invented Christian America* (New York: Basic Books, 2015), 6. Kruse's book locates the origins of the American movement to "Christianize" the state in corporate and evangelical Protestant push-back against the New Deal, and only secondarily

as a movement motivated by Cold War tensions. "The rites of our public religion originated not in a spiritual crisis, but rather in the political and economic turmoil of the Great Depression" (292). Kim Phillips-Fein traces the origins of Ronald Reagan's 1980 election, not to a post-1960s cultural conservative backlash, but to forty years of patient effort on the part of a "determined few" American businessmen to dismantle the New Deal. See *Invisible Hands: The Businessmen's Crusade Against the New Deal* (New York: W. W. Norton, 2009).

40 Quoted in Herzog, *Spiritual-Industrial Complex*, 78–79.

41 Herzog, 111.

42 Talk to Wildroot Executives, Biloxi, 1949, box 16, folder 12, JWR.

43 Walter Williams to Jean Wade Rindlaub, October 31, 1952, box 1, folder 14, JWR.

44 Walter Williams to Jean Wade Rindlaub, October 31, 1952. As Herzog explains, "Eisenhower would escalate the holy war Truman had started [and] preside over the most indelible codifications of American religious heritage. . . . With the possible exception of Abraham Lincoln, no president tied religion and social conflict together more effectively" (*Spiritual-Industrial Complex* 96).

45 Herzog, 92.

46 Quoted in Miller, *Piety Along the Potomac*, 44.

47 Miller, 20.

48 Miller, 9.

49 "United Fruit, Banana Cookbook Conference," November 12, 1956, box 18, folder 6, JWR.

50 "United Fruit, Banana Cookbook Conference," November 12, 1956.

51 "Great American Baking Revival," n.d., box 7, folder 11, JWR.

Chapter Ten

1 Henry C. Link, "Brands, A Major Contribution to Social Progress and World Harmony," n.d., box 15, folder 6, JWR.

2 J. McKeen Cattell, "The Psychological Corporation," *Annals of the American Academy of Political and Social Science* 110 (November 1923): 165–71.

3 Robert E. Gibby and Michael J. Zickar, "A History of the Early Days of Personality Testing in American Industry: An Obsession with Adjustment," *History of Psychology* 2, no. 3 (2008): 164–84.

4 Michael J. Zickar, "Using Personality Inventories to Identify Thugs and Agitators: Applied Psychology's Contribution to the War Against Labor," *Journal of Vocational Behavior* 59 (2001): 149–64. Elizabeth Lunbeck's *The Psychiatric Persuasion: Knowledge, Gender, and Power in Modern America* (Princeton, NJ: Princeton University Press, 1994), gives an excellent account of how industrial psychology tied modern masculinity to an unquestioning acceptance of the market-driven workplace.

5 Cattell, "Psychological Corporation."

6 Henry C. Link, *The Return to Religion* (New York: Macmillan, 1936), 48.

7 Link, *Return to Religion*, 73.

8 Bruce Barton, *The Man Nobody Knows* (Washington, DC: Ivan R. Dee, 2008), 36.

9 Barton, *Man Nobody Knows*, 33.

10 H. A. Overstreet, *Influencing Human Behavior* (New York: W. W. Norton, 1925), 3.

11 Dale Carnegie, *How to Win Friends and Influence People*, rev. ed. by Donna Dale Carnegie and Dorothy Carnegie (New York: Simon and Schuster, 1981), 42.

12 "Influencing Human Behavior—Overstreet," n.d., box 2, folder 11, JWR.

13 Link, *Return to Religion*, 131–32.

14 Quoted in Christopher Lane, *Surge of Piety: Norman Vincent Peale and the Remaking of American Religious Life* (New Haven, CT: Yale University Press), 5. For a biography of Peale, see Carol V. R. George, *God's Salesman: Norman Vincent Peale and the Power of Positive Thinking* (New York: Oxford University Press, 1993). The last ten years have seen a surge of literature documenting the complex relationship between evangelical Christianity and American business. In addition to Kevin Kruse, see Sarah Ruth Hammond, *God's Businessmen: Entrepreneurial Evangelicals in Depression and War*, ed. Darren Dochuk (Chicago: University of Chicago Press, 2017); Timothy E. W. Gloege, *Guaranteed Pure: The Moody Bible Institute, Business, and the Making of Modern Evangelicalism* (Chapel Hill: University of North Carolina Press, 2015); Kate Bowler, *Blessed: A History of the American Prosperity Gospel* (New York: Oxford University Press, 2013); Todd M. Brenneman, *Homespun Gospel: The Triumph of Sentimentality in Contemporary American Evangelicalism* (New York: Oxford University Press, 2014); and Moreton, *To Serve God and Walmart*.

15 Norman Vincent Peale, *The Power of Positive Thinking* (New York: Touchstone Books, 2015), 160, 6.

16 Peale, 41, 169.

17 Peale, 12–13.

18 Peale, 173, 175.

19 Intra-office memo to Lee Sherrill, from Jean Rindlaub, June 20, 1940, box 9, folder 5, JWR.

20 Assorted clippings, box 2, folder 11, JWR.

21 Peale clipping, box 2, folder 11, JWR.

22 "The New Togetherness," n.d., box 12, folder 7, JWR.

23 Speech given before Barcalo Manufacturing Company, January 6, 1956, box 18, folder 6, JWR.

24 Alex Osborn, *How to Think Up* (New York: McGraw-Hill, 1942), 2.

25 Osborn, *How to Think Up*, 29.

26 Osborn, *How to Think Up*, 26.

27 Intra-office memo from Jean Rindlaub to Alex Osborn, May 8, 1945, box 9, folder 5, JWR.

28 Speech for Alex Osborn, by Jean Rindlaub, December 17, 1947, box 16, folder 2, JWR.

29 Speech for Alex Osborn, by Jean Rindlaub, December 17, 1947.

30 Talk dated January 17, 1948, box 16, folder 2, JWR.

31 "How Are Your Personal Public Relations?" *Forecast for Home Economists*, June 1959, box 12, folder 7, JWR.

32 Talk to New Jersey State Dietetic Association, May 25, 1951, box 17, folder 5, JWR.

33 Talk to New Jersey State Dietetic Association, May 25, 1951.

34 "Keep Reaching," n.d., box 11, folder 12, JWR.

35 "Keep Reaching."

36 Jean Sprain Wilson, "Learn How to Worry Right," n.d., box 1, folder 5, JWR.

Chapter Eleven

1 "United Fruit, Banana Cookbook Conference," November 12, 1956, box 18, folder 6, JWR. Jean also gave talks for the United Fruit Food Forum Conferences in 1953 and 1954.

2 Newspaper clipping, "Edward Bernays Informs Food Forum Eating Habits Set by Cultural Pattern," n.d., box 1, folder 4, JWR.

3 "United Fruit Cookbook Conference," November 5, 1954, box 18, folder 3, JWR.

4 "United Fruit Cookbook Conference," November 5, 1954.

5 See Marcelo Bucheli, "United Fruit Company in Latin America," in *Banana Wars: Power, Production and History in the Americas*, ed. Steve Striffler and Mark Moberg (Durham, NC: Duke University Press, 2003).

6 The most detailed critical accounts of United Fruit Company's history can be found in Stephen Schlesinger and Stephen Kinzer, *Bitter Fruit: The Story of the American Coup in Guatemala*, expanded ed. (Boston: David Rockefeller Center for Latin American Studies, 1999); Peter Chapman, *Bananas: How the United Fruit Company Shaped the World* (Edinburgh: Canongate Books, 2007); and Thomas C. McCann, *An American Company: The Tragedy of United Fruit* (New York: Crown, 1956). A more sympathetic treatments of the company's role in Central America can be found in Frederick Upton Adams, *Conquest of the Tropics: The Story of the Creative Enterprises Conducted by the United Fruit Company* (New York: Doubleday, 1914).

7 Adams, *Conquest of the Tropics*, 53. Adams declares at several points throughout his book his intention to clear United Fruit—and American corporations more generally—of the Progressive charge that in their pursuit of profit, they ran roughshod over the rights of laborers at home and native citizens abroad. "There was no native agriculture in the American tropics to 'exploit'" before the arrival of United Fruit and other concerns of its type; rather, the Central American tropics "are productive just about in proportion as American initiative, American capital, and American enterprise make them productive" (36).

8 Schlesinger and Kinzer, *Bitter Fruit*, 81.

9 For a biography of Bernays, see Larry Tye, *The Father of Spin: Edward L. Bernays and the Birth of Public Relations* (New York: Henry Holt, 1998).

10 Edward Bernays, *Propaganda*, with an introduction by Mark Crispin Miller (New York: Ig Publishers, 2005), 37.

11 See Tye, *Father of Spin*, 162–64, and Schlesinger and Kinzer, *Bitter Fruit*, 82.

12 Studies of Carmen Miranda's cultural and political significance include Shari Roberts, "'The Lady in the Tutti-Frutti Hat': Carmen Miranda, a Spectacle of Ethnicity," *Cinema Journal* 23, no. 3 (Spring 1993): 3–23; James Mandrell, "Carmen Miranda Betwixt and Between: Or, Neither Here nor There," *Latin American Literary Review* 29, no. 57 (January–June 2001): 26–39; Kathryn Bishop-Sanchez, *Creating Carmen Miranda: Race, Camp and Transnational Stardom* (Nashville: Vanderbilt University Press, 2016); Maria José Canelo, "Producing Good Neighbors: Carmen Miranda's Body as Spectacular Pan-Americanism," *Revue Française d'études américaines* no. 139 (2014): 60–76.

13 As Virginia Scott Jenkins argues, bananas were introduced into the American diet at the same time as science was advancing in the fields of germ theory, calories,

and vitamins. See *Bananas: An American History* (Washington: Smithsonian Institution Press, 2000).

14 "No Siesta for Chiquita: How a Synthetic Senorita Educated and Expanded the Banana Market," *Sponsor*, February 1950, 40.

15 "No Siesta for Chiquita," 41.

16 Quoted in Jenkins, *Bananas*, 167.

17 Intra-office memo, Jean Rindlaub to Charlie Brower, March 4, 1954, box 14, folder 9, JWR.

18 "United Fruit Recipe Conference," November 6, 1953, box 18, folder 2, JWR.

19 Schlesinger and Kinzer, *Bitter Fruit*, 32.

20 Schlesinger and Kinzer, *Bitter Fruit*, 72.

21 Tye, *Spin*, 165.

22 Quoted in Schlesinger and Kinzer, *Bitter Fruit*, 75.

23 Schlesinger and Kinzer, 80.

24 Quoted in Tye, *Spin*, 156.

25 Schlesinger and Kinzer, 86.

26 Schlesinger and Kinzer, 86.

27 Schlesinger and Kinzer, 76.

28 Quoted in Schlesinger and Kinzer, 79.

29 In 1994, the CIA declassified documents relating to Operation Success, allowing historians to confirm what had long been suspected: the US engineering of the 1954 coup. Historian Nicholas Cullather provides a useful summary and timeline of Operation Success in his monograph *Operation PBSUCCESS: The United States and Guatemala, 1952–1954* (Washington DC: Center for the Study of Intelligence, Central Intelligence Agency, 1994). See also Richard H. Immerman, *The CIA in Guatemala: The Foreign Policy of Intervention* (Austin: University of Texas Press, 1982).

30 Schlesinger and Kinzer, *Bitter Fruit*, 111.

31 Schlesinger and Kinzer, 122.

32 Quoted in Immerman, *CIA in Guatemala*, 5.

33 See Cullather, *Operation PBSUCCESS*, 87–91.

34 "Article Ideas," box 11, folder 7, JWR.

35 See Tye, *Spin*, 178–79.

36 "Article Ideas."

Chapter Twelve

1 Betty Friedan, *The Feminine Mystique*, rev. ed., introduction by Gail Collins and afterword by Anna Quindlen (New York: W. W. Norton, 1997), 1.

2 For a detailed study of the rise of a conservative women's movement among California's suburban housewives in the 1950s, see Michelle M. Nickerson, *Mothers of Conservatism: Women and the Postwar Right* (Princeton, NJ: Princeton University Press, 2012). Catherine E. Rymph covers the fascinating intertwined history of feminism and conservatism within the Republican Party from 1920 through the 1970s in *Republican Women: Feminism and Conservatism from Suffrage through the Rise of the New Right* (Chapel Hill: University of North Carolina Press, 2006). R. Marie Griffith examines the role conservative Christian women played in bringing sex and gender into the political arena, consolidating "family values" as a central cultural component

of twentieth-century politics, in *Moral Combat: How Sex Divided American Christians and Fractured American Politics* (New York: Basic Books, 2017).

3   Nickerson, *Mothers of Conservatism*, 1.

4   Rymph, *Republican Women*, 215.

5   Letter from JWR to Jane Creel, July 19 1976, box 22, folder 11, JWR.

6   Nickerson, *Mothers of Conservatism*, 171.

7   Nickerson gives a useful historical summary of the decline of the Progressive middle-class social reform tradition of "maternalism" and the rise of what she calls "housewife populism" in *Mothers of Conservatism*, xiii–xxii.

8   Jane Addams, *Twenty Years at Hull House, with Autobiographical Notes* (New York: Macmillan, 1912), 167.

9   On the connection between women's social reform activism and the growth of the welfare state, see Molly Ladd-Taylor, *Mother-Work: Women, Child Welfare, and the State, 1890–1930* (Urbana: University of Illinois Press, 1994); Seth Koven and Sonya Michel, eds., *Mothers of a New World: Maternalist Politics and the Origins of Welfare States* (New York: Routledge, 1993).

10 See Nickerson, *Mothers of Conservatism*, chap. 1, "Patriotic Daughters and Isolationist Mothers: Conservative Women in the Early Twentieth Century," 1–31.

11 Nickerson, *Mothers of Conservatism*, 13.

12 See Rymph, *Republican Women*, chap. 4, "The Return of the Female Political Crusade," 98–130.

13 Barry M. Goldwater, *The Conscience of a Conservative* (Shepherdsville, KY: Victor, 1960), 69, 72.

14 Russel Kirk, *The Intelligent Woman's Guide to Conservatism* (New York: Devin-Adair, 1957), 45. See Nickerson, *Mothers of Conservatism*, chap. 5, "The 'Conservative Sex': Women and the Building of a Movement), 136–68.

15 *History and Minutes of the National Council of Women in the United States*, Organized in Washington, D.C., March 31, 1888, ed. Louise Barnum Robbins (Boston: E. B. Stillings, 1898), 239.

16 President's Commission on the Status of Women, *American Women: Report of the President's Commission on the Status of Women, 1963* (Washington, DC: Government Printing Office, 1963), 16.

17 "The Status of Women—and You," talk to Teaneck Presbyterian Church, March 16, 1964, box 20, folder 3, JWR.

18 "Status of Women—and You."

19 "Is There Any Room for *Women* in the Executive Suite?" Westover School, Middlebury, Connecticut, May 31, 1955, box 12, folder 7, JWR.

20 "You Can Help Change the Climate for Women," *Radcliffe Quarterly* 50, no. 1 (February 1966): 10–12, box 23, JWR.

21 "You Can Help Change the Climate for Women."

22 Anne Rindlaub Dow, n.d., typescript report on cost of homemaking, box 23, folder 7, JWR.

23 "You Can Help Change the Climate for Women," 12.

24 Quoted in "Women in the War on Poverty: Conference Proceedings" (Washington, DC: Women's Advisory Council on Poverty and the Office of Economic Opportunity, 1968), 26.

25 Speech, Churchwomen United, Teaneck, May Friendship Day, May 5, 1967, box 20, folder 6, JWR.

26 "The Golden Rule," n.d., box 2, folder 1, JWR.

27 Quoted in "Women in the War on Poverty: Conference Proceedings," 20.

28 "What One Woman Can Do About Poverty," n.d., box 23, folder 4, JWR.

29 Speech, "Churchwomen United," May 5, 1967.

30 Speech, "Churchwomen United," May 5, 1967.

31 Typed copy of material on "Welfare Myths," n.d., box 23, folder 4, JWR.

32 Speech, "Churchwomen United," May 5, 1967.

33 Henry Clark, *The Christian Case against Poverty*. (New York: Association Press, 1965), 86–87.

34 "What Can One Woman Do?" n.d., box 23, folder 4, JWR.

35 Intra-office memo from JWR to Bob Foreman, May 5, 1960.

36 Intra-office memo from JWR to Bob Foreman, May 5, 1960.

37 Letter from JWR to the Hon. Harrison Williams, June 19, 1968, box 23, folder 7, JWR.

38 Letter from JWR to Mrs. Jacobs, June 17, 1968, box 23, folder 7, JWR.

39 Letter from JWR to Mrs. Jacobs, July 31, 1968, box 23, folder 7, JWR.

40 Letter headed "Dear Rhetta and Corienne," April 13, 1964, box 23, folder 7, JWR.

41 Letter to "Millie," February 19, 1965, box 23, folder 7, JWR.

42 Arnold Forster and Benjamin R. Epstein, *Danger on the Right* (New York: Random House, 1964), 264.

43 Letter from JWR to Mrs. Jacobs, July 31, 1968.

Epilogue

1 Ad Age Course, Chicago, July 19, 1967, "How Advertising Looks to Me, Now That I Don't Write It Anymore," box 20, file 6, JWR.

2 Ad Age Course.

3 Speech to Pacific Coast Electrical Association, Coronado, CA, May 14 1958, "Never Underestimate the Power of a Woman," box 19, folder 3, JWR.

4 George W. Webber, *God's Colony in Man's World* (New York: Abington Press, 1960), 19.

5 Letter from JWR to Mrs. Jacobs, June 17, 1968, box 23, folder 7, JWR.

Index

Page numbers in italics refer to figures.

Adams, Frederick Upham, 194, 259n7
Addams, Jane, 31, 210, 212
Adorno, Theodor, 256n24
advertising: of cosmetics (*see* cosmetics); creating demand, need for, 32; democracy and, 88; ethics of, 101; by Jean for Batten Barton Durstine and Osborn (*see* Batten Barton Durstine and Osborn [BBDO]); Jean's belief in, 4; Jean's disenchantment with, 7; Jean's success in, reasons behind, 51–52; magical thinking in, 46–47; the makeover, magic of, 45–46; masculine and feminine branches of, ideological division between, 40; New Deal and, 106; postwar perspective, embrace of, 111–15; public image crafted by agencies, 39–40; public relations men in politics, 165–69, 174; public service, 117–18; rampant sexism in, 7; research for (*see* advertising/market research; opinion polling); soaps (*see* soaps); as a social good, 9–10, 40–41, 46, 62, 127, 129; on television (*see* television); "the woman's point of view," seeking out, 39; World War II, impact of (*see* World War II). *See also* marketing
Advertising Council, 117–18. *See also* War Advertising Council
Advertising Federation of America (AFA), 123
advertising industry, history of: advertising as progressive force, Frank Presbery on, 46; collaboration with government information campaigns during and after WWII, 107–10, 117–18; industry resistance to

federal regulation, 105–6; involvement with presidential campaigns, 162–66; patent medicine appeals and Christian conversion culture in early advertising practice, 50; patent medicine companies as first national advertisers, 46–49; rise of print media and spread of advertising, 48; trade card and almanacs as early advertising vehicles, 48–49; traveling medicine shows, 47–48 (*see also* patent medicine)
advertising/market research: by adwomen, 147–48; heterogeneity in vs. homogenization of opinion polls, 93–95; on housewives, 151–52, 229; housewives' fear of baking cakes, 132; ideological bias of public polling and, 95–99; "inspirational" messages higher rated than wartime messages, 111–12; "penetration" studies, 163; postwar research for Oneida, 119–20; psychology-based research, 174–75, 191–92; social scientific studies, use of, 99–101; "think up" technique/brainstorming sessions, 186–88. *See also* opinion polling
advertising strategy: corporate benevolence and the "human touch," 126; "heart-tug," playing on domestic sentiments and, 6, 130, 134; "homogenized," use of the term, 92–93; "love and kisses" copy, 140–41; "other-direction," use of, 99–101; peer acceptance, 91–92; "personality selling," television and, 137–38, 160; scare copy, 58–59; target audiences, recognition of population heterogeneity and, 94–95